MW01205793

PORTUGUESE
PHRASEBOOK·DICTIONARY

Alvino E. Fantini, Ph.D.
The Experiment in International Living
Brattleboro, Vermont

Beatriz Céspedes de Fantini, M.A.T.
School for International Training
Brattleboro, Vermont

Crown Publishers, Inc., New York

Copyright © 1993 by Crown Publishers, Inc.

Published by Crown Publishers, Inc., 201 East 50th Street, New York, New York 10022. Member of the Crown Publishing Group.

LIVING LANGUAGE, LIVING LANGUAGE TRAVELTALK, and colophon are trademarks of Crown Publishers, Inc.

Manufactured in the United States of America

Library of Congress Cataloging-in-Publication Data

Fantini, Alvino E., 1936–
    Living language traveltalk. Portuguese : phrasebook, dictionary /
Alvino E. Fantini, Beatriz Céspedes de Fantini.—1st ed.
        p.   cm.
    1. Portuguese language—Conversation and phrase books—English.
I. Céspedes de Fantini, Beatriz.   II. Title.
PC5073.F36   1992
469.83'421—dc20   92-42321
                                                                        CIP

ISBN 0-517-58756-4

ISBN 0-517-58755-6 (cassette)

10   9   8   7   6   5   4   3   2   1

First Edition

CONTENTS

ENGLISH-PORTUGUESE DICTIONARY 195

PORTUGUESE-ENGLISH DICTIONARY 235

ABOUT THE AUTHORS

Beatriz C. de Fantini   is a language teacher, author, and trainer who has conducted workshops over numerous years for language and cross-cultural educators in many parts of the world.

Alvino E. Fantini   is a linguist, educator, international consultant, and author who has worked with the U.S. Peace Corps in Brazil. He has directed the development of more than 30 language courses for classroom and self-instructional uses, as well as numerous guides for cross-cultural orientation.

ACKNOWLEDGMENTS

We are indebted to various individuals, organizations and resources for help in the preparation of this work. We thank Fodor's Travel Publications, Inc., for the following sources of travel and cultural information: *Fodor's 91: Brazil* and *Fodor's 91: Portugal*, available in bookstores nationwide.

We are especially grateful to The Experiment in International Living, an international, non-profit, educational exchange organization; to Sandra Sousa, Intercultura, Lisbon, Portugal; and to Carla Reichmann of São Paulo and Verónica Portela Lima of Bahia, Brazil, graduate students in the Master of Arts in Teaching Program, School for International Training, Brattleboro, Vermont, for reviewing the work for linguistic and cultural accuracy. We also thank Kathryn Mintz, Editorial Director, Jacqueline Natter, Editor, and Victoria Su, Editorial Assistant of the Living Language series at Crown Publishers. Lastly, we are indebted to Carla Alina Fantini-Céspedes, our daughter, who lent a helping hand throughout the project. **Dedicamos este livro muito especialmente a Carlina.**

PREFACE

Are you planning a trip to Brazil, Portugal, or another Portuguese-speaking area? If so, this book will help you make the most of your trip. The *Traveltalk*™ phrasebook/dictionary features more than 2,200 Portuguese expressions to use in the various situations you may encounter as a tourist. Each word has a phonetic transcription to help you with pronunciation.

No prior knowledge of Portuguese is necessary. All you have to do to make yourself understood is read the phonetics as you would any English sentence. In this program, pronunciation is based on the Portuguese spoken in São Paulo, Brazil. However, use of this book and cassette will enable you to communicate in Portugal as well. We recommend that you use the accompanying *Traveltalk*™ *Portuguese* cassette (with native speakers from Brazil), but this book is useful on its own, as it offers the following features:

Pronunciation Guide This section presents the phonetic transcription system for this book through the use of simple English examples and explanations. Reading through it first will help you learn how to pronounce the phrases in subsequent chapters.

Chapter 1: Useful Expressions Many common phrases are used repeatedly in a variety of contexts. For your convenience, these phrases have been grouped together in Chapter 1.

Chapters 2–13 reflect the full range of the visitor's experience. From arrival at the airport to saying farewell to new friends, *Traveltalk*™ provides a comprehensive resource for every important context of your visit.

Sample Dialogues in each chapter give you a sense of how the language sounds in conversation.

Travel Tips & Cultural Highlights Interspersed throughout the chapters are brief narratives highlighting cultural attractions in both Brazil and Portugal and offering insiders' tips for getting the most out of your visit.

General Information is given throughout. Essential facts are presented to ease your transition in a new setting.
- legal holidays
- metric conversion tables
- important signs
- common abbreviations
- clothing/shoe size conversion charts

Grammar Guide A concise and easy-to-follow grammar summary is included for those who would like to understand the structure of the language.

Two-way 1,600-Word Dictionary All of the key words presented in this book are listed in the English-Portuguese/Portuguese-English dictionary. The dictionary also provides a phonetic transcription of every Portuguese word and phrase.

The main focus of this *Traveltalk*™ is Brazil; however, much of the information will also apply to and be useful in Portugal and other Portuguese-speaking areas. You can of course use this book beforehand to prepare for your travels, but you will probably find it most useful "on the spot," so don't forget to include it when you pack for your trip. It's compact, handy, and small enough to fit easily into a handbag or pocket.

Boa sorte e boa viagem! (BOH-ah SOHR-chee ee BOH-ah vee-AH-zhehn) Good luck and have a good trip!

BEFORE YOU LEAVE

PASSPORTS & VISAS

As of this writing, Brazil requires tourist visas for both American and Canadian citizens. Visas are also required for citizens of Great Britain who are visiting Brazil for business purposes.

U.S. citizens need passports and visas—the latter are available from the nearest Brazilian consulate—for travel to or within Brazil. A tourist visa, valid for 90 days, is easily obtainable and free. A 2-by-3 inch passport photo, passport, and a round-trip ticket will secure your visa.

Passports must be valid for at least six months from the intended date of arrival in Brazil. When you receive your passport, be sure to write down its number, date, and place of issue on a separate piece of paper. If your passport is lost or stolen, notify either the nearest American consul or the Passport Office, Department of State, Washington, D.C., 20524, as well as the local Brazilian police.

Neither American nor British citizens need a visa to visit mainland Portugal, Madeira, or the Azores for stays of up to 60 days.

HEALTH CERTIFICATES

No vaccinations are required for entry into Brazil or Portugal unless the visitor is coming from an infected area. Because of frequent changes in the law, we suggest you check on this before you leave.

SOURCES OF INFORMATION

Brazil

Embratour, Brazil's National Tourism Authority, is located in Rio de Janeiro, at Rua Mariz e Barros 13, near Praça de Bandeira. In Rio, Varig Airlines at Avenida Rio Branco 128 can also provide information on travel in Brazil.

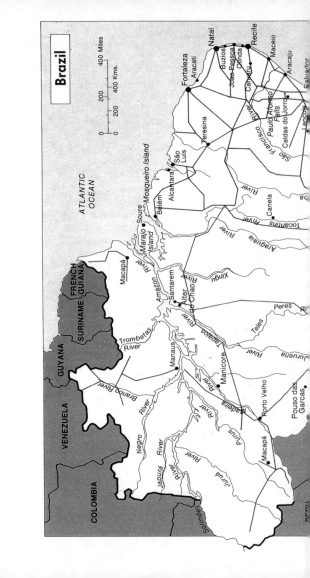

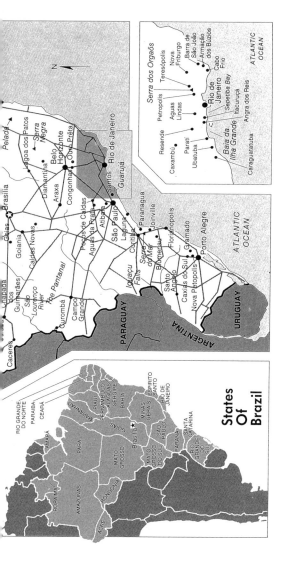

Serra dos Orgaõs

ATLANTIC OCEAN

Teresópolis
Nova Friburgo
Barra de São João
Armação dos Búzios
Petrópolis
Nova Lindas
Aguas Lindas
Cabo Frio
Rio de Janeiro
Sepetiba Bay
Itacuruçá
Resende
Baia da Ilha Grande
Angra dos Reis
Caxambú
Parati
Ubatuba
Caraguatatuba

Pelada
Lagoa dos Patos
Serra Negra
Belo Horizonte
Ouro Prêta
Rio de Janeiro
Guarujá
Diamantina
Araxa
Congonhas
Santos

Poços de Caldas
Águas da Prata
Atibaia
São Paulo
Laguna
Paranaguá
Joinville
Curitiba
Serra do Mar
Blumenau
Florianópolis
Caxias do Sul
Gramado
Porto Alegre
Santo Angelo
Nova Petropolis

Iguaçu Falls

Cáceres
Chapada dos...
Guimarães
São Lourenço River
The Pantanal
Goias
Brasilia
Goiania
Caldas Novas
Corumbá
Campo Grande

N

PARAGUAY
ARGENTINA
URUGUAY

ATLANTIC OCEAN

States Of Brazil

RORAIMA
AMAPÁ
PARÁ
AMAZONAS
MARANHÃO
PIAUÍ
CEARÁ
RIO GRANDE DO NORTE
PARAIBA
PERNAMBUCO
ALAGOAS
SERGIPE
BAHIA
ACRE
RONDÔNIA
MATO GROSSO
GOIÁS
Basília
MINAS GERAIS
ESPIRITO SANTO
RIO DE JANEIRO
MATO GROSSO DO SUL
SÃO PAULO
PARANÁ
SANTA CATARINA
RIO GRANDE DO SUL

Portugal

The Portuguese National Tourist Office can provide excellent information, brochures, and suggestions for helping you plan your trip in general. Casa de Portugal offices are located in New York at 590 Fifth Avenue, New York, NY 10036; in Toronto at 2180 Yonge Street, Toronto, Ontario M4S 2B9; and in London at New Bond Street House, 1-5 New Bond Street, London W1Y 0NP.

ABOUT THE PORTUGUESE LANGUAGE

Portuguese is a Romance language, along with French, Italian, Spanish, and Rumanian. These languages all have their origins in ancient Latin. The Iberian peninsula, which includes Spain and Portugal, was annexed by the Romans around 200 B.C. In later years, other conquerors or visitors such as the Greeks, Italians, French, and Arabs, also left their mark on the Portuguese language.

Today more than 100 million people speak Portuguese in various parts of the world: in Brazil, the fifth largest country in the world, and in Portugal, where the language is known as Luso Portuguese; also in Goa on the eastern coast of India, Macau on the southern China coast, Angola and Mozambique in Africa, the Azore Islands in the Atlantic Ocean, the Cabo Verde archipelago, and the islands of São Tomé and Príncipe. Even more surprising is that Portuguese is also commonly heard in certain parts of the United States, especially in areas of Massachusetts and Rhode Island. So you should be able to put this book to good use—not only abroad, but in the United States as well.

Portuguese explorers spread their language extensively during the 15th and 16th centuries and pockets of Portuguese speakers remain where the explorers landed. Christopher Columbus's historic voyage brought Spanish to the New World; Portuguese explorers soon followed. Portuguese eventually became the national language of Brazil, a country that accounts for about one-half of the size and population of South America. It is no wonder Brazilians are distressed when *norteamericanos* (nohr-chee-ah-meh-ree-KAH-noos), or North Americans, think Spanish is the language of Brazil instead of Portuguese. While Portuguese-speakers readily understand Spanish, Portuguese is not as easily understood by Spanish-speakers. In fact, its Slavic-sounding inflections and nasal sounds never fail to astonish anyone who is hearing Portuguese for the first time.

1

In the New World, Portuguese changed over the centuries, influenced by contact with the indigenous tongues. New words were borrowed or created for Native American things previously unknown to the colonists. Immigrants from other areas of Europe, as well as African slaves, further changed Brazilian Portuguese. Recently, English is also beginning to have a profound effect as contact increases between neighbors north and south. Some Portuguese words may already be familiar to you, e.g., *bossa nova*, *lambada*, *tanga*, and *carioca*. English words of Latin or Greek origin are often very similiar to Portuguese, especially in the written form. Consider Portuguese words like *aroma*, *hotel*, *perfume*, *professor*, *rádio*, *idéia*, *telefone*, which are either identical or similar enough to guess.

Portuguese varies slightly from country to country as well as within different parts of the same country. In Brazil, for example, there are often minor regional differences. The speech of Rio de Janeiro (whose inhabitants are called *cariocas*) is quite distinctive. Farther south, in São Paulo, and in the north, there are still other linguistic variations, but the language remains basically the same everywhere. Differences between Brazilian and Luso Portuguese (the Portuguese spoken in Portugal) in pronunciation, vocabulary, and grammar are probably no greater than those between British and American English. Happily, Portuguese follows the same general grammatical patterns everywhere, thanks to the efforts of academicians in Portugal and Brazil to maintain standards so that regional differences do not interfere with communication. At the time of this writing, a small number of differences in accents and spelling are still evolving in both Brazil and Portugal. However, these changes are minor and will not affect your ability to speak, understand, or be understood.

THE LANGUAGE OF THIS BOOK

As we mentioned, this book is based on Brazilian Portuguese and features the pronunciation of São Paulo, Brazil's largest city. However, significant variations from Brazilian vocabulary that are used in Portugal are indicated with a (P).

A GUIDE TO PRONUNCIATION

Each English word or phrase in this book is presented with its Portuguese translation and an easy-to-follow phonetic transcription that indicates the correct pronunciation. Simply read and pronounce the transcription as you would read English, and you will be speaking comprehensible Portuguese. However, some Portuguese sounds simply do not exist in English, so the transcriptions are only an approximate guide. To improve your pronunciation further, use the accompanying audio-cassette. It follows this text closely and gives you the opportunity to listen to and imitate native speakers like those you might encounter during your travels. Don't be afraid to practice your Portuguese with them; some may want to practice their English, but most will be flattered by your attempts to learn their language and will gladly help you.

ENGLISH-PORTUGUESE PRONUNCIATION CHART

The chart below is your guide to the transcriptions used in this book. Study it to see how Portuguese sounds are pronounced. With practice you will soon be able to follow the phonetics without having to consult this chart. Here are some general pronunciation guidelines:

1. Portuguese spelling is more consistent than English; once you learn the sounds, it will be easy to pronounce a word correctly just by reading it.
2. Pay special attention to vowels and vowel combinations. They are important to overall pronunciation of words and are crucial to making yourself understood.
3. Portuguese uses several nasal sounds, made by allowing air to escape through the nose as well as the mouth. Vowels are often nasalized before /m/ or /n/, as in *tem* or *homens*. This is also true of vowels written with a tilde (˜) above them, such as *vão*, *lições*, etc.
4. Word stress is indicated throughout the book by showing the stressed syllable in capital letters; for example, *turista* (too-REES-tah).

3

5. In Brazil, initial /r/ and double /rr/ are usually pronounced like English /h/, whereas in Portugal (and in some regions of Brazil bordering Spanish-speaking areas) they are trilled, as in Spanish.

6. In Brazil, /e/ and /o/ at the end of words are pronounced as /ee/ and /oo/, respectively. Examples: *breve* (BREH-vee) and *foto* (FOH-too). In Portugal (and some regions of Brazil), final /s/ is normally pronounced like /sh/, further distinguishing Luso-Portuguese from Brazilian speech in São Paulo.

Vowels

Portuguese Spelling	Approximate Sound in English	Phonetic Symbol	Example (Phonetic Transcription)
a	father	ah	casa (KAH-zah)
e	say	ay	chego (SHAY-goo)
also	met	eh	perto (PEHR-too)
i	beet	ee	lido (LEE-doo)
o	both	oh	foto (FOH-too)
u	booth	oo	uma (OO-mah)

Vowel Combinations

Diphthongs A diphthong is a double vowel combination that produces a single sound. Here is a list of frequent diphthongs and their pronunciation:

ai	ripe	ahy	pai (pahy)
au	now	ow	auto (OW-too)
ei	may	ay	cadeira (kah-DAY-rah)
eu		ay-oo	deu (DAY-oo)
ia	yacht	yah	diálogo (JYAH-loh-goo)
ie	yet	yeh	piedade (pyeh-DAH-jee)
io	Yolanda	yoh	Yolanda (yoh-LAHN-dah)

4

iu	y**ou**	ee-oo	**viu** (VEE-oo)
oi	soy sauce	oy	**noite** (NOY-chee)
ou	low	oh	**outro** (OH-troo)
ua	w**a**tch	wah	**água** (AH-gwah)
ue	w**e**t	weh	**suéter** (SWEH-tehr)
ui	w**e**	wee	**cuidar** (kwee-DAHR)
uo	qu**o**ta	woh	**quota** (KWOH-tah)

Consonants

Portuguese Spelling	Approximate Sound in English	Example (Phonetic Transcription)
b	similar to English	
c (before e/i)	s as in save	**cinema** (see-NAY-mah)
(before a/o/u)	k as in key	**casa** (KAH-zah)
ç (before a/o/u)	s as in save	**moço** (MOH-soo)
ch	sh as in shampoo	**chuva** (SHOO-vah)
d	similar to English, except before e and i, where it is usually pronounced like j	**morde** (MORH-jee) **aprendido** (ah-prehn-JEE-doo)
f	similar to English	
g (before a/o/u)	hard g as in go	**gato** (GAH-too)
(before e/i)	soft g as in measure	**geral** (zheh-ROW)
h	always silent, but like y when following n	**senhor** (sehn-YOHR)
j	s as in pleasure	**José** (zhoh-ZEH)
l	same as English, except in final positions, like u	**animal** (ah-nee-MOW)
lh	y as in yes	**filho** (FEEL-yoo)
m	like English, but more nasal	
n	similar to English	
nh	ny as in canyon	**senhor** (sehn-YOHR)
qu (before a/o)	qu as in quote	**quota** (KWOH-tah)

5

qu (before e/i)	k as in kite	**queixa** (KAY-shah)
r and rr	a breathy h as in hot in initial and mid-positions	**rosa** (<u>H</u>O-za)
		carro (KAH-<u>h</u>oo)
r	a breathy h in final positions; also sometimes trilled	**cantar** (kahn-TA<u>H</u>)
s	z as in zebra	**rosa** (HOH-<u>z</u>ah)
ss	s as in some	**passo** (PAH-soo)
t	similar to English, but often like ch before e and i	**noite** (NOY-<u>ch</u>ee)
		gentil (zhehn-<u>CH</u>EE-oo)
v	similar to English	
x	sh as in sheet; or	**caixa** (KAHY-<u>sh</u>ah)
	s as in see; or	**máximo** (MAH-<u>see</u>-moo)
	x as in wax	**táxi** (TAH<u>K</u>-see)
z	z as in zeal	**zebra** (<u>Z</u>E<u>H</u>-brah)

6

1. USEFUL EXPRESSIONS

GREETINGS AND GOOD-BYES

Good morning.	**Bom dia.**	bohn JEE-ah
Good afternoon.	**Boa tarde.**	BOH-ah TAHR-jee
Good evening.	**Boa noite.**	BOH-ah NOY-chee
Good night.	**Boa noite.**	BOH-ah NOY-chee
So long.	**Até logo.**	ah-TEH LOH-goo
See you soon.	**Até breve.**	ah-TEH BREH-vee
See you later.	**Até a vista.**	ah-TEH ah VEES-tah
	Até mais tarde.	ah-TEH mahys TAHR-jee
See you tomorrow.	**Até amanhã.**	ah-TEH ah-mahn-YOWN
Good-bye/Bye.	**Adeus!**	ah-DAY-oos!
	Tchau!	chow!
	Tchauzinho!	chow-ZEEN-yoo!

COURTESY

Please.	**Por favor./Faça favor.**	poor fah-VOHR/FAH-sah fah-VOHR
Thank you.	**Obrigado(-a).***	oh-bree-GAH-doo(-dah)*
You're welcome.	**De nada.**	jee NAH-dah
Excuse me (apology).	**Desculpe/Perdão.**	dehs-KOOL-pee/pehr-DOWN
Excuse me (request for permission).	**Com licença.**	kohn lee-SEHN-sah
It doesn't matter.	**Não importa.**	nown eem-POHR-tah

*In Portuguese, adjectives agree in gender and number with the nouns they modify. *Obrigado*, literally "(I am) obliged," agrees with the gender of the speaker. Thus, a male speaker would say, "Obrigado," and a female speaker would say, "Obrigada." Female endings appear in parentheses throughout this book.

APPROACHING SOMEONE FOR HELP

Excuse me . . .	**Desculpe-me. . .**	dehs-KOOL-pee mee . . .
• Sir.	• **senhor.**	• sehn-YOHR
• Madam.	• **senhora.**	• sehn-YOH-rah

• Miss/Ms.	• **senhorita.**	• sehn-yoh-REE-tah
	• **menina. (P)**	• meh-NEE-nah
Do you speak English?	**Fala inglês?**	FAH-lah een-GLAYS?
Do you understand?	**Você com-preende?**	voh-SAY kohm-pree-EHN-jee?
Do you understand English?	**Entende inglês?**	ehn-TEHN-jee een-GLAYS?
Yes./No.	**Sim./Não.**	seen/nown
I'm sorry.	**Sinto muito.**	SEEN-too MWEE-too
I don't speak Portuguese.	**Não falo portu-guês.**	nown FAH-loo pohr-too-GAYS
I don't understand.	**Não entendo.**	nown ehn-TEHN-doo
I understand a little.	**Compreendo um pouco.**	kohm-pree-EHN-doo oon POH-koo
I speak very little Portuguese.	**Falo pouquinho de português.**	FAH-loo poh-KEEN-yoo jee pohr-too-GAYS
Please speak slowly.	**Por favor, fale devagar.**	poor fah-VOHR, FAH-lee jee-vah-GAHR
Please repeat that.	**Por favor, repita isso.**	poor fah-VOHR, hay-PEE-tah EE-soo
May I ask a question?	**Uma pergunta, por favor.**	OO-mah pehr-GOON-tah, poor fah-VOHR
Can you help me?	**Pode me ajudar?**	POH-jee mee ah-zhoo-DAHR?
What does that mean?	**O que significa isso?**	oo keh seeg-nee-FEE-kah EE-soo?
How do you say that in Portuguese?	**Como se diz isso em português?**	KOH-moo see deez EE-soo ehn pohr-too-GAYS?
Can you translate?	**Pode traduzir?**	POH-jee trah-doo-ZEER?
Can you write it down?	**Pode escrevê-lo?**	POH-jee ehs-kray-VAY-loo?
Okay./Agreed.	**De acordo.**	jee ah-KOHR-doo
Of course.	**Pois não.**	poys nown

IDENTIFYING YOURSELF

I'm a tourist.	**Sou turista.**	soh too-REES-tah
We're tourists.	**Somos turistas.**	SOH-moos too-REES-tahs

8

I'm not from here.	**Não sou daqui.**	nown soh dah-KEE
I'm from the U.S.	**Sou dos Estados Unidos.**	soh doos ehs-TAH-doos oo-NEE-doos
I'm from . . .	**Sou de . . .**	soh jee . . .
• New York.	• **Nova Iorque.**	• NOH-vah YOHR-kee
• Philadelphia.	• **Filadélfia.**	• fee-lah-DEHL-fyah
• Chicago.	• **Chicago.**	• shee-KAH-goo
• California.	• **Califórnia.**	• kah-lee-FOHR-nyah
I'm American/North American.	**Sou americano (-a)/norte-americano(-a).**	soh ah-meh-ree-KAH-noo (-nah)/NOHR-chee-ah-meh-ree-KAH-noo(-nah)
We're Americans.	**Somos americanos.***	SOH-moos ah-meh-ree-KAH-noos(-nahs)

* Although there are some exceptions, most nouns and adjectives end in -o for male speakers, -a for females, with the corresponding plurals: -os, -as. Use -os when including both males and females.

QUESTION WORDS

Who?	**Quem?**	kehn?
What?/Which?	**(O) que?**	(oo) keh?
Which?/What?/ Whom?	**(O) qual?**	kwow?
Why?	**Porque?**	poor keh?
When?	**Quando?**	KWAHN-doo?
Where?	**Onde?**	OHN-jee?
Where from?	**De onde?**	jee OHN-jee?
Where to?	**Aonde?**	ah-OHN-jee?
How?	**Como?**	KOH-moo?
How much?	**Quanto?**	KWAHN-too?

CARDINAL NUMBERS

0	**zero**	ZEHR-oo
1	**um/uma**	oon/OO-mah
2	**dois/duas**	doys/DOO-ahs
3	**três**	trays
4	**quatro**	KWAH-troo
5	**cinco**	SEEN-koo
6	**seis**	says

7	**sete**	SEH-chee
8	**oito**	OY-too
9	**nove**	NOH-vee
10	**dez**	days
11	**onze**	OHN-zee
12	**doze**	DOH-zee
13	**treze**	TRAY-zee
14	**catorze**	kah-TOHR-zee
15	**quinze**	KEEN-zee
16	**dezesseis**	deh-zee-SAYS
17	**dezessete**	deh-zee-SEH-chee
18	**dezoito**	dehz-OY-too
19	**dezenove**	deh-zee-NOH-vee
20	**vinte**	VEEN-chee
21	**vinte e um/uma**	VEEN-chee ee oon/ OO-mah
22	**vinte e dois/ duas**	VEEN-chee ee doys/ DOO-ahs
23	**vinte e três**	VEEN-chee ee trays
30	**trinta**	TREEN-tah
40	**quarenta**	kwah-REHN-tah
50	**cinqüenta**	seen-KWEHN-tah
60	**sessenta**	seh-SEHN-tah
70	**setenta**	seh-TEHN-tah
80	**oitenta**	oy-TEHN-tah
90	**noventa**	noh-VEHN-tah
100	**cem**	sehn
101	**cento e um/uma**	SEHN-too ee oon/OO-mah
102	**cento e dois/ duas**	SEHN-too ee doys/ DOO-ahs
110	**cento e dez**	SEHN-too ee days
120	**cento e vinte**	SEHN-too ee VEEN-chee
200	**duzentos(-as)**	doo-ZEHN-toos(-tahs)
300	**trezentos(-as)**	tray-ZEHN-toos(-tahs)
400	**quatrocentos(-as)**	kwah-troo-SEHN-toos (-tahs)
500	**quinhentos(-as)**	keen-YEHN-toos(-tahs)
600	**seiscentos(-as)**	says-SEHN-toos(-tahs)
700	**setecentos(-as)**	seh-chee-SEHN-toos (-tahs)

800	**oitocentos(-as)**	oy-too-SEHN-toos(-tahs)
900	**novecentos(-as)**	noh-vee-SEHN-toos (-tahs)
1,000	**mil**	MEE-oo
2,000	**dois mil**	doys MEE-oo
3,000	**três mil**	trays MEE-oo
10,000	**dez mil**	days MEE-oo
1,000,000	**um milhão (de)**	oon meel-YOWN (jee)
2,000,000	**dois milhões (de)**	doys meel-YOWN-ees (jee)

Ordinal Numbers

first	**primeiro(-a)**	pree-MAY-roo(-rah)
second	**segundo(-a)**	seh-GOON-doo(-dah)
third	**terceiro(-a)**	tehr-SAY roo(-rah)
fourth	**quarto(-a)**	KWAHR-too(-tah)
fifth	**quinto(-a)**	KEEN-too(-tah)
sixth	**sexto(-a)**	SEHKS-too(-tah)
seventh	**sétimo(-a)**	SEH-chee-moo(-mah)
eighth	**oitavo(-a)**	oy-TAH-voo(-vah)
ninth	**nono(-a)**	NOH-noo(-nah)
tenth	**décimo(-a)**	DEH-see-moo(-mah)
eleventh	**décimo-primeiro(-a)**	DEH-see-moo-pree-MAY-roo(-rah)

QUANTITIES

half (of)	**meio(-a)**	MAY-oo(-ah)
half a pound	**meia libra**	MAY-ah LEE-brah
half a kilogram	**meio kilo**	MAY-oo KEE-loo
half an hour	**meia hora**	MAY-ah OH-rah
a quarter	**um quarto**	oon KWAHR-too
a third	**um terço**	oon TEHR-soo
a dozen	**uma dúzia**	OO-mah DOO-zee-ah
	uma duzena (P)	OO-mah doo-ZEH-nah
half a dozen	**méia dúzia**	MAY-ah DOO-żee-ah
ten percent	**dez por cento**	days poor SEHN-too
5.6%	**5,6 por centro**	SEEN-koo VEER-goh-lah says poor SEHN-too
once	**uma vez**	OO-mah vehz

11

twice	**duas vezes**	DOO-ahs VEH-zeez
the last time	**a última vez**	ah OOL-chee-mah vehz
a lot of, many	**muito, muitos (-as)**	MWEE-too, MWEE-toos(-tahs)
few, a few	**pouco, poucos (-as)**	POH-koo, POH-kohs (-kahs)
some	**algum, algumas**	ahl-GOON, ahl-GOO-mahs
enough	**bastante**	bahs-TAHN-chee
a pair of	**um par de**	oon pahr jee

ABOUT THE CURRENCY

Brazilian currency is known as the *cruzeiro* (kroo-ZAY-roo), abbreviated as *Cr$*. Brazil's currency continues to undergo serious devaluation due to inflation in recent years (e.g., 366% in 1987 alone), so you may also find *cruzados* and *cruzados novos*—former units of currency—still in circulation. Exchange rates, both *oficial* (official) and *paralelo* (parallel or "black market") are published daily in major newspapers under *cotação* (exchange rate). Banks and hotels pay the official rate, whereas *cambios* (exchanges) and stores pay slightly better rates.

In the Brazilian system of numerical notation, note that the role and position of the comma and period are exactly the opposite of the American system; therefore, something marked Cr$ 1.600,00 means Cr$ 1,600.00. Be careful not to be overcharged or shortchanged because of confusion.

Portugal's unit of currency is the *escudo* (ehsh-KOO-doh), with 100 *centavos* in each. The symbol for the *escudo* is $, written between the *escudo* and the *centavo* units—thus 100$50. Best exchange rates are usually obtained at banks; however, exchange offices often have more convenient schedules and generally take less time and paperwork. Remember to take your passport along when exchanging money. Some hotels also change money, but usually at a less favorable rate. In any case, it's a good idea to exchange some money before you leave the airport.

12

CREDIT CARDS AND TRAVELER'S CHECKS

Most major credit cards are accepted in Brazil and Portugal. All credit cards bill you back home in dollars at the official exchange rate on the day of the bank transaction. If the dollar is gaining over the *cruzeiro* or *escudo,* you will end up paying less; however, if the opposite is true, you will pay more. In Brazil, dollars can be changed at the "parallel" (see **Currency**, above) exchange up to 35% higher than the official rate, and this is perfectly legal.

Aside from credit cards, the best way to safeguard funds is to use traveler's checks. Normally you will receive slightly less when exchanging them than you would for cash. To exchange traveler's checks, you must present a passport and sign checks in the presence of the clerk. Outside of major cities in Brazil, it is sometimes more difficult to exchange checks than cash.

CHANGING MONEY

I'd like to change . . .	**Gostaria de trocar . . .**	gohs-tah-REE-ah jee troh-KAHR . . .
• some money.	• **algum dinheiro.**	• ahl-GOON jeen-YAY-roo
• some dollars.	• **dólares.**	• DOH-lah-rees
• this check.	• **este cheque.**	• EHS-chee SHEH-kee
• traveler's checks.	• **cheques de viagem.**	• SHEH-kees jee VYAH-zhehn
Do you accept . . .	**Aceita . . .**	ah-SAY-tah . . .
• personal checks?	• **cheques pessoais?**	• SHEH-kees peh-soh-AHYS?
• a bank draft?	• **um giro bancário?**	oon ZHEE-roo bahn-KAH-ryoo?
• a money order?	• **uma ordem de pagamento?**	• OO-mah OHR-dehn jee pah-gah-MEHN-too?
How much is the . . . worth?	**Quanto vale . . .**	KWAHN-too VAH-lee . . .
• dollar	• **o dólar?**	• oo DOH-lahr?
• cruzeiro	• **o cruzeiro?**	• oo kroo-ZAY-roo?
• escudo (P)	• **o escudo?**	• oh ehsh-KOO-doh?

13

Do you need . . .	**Precisa . . .**	pray-SEE-zah . . .
• my identification?	• **da minha iden-tificação?**	• dah MEEN-yah ee-dehn-tee-fee-kah-SOWN?
• my passport?	• **do meu passa-porte?**	• doo MAY-oo pah-sah-POHR-chee?
• other documents?	• **de outros docu-mentos?**	• jee OH-troos doh-koo-MEHN-toos?
Where do I sign?	**Onde assino?**	OHN-jee ah-SEE-noo?
May I have . . .	**Poderia me dar . . .**	poh-deh-REE-ah mee dahr . . .
• small bills?	• **notas miúdas?**	• NOH-tahs mee-OO-dahs?
• large bills?	• **notas grandes?**	• NOH-tahs GRAHN-jees?
• some large and small bills?	• **umas notas grandes e umas miúdas?**	• OO-mahs NOH-tahs GRAHN-jees ee OO-mahs mee-OO-dahs?
• some coins?	• **algumas moe-das?**	• ahl-GOO-mahs moh-EH-dahs?
• the change in coins?	• **o troco em moedas?**	oo TROH-koo ehn moh-EH-dahs?

TIPPING AND SERVICE CHARGES

In better restaurants in Brazil and Portugal, it is common to find service charges amounting to about 10–15% added to the bill. A tip (*uma gorjeta*/OO-mah gohr-ZHEH-tah) may be added to the service charge in accordance with the quality of the service provided. When no service charge is added to the bill, leave a 15% tip in better restaurants. In more ordinary restaurants and in smaller towns, a 10% tip is usually adequate.

Tips are given also for a variety of other services. The following chart will serve as a guide, but you may adjust amounts in accordance with the service provided, the place, and the size of the town.

Service	Brazil	Portugal
Waiter	15% & small change	15% & small change

14

Bellboy/porter	25–50¢/suitcase*	100–200 Es/ suitcase
Chambermaid	25–50¢/day*	500 Es/day
Taxi driver	10%	optional; 5–10%
Guide	$3/day*	$6/full day for 2
Barber/hairdresser	10–20%	100–200 Es
Shoeshine	small change	small change
Restroom attendant	small change	small change

*Because the exchange rates are constantly fluctuating in Brazil, the chart lists some tips in U.S. dollars.

PAYING THE BILL

The check, please?	**A conta, por favor?**	ah KOHN-tah, poor fah-VOHR?
Only one check, please.	**Um só cheque, por favor.**	oon soh SHEH-kee, poor fah-VOHR
Please give us separate checks.	**Por favor, dê-nos cheques separados.**	poor fah-VOHR, DAY-noos SHEH-kees seh-pah-RAH-doos
Is service included?	**Está incluido o serviço?**	ehs-TAH een-kloo-EE-doo oo sehr-VEE-soo?
I think there's a mistake.	**Acho que tem um erro.**	AH-shoo keh tehn oon EH-hoo
Do you accept . . .	**Aceita . . .**	ah-SAY-tah . . .
• credit cards?	• **cartões de crédito?**	• kahr-TOWN-ees jee KREH-jee-too?
• traveler's checks?	• **cheques de viagem?**	• SHEH-kees jee VYAH-zhehn?
• dollars?	• **dólares?**	• DOH-lah-rees?
This is for you.	**Isto é para o senhor (a senhora).**	EES-too eh PAH-rah oo sehn-YOHR (ah sehn-YOH-rah)
Keep the change.	**Guarde o troco.**	GWAHR-jee oo TROH-koo

15

TIME AND TIME EXPRESSIONS

Telling Time

What time is it?	**Que horas são?**	keh OH-rahs sown?
At what time?	**A que horas?**	ah keh OH-rahs?
It's . . .	**É . . .**	eh . . .
• noon.	• **meio-dia.**	• MAY-oo-jee-ah
• midnight.	• **meia-noite.**	• may-ah-NOY-chee
• one o'clock.	• **uma hora.**	• OO-mah OH-rah
• 1:15	• **uma e quinze.**	• OO-mah ee KEEN-zee
• 1:30.	• **uma e meia.**	• OO-mah ee MAY-ah
• 1:45.	• **uma e quarenta e cinco.**	• OO-mah ee kwah-REHN-tah ee SEEN-koo
It's . . .	**São . . .**	sown . . .
• two o'clock.	• **duas (horas).**	• DOO-ahs (OH-rahs)
• two o'clock in the morning.	• **duas da manhã.**	• DOO-ahs dah mahn-YOWN
• two o'clock in the afternoon.	• **duas da tarde.**	• DOO-ahs dah TAHR-jee
• eight o'clock at night.	• **oito da noite.**	• OY-too dah NOY-chee
• nearly ten.	• **quase dez.**	• KWAH-zee days
• almost eleven.	• **quase onze.**	• KWAY-zee OHN-zee

Time Expressions

now	**agora**	ah-GOH-rah
on time	**(está) na hora**	ehs-TAH nah OH-rah
earlier	**mais cedo**	mahys SAY-doo
later	**mais tarde**	mahys TAHR-jee
before 10:30	**antes das dez e trinta**	AHN-chees dahs dehz ee TREEN-tah
after 8:00	**depois das oito**	jee-POYS dahs OY-too
since 9:00	**desde as nove**	DEHZ-jee ahs NOH-vee
soon	**logo**	LOH-goo
five minutes ago	**há cinco minutos atrás**	ah SEEN-koo mee-NOO-toos ah-TRAHS

16

in five seconds	**em cinco segundos**	ehn SEEN-koo seh-GOON-doos
morning	**amanhã**	ah-mahn-YOWN
afternoon	**tarde**	TAHR-jee
night	**noite**	NOY-chee
midnight	**meianoite**	may-ah-NOY-chee
this morning	**esta manhã**	EHS-tah mahn-YOWN
tomorrow morning	**amanhã de manhã**	ah-mahn-YOWN jee mahn-YOWN
the day after tomorrow	**depois da manhã**	jee-POYS dah mahn-YOWN
yesterday	**ontem**	OHN-tehn
yesterday morning	**ontem de manhã**	OHN-tehn jee mahn-YOWN
the day before yesterday	**ante ontem**	ahn-chee-OHN-tehn
in a week	**numa semana**	NOO-mah say-MAH-nah
next week	**a semana que vem**	ah say-MAH-nah keh vehn
last week	**a semana passada**	ah say-MAH-nah pah-SAH-dah
next month	**o mês seguinte**	oo mays say-GEEN-chee
last month	**o mês passado**	oo mays pah-SAH-doo
all year	**o ano todo**	oo AH-noo TOH-doo
last year	**o ano passado**	oo AH-noo pah-SAH-doo

THE 24-HOUR CLOCK

In normal conversation, Portuguese speakers generally express time using a 12-hour clock, as we do, but for official listings, like transportation schedules, business hours, and theater times, the 24-hour system (our ''military time'') is used. After 12 noon, just keep counting: 1:00 P.M. becomes 12 plus 1 = 13.00, or *treze horas;* 12 midnight becomes 24.00, or *vinte e quatro horas*. Once you pass 12 noon, you can convert official time back to the 12-hour system by subtracting 12. A typical evening show time, 8:30 P.M., would be 20.30, *vinte e meia*. Note that in place of the colon, a decimal point is used. Use this chart for quick reference:

Official Time Chart

1 A.M.	01.00	**uma hora**	OO-mah Oh-rah
2 A.M.	02.00	**duas horas**	DOO-ahs OH-rahs
3 A.M.	03.00	**três horas**	trays OH-rahs
4 A.M.	04.00	**quatro horas**	KWAH-troo OH-rahs
5 A.M.	05.00	**cinco horas**	SEEN-koo OH-rahs
6 A.M.	06.00	**seis horas**	says OH-rahs
7 A.M.	07.00	**sete horas**	SEH-chee OH-rahs
8 A.M.	08.00	**oito horas**	OY-too OH-rahs
9 A.M.	09.00	**nove horas**	NOH-vee OH-rahs
10 A.M.	10.00	**dez horas**	days OH-rahs
11 A.M.	11.00	**onze horas**	OHN-zee OH-rahs
12 noon	12.00	**doze horas**	DOH-zee OH-rahs
1 P.M.	13.00	**treze horas**	TREH-zee OH-rahs
2 P.M.	14.00	**catorze horas**	kah-TOHR-zee OH-rahs
3 P.M.	15.00	**quinze horas**	KEEN-zee OH-rahs
4 P.M.	16.00	**dezesseis horas**	day-zee-SAYS OH-rahs
5 P.M.	17.00	**dezessete horas**	day-zee-SEH-chee OH-rahs
6 P.M.	18.00	**dezoito horas**	days-OY-too OH-rahs
7 P.M.	19.00	**dezenove horas**	day-zee-NOH-vee OH-rahs
8 P.M.	20.00	**vinte horas**	VEEN-chee OH-rahs
9 P.M.	21.00	**vinte e uma horas**	VEEN-chee ee OO-mah OH-rahs
10 P.M.	22.00	**vinte e duas horas**	VEEN-chee ee DOO-ahs OH-rahs
11 P.M.	23.00	**vinte e três horas**	VEEN-chee ee trays OH-rahs
12 midnight	24.00	**vinte e quatro horas (also: meia-noite)**	VEEN-chee ee KWAH-troo OH-rahs MAY-yah NOY-chee

18

2. AT THE AIRPORT

WELCOME

Benvindos ao Brasil! Welcome to Brazil . . . and Portugal! Going through customs at airports in Brazil and Portugal should pose no problems. In general, visitors from abroad may bring duty-free items for personal use into Brazil without declaring them in customs. In addition to clothing and jewelry, this applies to cameras, hair dryers, electric razors, and other electronic equipment. Other items require justification, and we advise registering such items with the Brazilian Consulate at home before you leave. Carry purchase receipts with you, especially if items are in their original packaging. You are also allowed to take in $300 worth of presents and up to $300 worth of any items bought elsewhere.

Likewise, when planning a trip to Portugal, you may bring most possessions for personal use, such as typewriters, cameras, movie cameras, video cameras, camping equipment, and sports equipment. If these items are expensive, it is wise, again, to keep their receipts with your personal documents as proof that you bought them at home.

Here's a typical dialogue you may hear at the airport:

DIALOGUE: PASSPORT CONTROL/IMMIGRATION (*O CONTROLE DE PASSAPORTES*)

Empregado de imigração:	**Bom dia. Posso ver o seu passa-porte?**	bohn JEE-ah. POH-soo vehr oo SAY-oo pah-sah-POHR-chee?
Turista:	**Sim, aqui está.**	seen, ah-KEE ehs-TAH.
Empregado:	**O senhor (A senhora) é norte-americano(-a)?**	oo sehn-YOHR eh nohr-chee-ah-meh-ree-KAH-noo?
Turista:	**Sou, sim.**	soh, seen.
Empregado:	**Quanto tempo vai ficar no país?**	KWAHN-too TEHM-poo vahy fee-KAHR noh pah-EES?

19

Turista:	Vou ficar aqui por três semanas.	voh fee-KAHR ah-KEE poor trays say-MAH-nahs.

. . . .

Officer	Hello. Can I see your passport, please?
Tourist:	Yes, here it is.
Officer:	Are you North American?
Tourist:	Yes, I am.
Officer:	How long will you stay in the country?
Tourist:	I'll be here for three weeks.

IMMIGRATION AND CUSTOMS

What is your nationality?	**Qual é a sua nacionalidade?**	kwow eh ah SOO-ah nah-syoh-nah-lee-DAH-jee?
I'm . . .	**Sou . . .**	soh . . .
• American.	• **norte-americano(-a).**	• nohr-chee-ah-meh-ree-KAH-noo(-nah)
• Canadian.	• **canadense.** **canadiano(-a). (P)**	• kah-nah-DEHN-see kah-nah-DYAH-noh (-nah)
• English.	• **inglês(-a).**	• een-GLAYS(-ah)
What's your name?	**Qual é o seu nome?**	kwow eh oo SAY-oo NOH-mee?
My name is . . .	**O meu nome é . . .**	oo MAY-oo NOH-mee eh
Where will you be staying?	**Onde vai ficar?**	OHN-jee vahy fee-KAHR?
I am staying at the Rex hotel.	**Vou ficar no ho-tel Rex.**	voh fee-KAHR noo oh-TAY-oo hehks
Are you on vacation?	**Está de férias?**	ehs-TAH jee FEH-ryahs?
I'm just passing through.	**Estou só de pas-sagem.**	ehs-TOH soh jee pah-SAH-zhehn
I'm here on a business trip.	**Estou aqui em viagem de ne-gócios.**	ehs-TOH ah-KEE ehn VYAH-zhehn jee neh-GOH-syoos

20

I'll be here for . . .	**Vou ficar por . . .**	voh fee-KAHR poor . . .
• a few days.	**• uns dias.**	• oons JEE-ahs
• a week.	**• uma semana.**	• OO-mah say-MAY-nah
• several weeks.	**• algumas sema-nas.**	• ahl-GOO-mahs say-MAH-nahs
• a month.	**• um mês.**	• oon mays
Do you have anything to declare?	**Tem alguma coisa para declarar?**	tehn ahl-GOO-mah KOY-zah PAH-rah deh-klahr-AHR?
I have nothing to declare.	**Não tenho nada para declarar.**	nown TEHN-yoo NAH-dah PAH-rah deh-klahr-AHR
Can you open your bag?	**Pode abrir a sua mala?**	POH-jee ah-BREER ah SOO-ah MAH-lah?
Of course.	**Pois não.**	poys nown
What are these?	**O que são istos?**	oo keh sown EES-toos?
They're . . .	**São . . .**	sown . . .
• personal items.	**• objetos pes-soais.**	• oh-bee-ZHEH-toos peh-soh-AHYS
• gifts.	**• presentes.**	• pray-SEHN-chees
Do I have to pay duty?	**Devo pagar alguma taxa?**	DEH-voo pah-GAHR ahl-GOO-mah TAH-shah?
Yes./No.	**Sim./Não.**	seen/nown
Have a nice stay!	**Boa estadia!**	BOH-ah ehs-tah-JEE-ah!

LUGGAGE AND PORTERS

I need . . .	**Preciso de . . .**	pray-SEE-zoo jee . . .
• a porter.	**• um carregador.**	• oon kah-hay-gah-DOHR
• a baggage cart.	**• um carrinho para as malas.**	• oon kah-HEEN-yoo PAH-rah ahs MAH-lahs
Here is my luggage.	**Aqui estão as minhas malas.**	ah-KEE ehs-TOWN ahs MEEN-yahs MAH-lahs.
Take the bags . . .	**Leve as malas . . .**	LAY-vee ahs MAH-lahs . . .
• to the taxi.	**• para o taxi.**	• PAH-rah oo TAHK-see

21

• to the bus.	• ao ônibus. ao autocarro (P).	• ow OH-nee-boos ow ow-toh-KAH-rroh
• to the sidewalk. Please be careful!	• à calçada. Tehna cuidado, por favor!	• ah kahl-SAH-dah TEHN-ya kwee-DAH-doo, poor fah-VOHR!
How much is it?	Quanto custa?	KWAHN-too KOOS-tah?

AIRPORT TRANSPORTATION AND SERVICES

When arriving in São Paulo, Brazil, you'll see many red-and-white taxis ready to take you downtown from the airport; these trips are usually quite inexpensive. In both Rio and São Paulo, you can also take regular metered cabs, which are quite reasonable within the center-city area. In Rio, vouchers are issued for airport taxis, with set prices based on your destination. You can also rent a car from one of the agencies.

Do you know where . . . is?	Sabe onde fica	SAH-bee OHN-jee FEE-kah . . .
• American	• American?	• oh-MEH-ree-kahn?
• Varig	• Varig?	• VAH-ree-gee?
• Cruzeiro do Sul	• Cruzeiro do Sul?	• kroo-ZAY-roo doo sool?
Where is . . .	Onde fica . . .	OHN-jee FEE-kah . . .
• an information booth?	• o balcão de in- formações?	• oo bahl-KOWN jee een-fohr-mah-SOWN-ees?
• the ticket counter?	• o balcão de passagens?	• oo bahl-KOWN jee pah-SAH-zhehns?
• the luggage check- in?	• o check-in da bagagem?	• oo SHEHK-een dah bah-GAH-zhehn?
• the place to pay the airport tax?	• o lugar para pagar a taxa de embarque?	• oo loo-GAHR PAH-rah pah-GAHR ah TAH-shah jee ehm-BAHR-kee?
• the lost baggage office?	• a seção de bagagem per- dida?	• ah seh-SOWN jee bah-GAH-zhehn pehr-DEE-dah?

22

• the duty-free shop?	• **o duty free?**	• oo DOO-tee free?
• the money exchange?	• **a casa de câmbio?**	• ah KAH-zah jee KAHM-byoo?
• a car rental agency?	• **a agência de alugar carros?**	• ah ah-ZEHN-syah jee ah-loo-GAHR KAH-hoos?
• the bus stop?	• **o ponto do ônibus?**	• oo POHN-too doo OH-nee-boos?
• the taxi stand?	• **o ponto de taxi?**	• oo POHN-too jee TAHK-see?

FLIGHT ARRANGEMENTS

Is there a direct flight to Brasilia?	**Tem um vôo direto para Brasilia?**	tehn oon VOH-oo jee-RAY-too PAH-rah brah-ZEE-lyah?
Do I have to change planes?	**Devo trocar de aviões?**	DEH-voo troh-KAHR jee ah-vee-OYN-ees?
How many stops are there?	**Quantas escalas faz?**	KWAHN-tahs ehs-KAH-lahs fahz?
Can I make a connection to Bahia?	**Posso fazer conexão para Bahia?**	POH-soo fah-ZEHR koh-nehk-SOWN PAH-rah bah-EE-ah?
When does it leave?	**A que horas parte?**	ah keh OH-rahs PAHR-chee?
What's the arrival time?	**A que horas chega?**	ah keh OH-rahs SHAY-gah?
Please give me . . .	**Por favor, me dê . . .**	poor fah-VOHR, mee DAY . . .
• a one-way ticket.	• **um bilhete só de ida.**	• oon beel-YEH-chee soh jee EE-dah
• a round-trip ticket.	• **um bilhete de ida e volta.**	• oon beel-YEH-chee jee EE-dah ee VOHL-tah
• a seat in first class.	• **um assento em primeira classe.**	• oon ah-SEHN-too ehn pree-MAY-rah KLAH-see
• a seat in tourist class.	• **um assento em classe turista.**	• oon ah-SEHN-too ehn KLAH-see too-REES-tah

23

English	Portuguese	Pronunciation
• a seat for non-smokers.	• um assento para não fumantes.	oon ah-SEHN-too PAH-rah nown foo-MAHN-chees
• a window seat.	• um assento na janela.	oon ah-SEHN-too nah zhah-NEH-lah
• an aisle seat.	• um assento no corredor.	oon ah-SEHN-too noo koh-hay-DOHR
What's my seat number?	Qual é o numero do meu assento?	kwow eh oo NOO-meh-roo doo MAY-oo ah-SEHN-too?
What's the flight number?	Qual é o numero do vôo?	kwow eh oo NOO-meh-roo doo VOH-oo?
What gate does it leave from?	De qual portão sai?	jee kwow pohr-TOWN sahy?
I'd like to . . . my reservation.	Gostaria de . . . a minha reserva.	gohs-tah-REE-ah jee . . . ah MEEN-yah hay-ZEHR-vah
• confirm	• confirmar	• kohn-feer-MAHR
• change	• trocar	• troh-KAHR
• cancel	• cancelar	• kahn-seh-LAHR

COMMON AIRPORT SIGNS AND TERMS

Portuguese	Pronunciation	English
linhas nacionais	LEEN-yahs nah-syoh-NAHYS	national airlines
linhas internacionais	LEEN-yahs een-tehr-nah-syoh-NAHYS	international airlines
vôos nacionais	VOH-oos nah-syoh-NAHYS	national flights
vôos internacionais	VOH-oos een-tehr-nah-syoh-NAHYS	international flights
vôo direto	VOH-oo jee-RAY-too	direct flight
vôo com escalas	VOH-oo kohn ehs-KAH-lahs	flight with stops
so ida	soh EE-dah	one-way flight
viagem de ida e volta	VYAH-zhehn jee EE-dah ee VOHL-tah	round trip

saidas	sah-EE-dahs	departures
chegadas	sheh-GAH-dahs	arrivals
primeira classe	pree-MAY-rah KLAH-see	first class
classe turista	KLAH-see too-REES-tah	tourist class
numero de vôo	NOO-meh-roo jee VOH-oo	flight number
portão de embarque	pohr-TOWN jee ehm-BAHR-kee	departure gate
numero de assento	NOO-meh-roo jee ah-SEHN-too	seat number
assento na janela	ah-SEHN-too nah zhah-NEH-lah	window seat
assento no corredor	ah-SEHN-too noo koh-heh-DOHR	aisle seat
seção de fumantes	seh-SOWN jee foo-MAHN-chees	smoking section
proibido fumar	proh-ee-BEE-doo foo-MAHR	no smoking
não fume	nown FOO-mee	no smoking
bagagem de mão	bah-GAH-zhehn jee mown	hand luggage
etiquetas	eh-tee-KEH-tahs	luggage tags

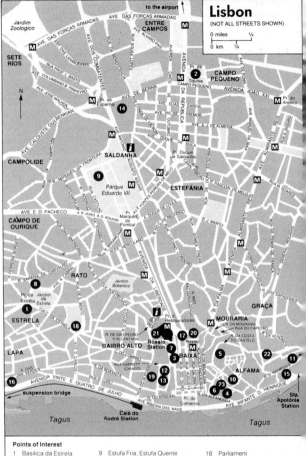

to the airport

Lisbon
(NOT ALL STREETS SHOWN)

0 miles   ¼
0 km   ¼

Jardim Zoologico

ENTRE CAMPOS

SETE RÍOS

Pr. de Touros
CAMPO PEQUENO

CAMPO PEQUENO

Pr. de Espanha

SALDANHA

CAMPOLIDE

Parque Eduardo VII

ESTEFÂNIA

CAMPO DE OURIQUE

Pr. Marquês de Pombal

Jardim Botânico

RATO

Pr. da Estrela
Jardim da Estrela

ESTRELA

Pr. dos Restauradores

GRAÇA

MOURARIA

LAPA

BAIRRO ALTO

Rossio Station

Rossio

BAIXA

ALFAMA

suspension bridge

Cais do Sodré Station

Pr. do Comércio

Sta. Apolónia Station

Tagus

Tagus

Points of Interest

1 Basílica da Estrela
2 Bullring
3 Carmo Elevator
4 Casa dos Bicos
5 Castelo de São Jorge
6 Conceição Velha
7 Convento do Carmo; Arqueológico
8 English Church and Cemetery
9 Estufa Fria; Estufa Quente
10 Fundação Ricardo Espírito Santo
11 Madre de Deus Tile Museum
12 Mártires Church
13 Museu de Arte Contemporanea
14 Museu C. Gulbenkian
15 Museu Militar
16 Museu Nacional de Arte Antiga
17 National Theater
18 Parliament
19 São Carlos Opera House
20 São Domingos
21 São Roque; Museu de Arte Religiosa
22 São Vicente
23 Sé (Cathedral)
ℹ️ Tourist Information
Ⓜ Metro Station

3. FINDING YOUR WAY

DIALOGUE: TAKING A TAXI (*TOMANDO UM TAXI*)

Turista:	**Está livre?**	ehs-TAH LEEV-ree?
Chofer:	**Sim, aonde o senhor (a senhora) vai?**	seen, ah-OHN-jee oo sehn-YOHR vahy?
Turista:	**Para o aeroporto.**	PAH-rah o ah-eh-roh-POHR-too.
Chofer:	**Bom.**	bohn.
Turista:	**Quanto tempo leva?**	KWAN-too TEHM-poo lay-vah?
Chofer:	**Uns vinte minutos.**	oons VEEN-chee mee-NOO-toos.
Turista:	**Está bem. Obrigado(-a).**	ehs-TAH behn. oh-bree-GAH-doo.

. . . .

Tourist:	Is this taxi free?
Driver:	Yes, where are you going?
Tourist:	To the airport.
Driver:	Fine.
Tourist:	How long does it take?
Driver:	About twenty minutes.
Tourist:	That's fine. Thank you.

Taxis are usually identified by a logo on the door or a light on top; sometimes they are distinguished by their color or special license plates. Taxis are normally found at airports near baggage claim areas, at hotels, and in other downtown areas. Some taxis charge by zones and display a map showing the fares by zone. Others use meters. In Brazil, the meters register "UT's" (taximeter units), which are keyed to a table that must be affixed to the left rear window. Pay the amount that corresponds to what appears on the meter plus any tip you wish to give.

27

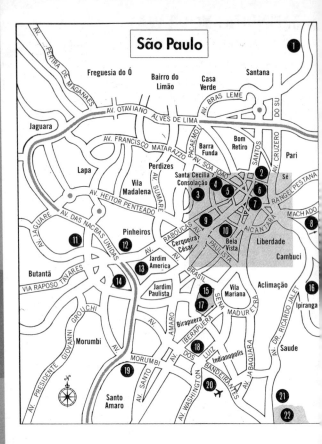

São Paulo

Freguesia do Ó

Bairro do Limão

Casa Verde

Santana

Jaguara

Barra Funda

Bom Retiro

Pari

Lapa

Perdizes

Santa Cecília Consolação

Sé

Vila Madalena

Jardim América

Pinheiros

Cerqueira César

Bela Vista

Liberdade

Cambuci

Butantã

Jardim Paulista

Vila Mariana

Aclimação

Ipiranga

Morumbi

Birapuera Iberapuera

Indianópolis

Saude

Santo Amaro

Don't be surprised if an additional fee is charged for driving you up steep hills, such as the Corcovado, although some Rio taxi drivers refuse to climb hills.

In Portugal, most taxis are black with green roofs. Drivers are skillful and know their way through the maze of twisting back streets. Best of all, fares are reasonable compared with other countries. Ask about any special charges for bags or supplemental fees after certain hours.

Is there a taxi stand nearby?	**Tem um ponto de taxis por aqui?**	tehn oon PON-too jee TAK-sees poor ah-KEE?
Please call me a taxi.	**Por favor, me chame um taxi.**	poor fah-VOHR, mee SHAH-mee oon TAHK-see
Is this taxi . . .	**Está . . .**	ehs-TAH . . .
• free?	• **livre?**	• LEEV-ree?
• occupied?	• **ocupado?**	• oh-koo-PAH-doo?
Please take me . . .	**Por favor, me leve . . .**	poor fah-VOHR, mee LEH-vee . . .
• to the hotel Rex.	• **ao hotel Rex.**	• ow oh-TAY-oo hehks
• to the station.	• **à estação.**	• ah ehs-tah-SOWN
• to the airport.	• **ao aeroporto.**	• ow ah-eh-roh-POHR-too
• to the main square.	• **à praça principal.**	• ah PRAH-sah preen-see-POW
• to the center.	• **ao centro.**	• ow SEHN-troo
• to . . . Street.	• **para a rua . . .**	• PAH-rah ah HOO-ah . . .
• to . . . Avenue.	• **para a avenida . . .**	• PAH-rah ah ah-veh-NEE-dah . . .
Please stop over there.	**Por favor, pare ali.**	poor fah-VOHR, PAH-ree ah-LEE
Do you know this address?	**Conhece este endereço?**	kohn-YEH-see EHS-chee ehn-deh-RAY-soo?
I'm in a hurry.	**Estou com pressa.**	ehs-TOH kohn PREH-sah
How long will it take?	**Quanto tempo vai levar?**	KWAHN-too TEHM-poo vahy lay-VAHR?
meter	**taximetro**	tahk-SEE-meh-troo
fare	**tarifa**	rah-REE-fah

29

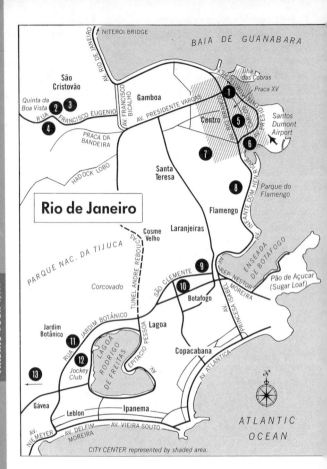

Rio de Janeiro

NITEROI BRIDGE

BAIA DE GUANABARA

Ilha
das Cobras

Praca XV

São
Cristovão

Gamboa

Santos
Dumont
Airport

Quinta da
Boa Vista

Centro

RUA FRANCISCO EUGENIO

PRACA DA
BANDEIRA

HADOCK LOBO

Santa
Teresa

Parque do
Flamengo

Flamengo

Laranjeiras

PARQUE NAC. DA TIJUCA

Cosme
Velho

Corcovado

ENSEADA
DE BOTAFOGO

Pão de Açúcar
(Sugar Loaf)

SÃO CLEMENTE

Botafogo

Jardim
Botânico

JARDIM BOTÂNICO

Lagoa

LAGOA
RODRIGO
DE FREITAS

Copacabana

Jockey
Club

Gávea

Leblon

Ipanema

AV. NIEMEYER

AV. DELFIM
MOREIRA

AV. VIEIRA SOUTO

AV. ATLANTICA

ATLANTIC
OCEAN

CITY CENTER represented by shaded area.

AV. RIO DE JANEIRO

AV. FRANCISCO BICALHO

AV. PRESIDENTE VARGAS

TUNEL ANDRE REBOUÇAS

EPITACIO PESSOA

AV. REP. NESTOR MOREIRA

AV. PRINCESA ISABEL

AV. INFANTE DOM HENRIQUE

| fixed rate | **tarifa fixa** | tah-REE-fah FEEK-sah |
| tip | **gorjeta** | gohr-ZHEH-tah |

BUSES

Bus transportation is available throughout most of Brazil, and a good network of highways connects major cities. However, you usually can't buy a direct ticket for a trip between two distant points; instead it's more common to buy a ticket from city to city along your route. On heavily traveled routes, service is frequent and inexpensive. For example, between Rio and São Paulo (6½ to 7 hours), there is a bus every half-hour all day long. For intra-urban transportation, taxis are convenient, or you may take comfortable air-conditioned buses. When you ride a bus within Rio, you must get on at the rear and leave at the front. Buses stop only if you pull the cord. Keep change handy, as drivers sometimes claim they don't have any. There are regularly marked bus stops. However, keep in mind that the metro (see below) from Botafogo to Zona Norte is the quickest way to get around downtown Rio.

In Portugal, city bus transportation is nationalized. There are several intercity bus lines. The best known system is called *Rodoviário Nacional*, which has various terminals in Lisbon and provides service throughout Portugal. Many tourist offices as well as hotels also offer bus trips.

Where's the . . .	**Onde fica . . .**	OHN-jee FEE-kah . . .
• the bus stop?	• **o ponto de ôni-bus?**	• oo POHN-too jee OH-nee-boos?
	a paragem de autocarro? (P)	ah pah-RAH-zhehn deh ow-toh-KAH-rroh?
• the bus station?	• **a estação de ônibus?**	• ah ehs-tah-SOWN jee OH-nee-boos?
What bus line goes . . .	**Qual linha vai . . .**	kwow LEEN-yah vahy . . .
• north?	• **ao norte?**	• ow NOHR-chee?
• south?	• **ao sul?**	• ow sool?
• east?	• **ao leste?**	• ow LEHS-chee?
• west?	• **ao oeste?**	• ow oh-EHS-chee?

31

What bus do I take to go . . .	**Qual ônibus tomo para ir . . .**	kwow OH-nee-boos TOH-moo PAH-rah eer . . .
• to Rio de Janeiro?	• **ao Rio de Janeiro?**	• ow HEE-oo jee zhah-NAY-roo?
• to Santos?	• **a Santos?**	• ah SAHN-toos?
• to Coimbra?	• **a Coimbra? (P)**	• ah KWEEM-brah?
• to Oporto?	• **ao Porto? (P)**	• ow POHR-toh?
• to the airport?	• **ao aeroporto?**	• ow ah-eh-roh-POHR-too?
How many stops does this bus make?	**Quantas paradas este ônibus faz?**	KWAHN-tahs pah-RAH-dahs EHS-chee OH-nee-boos fahz?
How long does it take to get to . . . ?	**Quanto tempo leva para chegar até . . . ?**	KWAHN-too TEHM-poo LAY-vah PAH-rah eer ah-TEH . . . ?
How much is the fare?	**Quanto é a passagem?**	KWAHN-too eh ah pah-SAH-zhehn?
Should I pay when I get on?	**Devo pagar ao entrar?**	DEH-voo pah-GAHR ow ehn-TRAHR?
Where do I get the bus to return?	**Onde se toma o ônibus para voltar?**	OHN-jee see TOH-mah oo OH-nee-boos PAH-rah vohl-TAHR?
How often do the return buses come?	**Com que freqüência tem ônibus para voltar?**	kohn kee fray-KWEHN-syah tehn OH-nee-boos PAH-rah vohl-TAHR?
Which is the closest stop to . . . ?	**Qual é a parada mais perto do(da) . . . ?**	kwow eh ah pah-RAH-dah mahys PEHR-too doo(dah) . . . ?
I would like . . .	**Gostaria de . . .**	gohs-tah-REE-ah jee . . .
• a ticket.	• **uma passagem.**	• OO-mah pah-SAH-zhehn
• a receipt.	• **um recibo.**	• oon hay-SEE-boo
• a reserved seat.	• **um assento numerado.**	• oon ah-SEHN-too noo-meh-RAH-doo
• first-class.	• **primeira classe.**	• pree-MAY-rah KLAH-see
• second-class.	• **segunda classe.**	• say-GOON-dah KLAH-see
• a direct bus.	• **um ônibus direto.**	• oon OH-nee-boos jee-RAY-too

• an express bus.	• **um ônibus ex-presso.**	• oon OH-nee-boos ehks-PRAH-soo
• ticketed luggage.	• **bagagem re-gistrada.**	• bah-GAH-zhehn heh-jees-TRAH-dah

THE METRO

The metro (subway systems) of São Paulo and Lisbon are quite efficient. If you plan to spend time in these cities, you may want to learn to get around by subway since it will save you time and easily get you to the most important attractions. Like most subways anywhere, the metro tends to be crowded, especially at rush hours. So plan your day to avoid the rush.

Where can I buy a token?	**Onde posso comprar uma ficha?**	OHN-jee POH-soo kohm-PRAHR OO-mah FEE-shah?
How much are they?	**Quanto custam?**	KWAHN-too KOOS-tahn?
Is there a map for the metro?	**Tem um mapa do metrô?**	tehn oon MAH-pah doo meh-TROH?
Which train do I take to go to . . . ?	**Qual trem tomo para . . . ?**	kwow trehn TOH-moo PAH-rah . . . ?
Can you tell me when we arrive at . . . ?	**Me avise quando che-garmos a . . . ?**	mee ah-VEE-zee KWAHN-doo shay-GAHR-moos ah . . . ?

TRAINS AND TRAMS

In Brazil, train service between Rio and São Paulo is comfortable and inexpensive. There is also excellent regional service from São Paulo on the Paulista and Sorocabana lines, from São Paulo to Brasilia, and from Rio to Belo Horizonte. However, most service to other areas of Brazil is inferior to air travel.

The railway system in Portugal is surprisingly extensive for such a small country. Trains are clean and leave on time, but some of those away from the main Lisbon-Oporto line are slow, old-fashioned, and infrequent. Expresses between Lisbon and Oporto are non-stop and have restaurant or buffet facilities.

33

They are first class and require supplementary fares and reservations. A secondary route between Lisbon and Oporto travels along the coast through unspoiled country via Leiria and Figueira da Foz. There is also a daily train between Oporto and Braga. Be sure to buy tickets at the station as there is a huge surcharge if you buy them on the train. Portuguese Railroads (CP) are covered by the Eurail pass, which can be purchased for unlimited travel during specific periods of time.

Lisbon's tram service is one of the best in Europe, and it is the most amusing way of getting around in the city. You can buy books of 20 tickets at a reduced price; each book is good for seven days on all trams and buses. This very efficient tramway system was built at the end of the last century and is a fascinating reminder of days gone by.

Where is the train station?	**Onde fica a estação de trem (comboio) (P)?**	OHN-jee FEE-kah ah ehs-tah-SOWN jee trehn (kom-BOH-yoh)?
Where is the ticket window?	**Onde fica a bilheteria?**	OHN-jee FEE-kah ah beel-yeh-teh-REE-ah?
When does the train for Vitória leave?	**Quando sai o trem para Vitória?**	KWAHN-doo sahy oo trehn PAH-rah vee-TOH-ryah?
Is it a . . . train?	**É um trem . . .**	eh oon trehn . . .
• local	• **local?**	• loh-KOW?
• express	• **expresso?**	• ehks-PRAY-soo?
• through	• **direto?**	• jee-RAY-too?
What train do I take to get to . . . ?	**Qual trem tomo para ir a . . . ?**	kwow trehn TOH-moo PAH-rah eer ah . . . ?
When does it arrive at . . . ?	**Quando chega a . . . ?**	KWAHN-doo SHEH-gah ah . . . ?
Do I need to change trains?	**Preciso trocar de trem?**	pray-SEE-zoo troh-KAHR jee trehn?
When does the train . . .	**Quando o trem . . . ?**	KWAHN-doo oo trehn . . . ?
• leave?	• **sai?**	• sahy
• arrive?	• **chega?**	• SHEH-gah

34

Is the train . . .	**O trem está . . .**	oo trehn ehs-TAH . . .
• on time?	• **na hora?**	• nah OH-rah?
• late?	• **atrasado?**	• ah-trah-ZAH-doo?
From what platform does it leave?	**Sai de qual plataforma?**	sahy jee kwow plah-tah-FOHR-mah?
Does this train stop at . . .	**Este trem para em . . .**	EHS-chee trehn PAH-rah ehn . . .
• Campinas?	• **Campinas?**	• kahm-PEE-nahs?
• Minas?	• **Minas?**	• MEE-nahs?
• Oporto?	• **Porto? (P)**	• POHR-toh?
Is there a . . .	**Tem . . .**	tehn . . .
• baggage check?	• **entreque de bagagem?**	• ehn-TREH-gee jee bah-GAH-zhehn?
• dining car?	• **carro-restau-rante?**	• KAH-hoo hehs-tow-RAHN-chee?
• sleeping car?	• **vagão-leito?**	• vah-GOWN LAY-too?
I'd like a . . . ticket.	**Gostaria de um bilhete de . . .**	gohs-tah-REE-ah jee oon beel-YEH-chee jee . . .
• round-trip	• **ida e volta.**	• EE-dah ee VOHL-tah
• one-way	• **ida.**	• EE-dah
• first-class	• **primeira classe.**	• pree-MAY-rah KLAH-see
• second-class	• **segunda classe.**	• say-GOON-dah KLAH-see
Is this seat taken?	**Este lugar está ocupado?**	EHS-chee loo-GAHR ehs-TAH oh-koo-PAH-doo?
Excuse me, I believe this is my seat.	**Perdão, acho que este é o meu lugar.**	pehr-DOWN, AH-shoo kee EHS-chee eh oo MAY-oo loo-GAHR
Sorry, this seat is occupied.	**Perdão, este lugar está ocu-pado.**	pehr-DOWN, EHS-chee loo-GAHR ehs-TAH oh-koo-PAH-doo
No, it's not occu-pied.	**Não, não está ocupado.**	nown, nown ehs-TAH oh-koo-PAH-doo

DIRECTIONS

Do you have a map of the city?	**Tem mapa da cidade?**	tehn MAH-pah dah see-DAH-jee?

35

English	Portuguese	Pronunciation
Can you show me on the map?	**Pode me mostrar no mapa?**	POH-jee mee mohs-TRAHR noo MAH-pah?
I'm lost.	**Estou perdido (-a).**	ehs-TOH pehr-DEE-doo(-dah)
Where is . . .	**Onde fica . . .**	OHN-jee FEE-kah . . .
• the hotel Rex?	• **o hotel Rex?**	• oo oh-TAY-oo hehks?
• . . . Street?	• **a rua . . . ?**	• ah HOO-ah . . . ?
• . . . Avenue?	• **a avenida . . . ?**	• ah ah-veh-NEE-dah . . . ?
How can I get . . .	**Como posso ir . . .**	KOH-moo POH-soo eer . . .
• to the station?	• **à estação?**	• ah ehs-tah-SOWN?
• to the bus stop?	• **ao ponto de ônibus?**	• ow POHN-too jee OH-nee-boos?
• to the ticket office?	• **à bilheteria? à bilheteira? (P)**	• ah beel-yeh-teh REE-yah? ah beel-yeh-TAY-rah?
• to the subway entrance?	• **à entrada do metrô?**	• ah ehn-TRAH-dah doo meh-TROH?
• to the airport?	• **ao aeroporto?**	• ow ah-eh-roh-POHR-too?
straight ahead	**direto**	dee-RAY-too
to the right	**à direita**	ah jee-RAY-tah
to the left	**à esquerda**	ah ehs-KEHR-dah
a block away	**no próximo quarteirão**	noh PROHK-see-moh kwahr-tay-ROWN
on the corner	**na esquina**	nah ehs-KEE-nah
on the square	**na praça**	nah PRAH-sah
facing, opposite	**em frente**	ehn-FREHN-chee
across	**do outro lado**	doo OH-troo LAH-doo
next to	**ao lado**	ow LAH-doo
near	**perto**	PEHR-too
far	**longe**	LOHN-zhee

COMMON PUBLIC SIGNS

Portuguese	Pronunciation	English
entrada	ehn-TRAH-dah	entrance
saida	sah-EE-dah	exit
ponto	POHN-too	bus or taxi stop
aberto	ah-BEHR-too	open

fechado	fay-SHAH-doo	closed
para baixo	PAH-rah BAHY-shoo	down
para cima	PAH-rah SEE-mah	up
empurre	ehm-POO-hee	push
puxe	POO-shee	pull
pare	AHL-too	stop
perigo	peh-REE-goo	danger
proibido	proh-ee-BEE-doo	no passage
serviço	sehr-VEE-soo	service
privado	pree-VAH-doo	private
damas	DAH-mahs	women
senhoras	sehn-YOH-rahs	women
mulheres	mool-YEH-rees	women
senhores	sehn-YOH-rees	men
homens	OH-mehns	men
lavabo	lah-VAH-boo	bathroom
agua não potavel	AH-gwah nown poh-TAY-vay-oo	not drinking water
proibido fumar	proh-ee-BEE-doo foo-MAHR	no smoking
proibido tirar fotografias	proh-ee-BEE-doo chee-RAHR foh-toh-grah-FEE-ahs	no photographs
proibido jogar objetos pela janela	proh-ee-BEE-doo joh-GAHR oh-bee-ZHEH-toos PEH-lah zhah-NAY-lah	do not throw objects out of window
saida de emergencia	sah-EE-dah jee eh-mehr-ZHAYN-syah	emergency exit

37

4. ACCOMMODATIONS

SELECTING ACCOMMODATIONS

In most cases, it's best to make hotel reservations in advance, especially if an important holiday or celebration is taking place in the area. Your travel agency can help with arrangements.

In Brazil, you will find different price categories of accommodations that don't always reflect the quality of a hotel. Hotels are classified as Super Deluxe, Deluxe, Expensive, Moderate, and Inexpensive. As of this writing, Super Deluxe hotels begin at $100.00 per night; Deluxe are $75 to $100; Expensive, Moderate, and Inexpensive range from $30 to $75 or less. Continental breakfast is generally included in the room rate of all hotels. Advance reservations should always be made at Expensive and Super Deluxe hotels. Unless you are traveling with a tour, for trips during Carnival (see p. 161) you will need to reserve a room in the best hotels at least a year before. Motels in Brazil differ from those in the U.S.; they are only for couples engaging in amorous interludes and are rented out for short periods of time.

In Rio, luxury hotels are concentrated in Copacabana, Ipanema, Leblon, and São Conrado. The cost of a hotel is directly related to its location and its ocean view; beachfront hotels are generally more expensive. Rooms are also classified as Standard, Superior, or Deluxe as a function of their location within the hotel. Because of its international business atmosphere, São Paulo has hundreds of hotels from which to choose. Categories are similar to those in Rio, with continental breakfast normally included. Brasilia, although the capital city, does not have the same range of accommodations as do Rio and São Paulo. The new Hilton chain will be the first Deluxe hotel in Brasilia. Other good hotels exist; however, they are neither in the same price range nor of the same quality as those found in the two major cities. In most other cities, you should be able to find boarding houses, pensions, and *pousadas* (poh-ZAH-dahs) in addition to hotels.

In Portugal, hotels are graded into categories, from one to five stars (Deluxe), based on quality and price. There are also Bed and Breakfasts divided into categories of Deluxe, Expensive, Moderate, and Inexpensive. Service and tourist taxes are usually included in hotel rates. Pensions (*pensões*/pehn-SOWN-ehsh) and *residências* (rray-see-DEHN-syahsh) can also be found, usually providing breakfast. Other pension-like establishments are the *albergarias* (ahl-behr-gah-REE-ahsh). Country-house Tourism (*turismo de habitação*/too-REEZ-moh day ah-bee-tah-SOWN) arranges visits in private country houses. *Pousadas* (poh-SAH-dahsh), which are government controlled, are usually historic buildings found outside town, and generally fall into the Expensive or even Deluxe price category. These attractive inns offer tourists a chance to rest in typical Portuguese surroundings with excellent service and comfort. Finally, students often stay at Youth Hostels (*Pousadas de Juventude*/poh-ZAH-dahsh day zhoo-vehn-TOO-deh). These are open to young travelers of all nationalities, provided they have valid membership cards bearing the current year's stamp of a Youth Hostel Association belonging to the International Federation of Youth Hostels.

TYPES OF ACCOMMODATIONS

albergaria (P)	ahl-behr-gah-REE-ah	guest house
hotel	oh-TAY-oo	hotel
pensão	pehn-SOWN	pension
pousada	poh-ZAH-dah	inn
pousada de juventude (P)	poh-ZAH-dah day zhoo-vehn-too-deh	youth hostel
residência de estudantes	hay-see-DAYN-syah jee ehs-too-DAHN-chees	student residence
turismo de habitação (P)	too-REEZ-moh deh ah-bee-tah-SOWN	country house

39

DIALOGUE: AT THE HOTEL (*HOTEL*)

Turista:	**Gostaria de um quarto simples, por favor.**	gohs-tah-REE-ah jee oon KWAR-too SEEM-plees, poor fah-VOHR.
Recepcionista:	**Por quanto tempo?**	poor KWAHN-too TEHM-poo?
Turista:	**Por quatro noites. Quanto custa por noite?**	poor KWAH-troo NOY-chees. KWAH-too KOOS-tah poor NOY-chee?
Recepcionista:	**Custa Cr$ 75.000 por noite**	KOOS-tah seh-TEHN-tah-SEEN-koo kroo-ZAY-roos poor NOY-chee.
Turista:	**Está bem. Posso-me registrar?**	ehs-TAH behm. POH-soo mee hay-jees-TRAHR?
Recepcionista:	**Sim. Preencha este formulário, por favor.**	seen. PREHN-shah EHS-chee fohr-moo-LAH-ryoo, poor fah-VOHR.
Turista:	**Pois não! Obrigado.**	poys nown. oh-bree-GAH-doo.

. . . .

Tourist:	I'd like a single room, please.
Clerk:	For how long?
Tourist:	For four nights. How much is it per night?
Clerk:	It's 75,000 *cruzeiros* per night.
Tourist:	Fine. May I register?
Clerk:	Yes. Please fill out this form.
Tourist:	Of course. Thank you.

GENERAL HOTEL EXPRESSIONS

I would like a room for . . .	**Gostaria de um quarto por . . .**	gohs-tah-REE-ah jee oon KWAHR-too poor . . .

40

English	Portuguese	Pronunciation
• one night.	• **uma noite.**	• OO-mah NOY-chee
• two nights.	• **duas noites.**	• DOO-ahs NOY-chees
• a week.	• **uma semana.**	• OO-mah seh-MAH-nah
• two weeks.	• **duas semanas.**	• DOO-ahs seh-MAH-nahs
• one person.	• **uma pessoa.**	• OO-mah peh-SOH-ah
• two people.	• **duas pessoas.**	• DOO-ahs peh-SOH-ahs
How much is it for . . .	**Quanto é por . . .**	KWAHN-too eh poor . . .
• a day?	• **dia?**	• JEE-ah?
• a week?	• **uma semana?**	• OO-mah seh-MAH-nah?
Does that include tax?	**Inclui impostos?**	een-KLOO-ee eem-POHS-toos?
I have a reservation.	**Tenho uma reserva.**	TEHN-yoo OO-mah hay-ZEHR-vah
I don't have a reservation.	**Não tenho reserva.**	nown TEHN-yoo hay-ZEHR-vah
Do you have a room with . . .	**Tem quarto com . . .**	tehn KWAHR-too kohn . . .
• a private bath?	• **banheiro privativo?**	• bahn-YAY-roo pree-vah-CHEE-voo?
• air conditioning?	• **ar acondicionado?**	• ahr ah-kohn-dee-syo-NAH-doo?
• heat?	• **aquecimento?**	• ah-keh-see-MEHN-too?
• television?	• **televisão?**	• teh-lay-vee-ZOWN?
• hot water?	• **água quente?**	• AH-gwah KEHN-chee?
• a balcony?	• **terraço?**	• teh-HAH-soo
• a view facing the street?	• **vista para a rua?**	• VEES-tah PAH-rah ah HOO-ah?
• a view facing the ocean?	• **vista para o mar?**	• VEES-tah PAH-rah oo mahr?
Does the hotel have . . .	**O hotel tem . . .**	oo oh-TAY-oo tehn . . .
• a restaurant?	• **restaurante?**	• hehs-tah-oo-RAHN-chee?
• a bar?	• **bar?**	• bahr?
• a swimming pool?	• **piscina?**	• pee-SEE-nah?

41

• room service?	• **serviço de quarto?**	• sehr-VEE-soo jee KWAHR-too?
• a garage?	• **garagem?**	• gah-RAH-zhehn?
• a safety deposit box?	• **um cofre?**	• oon KOH-free?
• laundry service?	• **serviço de lavanderia?**	• sehr-VEE-soo jee lah-vahn-deh-REE-ah?
May I have . . .	**Poderia ter . . .**	poh-deh-REE-ah tehr . . .
• meals included?	• **refeições incluidas?**	• hay-fay-SOWN-ees een-kloo-EE-dahs?
• no meals included?	• **sem refeições?**	• sehn hay-fay-SOYN-ees?
• an extra bed?	• **uma cama extra?**	• OO-mah KAH-mah EHKS-trah?
• a baby crib?	• **um berço para o bebê?**	• oon BEHR-soo PAH-rah oo beh-bay?
• another towel?	• **outra toalha?**	• OH-trah TWAHL-yah?
• soap?	• **sabão?**	• sah-BOWN?
• clothes hangers?	• **cabides de roupa?**	• kah-BEE-jees jee HOW-pah?
• another blanket?	• **outro cobertor?**	• OH-troo koh-behr-TOHR?
• drinking water?	• **água potável?**	• AH-gwah poh-TAH-vay-oo?
• toilet paper?	• **papel higiênico?**	• pah-PAY-oo ee-ZHYAY-nee-koo?
This room is very . . .	**Este quarto é muito . . .**	EHS-chee KWAHR-too eh MWEE-too . . .
• small.	• **pequeno.**	• peh-KEH-noo
• cold.	• **frio.**	• FREE-oo
• hot.	• **quente.**	• KEHN-chee
• dark.	• **escuro.**	• ehs-KOO-roo
• noisy.	• **barulhento.**	• bah-rool-YEHN-too
The . . . does not work.	**Não funciona . . .**	nown foon-SYOH-nah . . .
• light	• **a luz.**	• ah looz
• heat	• **o aquecimento.**	• oo ah-keh-see-MEHN-too
• toilet	• **o vaso. a sanita. (P)**	• oo VAH-zoo ah sah-NEE-tah

English	Portuguese	Pronunciation
• air conditioner	• o ar acondicionado.	oo ahr ah-KOHN-dee-syoh-NAH-doo
• key	• a chave.	ah SHAH-vee
• lock	• a fechadura.	ah feh-shah-DOO-rah
• fan	• o ventilador.	oo vehn-chee-lah-DOHR
• outlet	• a tomada.	ah toh-MAH-dah
• television	• a televisão.	ah teh-lay-vee-ZOWN
May I change to another room?	Poderia trocar de quarto?	poh-deh-REE-ah troh-KAHR jee KWAHR-too?

HOTEL SERVICES

English	Portuguese	Pronunciation
Is there . . .	Tem . . .	tehn . . .
• room service?	• serviço de quarto?	• sehr-VEE-soo jee KWAHR-too?
• laundry service?	• serviço de lavanderia?	• sehr-VEE-soo jee lah-vahn-deh-REE-ah?
• a beauty parlor?	• um salão de beleza? um cabeleireiro? (P)	• oon sah-LOWN jee ben-LAY-zah? kah-beh-lay-RAY-roh?
• a barbershop?	• um barbeiro?	• oon bahr-BAY-roo?
• a baby-sitter?	• uma babá? uma babysitter? (P)	• OO-mah bah-BAH? OO-mah bay-bee-SEE-tehr?
• a gift shop?	• uma loja de presentes?	• OO-mah LOH-zhah jee pray-ZEHN-chees?
I wish to place an order for room . . .	Desejo fazer um pedido para o quarto . . .	deh-ZEH-zhoo fah-ZEHR oon peh-JEE-doo PAH-rah oo KWAHR-too . . .
Do you have a laundry list?	Tem uma lista de lavanderia?	tehn OO-mah LEES-tah jee lah-vahn-deh-REE-ah?
Laundry list:	Lista de lavanderia:	LEES-tah jee lah-vahn-deh-REE-ah
• ladies' garments	• roupas de senhoras	• HOH-pahs jee sehn-YOH-rahs

43

English	Portuguese	Pronunciation
• a blouse	• **uma blusa**	• OO-mah BLOO-zah
• a skirt	• **uma sáia**	• OO-mah SAH-yah
• stockings	• **meia-calças collants (P)**	• MAY-yah KOW-sahs koh-LAHNTS
• underclothes	• **roupas íntimas**	• HOH-pahs EEN-chee-mahs
• men's clothes	• **roupas de homem**	• HOH-pahs jee OH-mehn
• a tie	• **uma gravata**	• OO-mah grah-VAH-tah
• a shirt	• **uma camisa**	• OO-mah kah-MEE-zah
• a jacket	• **um paletó uma jaqueta (P)**	• oon pah-lay-TOH OO-mah zha-KEH-tah
• a pair of pants	• **calças**	• KOW-sahs
• a suit	• **um terno**	• oon TEHR-noo
• an undershirt	• **uma camiseta**	• OO-mah kah-mee-ZEH-tah
• undershorts	• **cuecas**	• KWEH-kahs
• socks	• **meias**	• MAY-yahs

For a more complete list of clothing, see Chapter 12: Shopping

English	Portuguese	Pronunciation
I need these clothes for . . .	**Preciso destas roupas para . . .**	pray-SEE-zoo DEHS-tahs HOH-pahs PAH-rah
• later.	• **mais tarde.**	• mahys TAHR-jee
• tonight.	• **esta noite.**	• EHS-tah NOY-chee
• tomorrow.	• **amanhã.**	• ah-mahn-YOWN
• the day after tomorrow.	• **depois-de-amanhã.**	• jee-POYS jee ah-mahn-YOWN
Can you . . . my clothes?	**Pode . . . a minha roupa?**	POH-jee . . . ah MEEN-yah HOH-pah?
• wash	• **lavar**	• lah-VAHR
• dry	• **secar**	• seh-KAHR
• iron	• **passar**	• pah-SAHR
• dry-clean	• **lavar a seco**	• lah-VAHR ah SAY-koo
• starch	• **engomar**	• ehn-goh-MAHR

• iron without starch	• **passar sem goma**	• pah-SAHR sehn GOH-mah
Can you recommend a baby-sitter?	**Pode recomendar uma babá?**	POH-jee hay-koh-mehn-DAHR OO-mah bah-BAH?
How much do you charge?	**Quanto você cobra?**	KWAHN-too voh-SAY KOH-brah?
Can you stay until midnight?	**Pode ficar até meianoite?**	POH-jee fee-KAHR ah-TEH MAY-yoh NOY-chee?

USING THE HOTEL TELEPHONE

Operator	**Telfonista**	teh-leh-foh-NEES-tah
May I have an outside line, please?	**Pederia ter uma linha, por favor?**	poh-deh-REE-ah tehr OO-mah LEEN-yah, poor fah-VOHR?
I would like to make . . .	**Gostaria de fazer . . .**	gohs-tah-REE-ah jee fah-ZEHR . . .
• an international call.	• **uma chamada internacional.**	• OO-mah shah-MAH-dah EEN-tehr-nah-syoh-now
• a collect call.	• **uma chamada a cobrar.**	• OO-mah shah-MAH-dah ah koh-BRAHR
• a call with time and charges.	• **uma chamada com tempo e custo.**	• OO-mah shah-MAH-dah kohn TEHM-poo ee KOOS-too
• a person-to-person call.	• **uma chamada pessoa a pessoa.**	• OO-mah shah-MAH-dah peh-SOH-ah ah peh-SOH-ah
• a credit card call.	• **uma chamada com cartão de crédito.**	• OO-mah shah-MAH-dah kohn kahr-TOWN jee KREH-dee-too
Please connect me with . . .	**Por favor, preciso falar com . . .**	poor fah-VOHR, pray-SEE-zoo fah-LAHR kohn . . .
• room 203.	• **o quarto duzentos e três.**	• oo KWAHR-too doo-ZEHN-toos ee trays

45

• the reception desk.	• **a recepção.**	• ah hay-sehp-SOWN
• the dining room.	• **o restaurante.**	• oo hehs-tow-RAHN-chee
• telephone number . . .	• **o número . . .**	• oo NOO-meh-roo
• room service.	• **o serviço de quarto.**	• oo sehr-VEE-soo jee KWAHR-too

5. SOCIALIZING

MEETING PEOPLE

Meeting people and discovering a new culture through personal contacts can be some of the most rewarding travel experiences. An open mind, tolerance, and curiosity will help foster good relationships, and showing an interest in your hosts will undoubtedly be your best entrée into Brazilian and Portuguese cultures!

ABOUT THE BRAZILIAN PEOPLE

Brazilians are known to be some of the most relaxed and fun-loving people in the world. They love to meet people and you should feel at home with them immediately. In addition, there are few other countries where you can find such a great variety of skin tones; like the United States, Brazil owes a great deal to the different waves of immigrants who made their lives there.

Within Brazil, manners change from place to place and often with social class as well. Behaviors that English-speakers might find impolite may constitute the normal way of doing things in Brazil, and vice-versa. For example, to get someone's attention in a restaurant, it is common to snap one's fingers, hiss, or make a *sshh*ing sound (as if you were trying to tell someone to be quiet). Also, it is considered in bad taste for a waiter to bring the check before the customer asks for it. These are just two of many habits that non-natives may find "peculiar."

Be aware of cultural differences when interpreting Brazilian body language, too. For example, when a Brazilian snaps his or her fingers several times in succession, it does not mean something was easy or instantaneous, but rather that it happened a long time ago. Tugging an earlobe is a sign of approval. To signal "come here," Brazilians open and close the hand, palm down, as if waving goodbye to the ground, without fluttering the fingers. And keep in mind that the American "A-OK" sign, formed by making a circle with the thumb and forefinger, is an obscene gesture in Brazil. Brazilians are generally more physical and display their emotions more than Americans or Brit-

47

ish, even with people they don't know well. For example, women greet each other and their male friends with kisses on both cheeks, and men often embrace.

Finally, time does not have the same cultural importance for Brazilians as it does for Americans and Europeans, and punctuality is definitely not a concern for Brazilians.

ABOUT THE PORTUGUESE PEOPLE

In Portugal, visitors are often struck immediately by the amiable disposition, gentleness, patience, and courtesy characteristic of the Portuguese people. From police officers to local citizens of all ages, people will often go out of their way to help a foreigner. While the Portuguese tend to be more formal than Brazilians, you will quickly see that they are open, friendly, and good-natured. Brazilian character is marked by a Celtic melancholy that they call *saudade* (sow-DAH-deh): a sadness and nostalgia for past things and a yearning for things that will never be. This nostalgia is best reflected in their most popular music genre, known as the *fado* (FAH-doh), described in Chapter 13.

DIALOGUE: MAKING FRIENDS (*FAZER AMIGOS*)

Turista:	**Bom dia, senhor.* Poderia-me apresentar? Sou Julie Adams.**	bohn JEE-ah, sehn-YOHR. poh-deh-REE-ah mee ah-pray-zehn-TAHR? soh Julie Adams.
Sr. Silva:	**Muito prazer, senhora.* Eu sou João Silva.**	MWEE-too prah-ZEHR, sehn-YOH-rah. AY-oo soh joh-OWN SEEL-vah
Turista:	**Muito prazer.**	MWEE-too prah-ZEHR.
Sr. Silva:	**Está aqui de férias?**	ehs-TAH ah-KEE jee FEH-ryahs?
Turista:	**Sim. Vou ficar aqui por três semanas.**	seen. voh fee-KAHR ah-KEE poor trays seh-MAH-nahs.

| Sr. Silva: | Que bom! Espero que goste do Brasil. | keh bohn! ehs-PEH-roo keh GOHS-chee jee brah-ZEE-oo. |
| Turista: | Obrigada. Até logo, senhor. | oh-bree-GAH-doo! ah-TEH LOH-goo, sehn-YOHR. |

. . . .

Tourist:	Hello! May I introduce myself? I'm Julie Adams.
Mr. Silva:	Pleased to meet you. I'm João Silva.
Tourist:	Pleased to meet you.
Mr. Silva:	Are you here on vacation?
Tourist:	Yes. I'll be here for three weeks.
Mr. Silva:	How nice! I hope you enjoy Brazil.
Tourist:	Thank you. So long, sir.

* In Brazil, use the titles *senhor, senhora,* and *senhorita* to show respect, especially when speaking to people who are not close friends. These titles may be used with the last name, or alone. Note that *menina* is used in Portugal for young girls up to about 16 years of age, instead of *senhorita.*

INTRODUCTIONS AND GREETINGS

Allow me to introduce myself.	**Permita que me apresente.**	pehr-MEE-tah keh mee ah-pray-ZEHN-chee
I am . . .	**Sou . . .**	soh . . .
My name is . . .	**Chamo-me . . .**	CHAH-moo-mee . . .
• John.	• **João.**	• joh-OWN
• Joan.	• **Joana.**	• joh-AH-nah
• Mr. Silva.	• **Sr. Silva.**	• sehn-YOHR SEE-oo-vah
• Ana Silva.	• **Ana Silva.**	• AH-nah SEEL-vah
I'd like to introduce you . . .	**Gostaria de apresentá-lo . . .**	gohs-tah-REE-ah jee ah-pray-sehn-TAH-loo . . .
• to Mr. Silva.	• **ao senhor Silva.**	• ow sehn-YOHR SEE-oo-vah
• to Mrs. Silva.	• **à senhora Silva.**	• ah sehn-YOH-rah SEE-oo-vah

49

• to Miss/Ms. . . .	• à senhorita . . .	• ah zehn-yoh-REE-tah . . .
Allow me to introduce you to . . .	Permita-me apresentá-lo a . . .	pehr-MEE-tah-mee ah-pray-sehn-TAH-loo ah . . .
What's your name?	Como é o seu nome?	KOH-moh eh oo SAY-oo NOH-mee?
Pleased to meet you.	Prazer.	prah-ZEHR
This is . . .	E . . .	eh . . .
• my husband.	• o meu marido.	• oo MAY-oo mah-REE-doo
• my wife.	• a minha esposa. a minha mulher. (P)	• ah MEEN-yah ehs-POH-zah ah MEEN-yah mool-YEHR
• my friend (male).	• o meu amigo.	• oo MAY-oo ah-MEE-goo
• my friend (female).	• a minha amiga.	• ah-MEEN-yah ah-MEE-gah
How are you?	Como vai?	KOH-moo vahy?
Fine, thanks.	Bem, obrigado (-a).	behn, oh-bree-GAH-doo(-dah)
And you?	E você?*	ee voh-SAY?*

* In Brazil, *você* is used only for persons you know well. Otherwise be sure to use the titles of address—*o senhor, a senhora,* etc.—when addressing all other persons as ''you.''

FIRST CONTACT

Where do you live?	Onde mora?	OHN-jee MOH-rah?
I live . . .	Moro . . .	MOH-roo . . .
• in the United States.	• nos Estados Unidos.	• noos ehs-TAH-doos oo-NEE-doos
• in England.	• na Inglaterra.	• nah een-glah-TEH-hah
• in Canada.	• no Canadá.	• noo kah-nah-DAH
• in New York.	• em Nova Iorque.	• en NOH-vah YOHR-kee
• in California.	• na Califórnia.	• nah kah-lee-FOHR-nyah

English	Portuguese	Pronunciation
That's in the . . .	Fica no . . .	FEE-kah noo . . .
• north.	• norte.	• NOHR-chee
• south.	• sul.	• sool
• east.	• leste.	• LEHS-chee
• west.	• oeste.	• oh-EHS-chee
That's near . . .	E perto . . .	eh PEHR-too . . .
• the coast.	• da costa.	• dah KOHS-tah
• Canada.	• do Canadá.	• doo kah-nah-DAH
• the border.	• da fronteira.	• dah frohn-TAY-rah
• the ocean.	• do mar.	• doo mahr
• the mountains.	• das montanhas.	• dahs mohn-TAHN-yahs
How long will you be here?	Quanto tempo vai ficar aqui?	KWAHN-too TEHM-poo vahy fee-KAHR ah-KEE?
I'll be here for . . .	Vou ficar aqui por . . .	voh fee-KAHR ah-KEE poor . . .
• a week.	• uma semana.	• OO-mah say-MAH-nah
• another week.	• mais uma semana.	• mahyz OO-mah say-MAH-nah
• three weeks.	• três semanas.	• trays say-MAH-nahs
• a short while.	• pouco tempo.	• POH-koo TEHM-poo
• a long time.	• muito tempo.	• MWEE-too TEHM-poo
What hotel are you staying at?	Em que hotel vai ficar?	ehn keh oh-TAY-oo vahy fee-KAHR?
I am at the . . . Hotel.	Vou ficar no Hotel . . .	voh fee-KAHR no oh-TAY-oo . . .
How do you like . . .	Gosta . . .	GOHS-tah . . .
• Brazil?	• do Brasil?	• doo brah-ZEE-oo?
• Portugal?	• de Portugal?	• jee pohr-too-GOW?
• Bahia?	• da Bahia?	• da bah-EE-ah?
I like it very much.	Gosto muito.	GOHS-too MWEE-too.
I just arrived.	Acabei de chegar.	ah-kah-BAY jee shay-GAHR
I'm not sure yet.	Não tenho certeza ainda.	nown TEHN-yoo sehr-TAY-zah ah-EEN-dah
I like the people very much.	Gosto muito do povo.	GOHS-too MWEE-to doo POH-voo
I like the countryside.	Gosto do campo.	GOHS-too doo KAHM-poo

Everything is so . . .	Tudo é tão . . .	TOO-doo eh town . . .
• interesting.	• interessante.	• een-teh-ray-SAHN-chee
• different.	• diferente.	• dee-feh-REHN-chee
• pretty.	• bonito.	• boh-NEE-too

THE FAMILY

I'm traveling with/ without my family.	Estou viajando com/sem a minha família.	ehs-TOH vee-ah-ZHAHN-doo kohn/sehn ah MEEN-yah fah-MEEL-yah
My family lives in New York.	A minha família mora em Nova Iorque.	ah MEEN-ya fah-MEEL-yah MOH-rah ehn NOH-vah YOHR-kee
My family is spread out in different places.	A minha família está espalhada em lugares diferentes.	ah MEEN-yah fah-MEEL-yah ehs-TAH ehs-pahl-YAH-dah ehn loo-GAH-rees dee-feh-REHN-chees
I have a . . .	Tenho uma família . . .	TEHN-yoo OO-mah fah-MEEL-yah . . .
• big family.	• grande.	• GRAHN-jee
• small family.	• pequena.	• peh-KEH-nah
I have many relatives.	Tenho muitos parentes.	TEHN-yoo MWEE-toos pah-REHN-chees
I have . . .	Tenho . . .	TEHN-yoo . . .
• a husband.	• um marido.	• oon mah-REE-doo
• a wife.	• uma esposa.	• OO-mah ehs-POH-zah
• a son.	• um filho.	• oon FEEL-yoo
• a daughter.	• uma filha.	• OO-mah FEEL-yah
• two children.	• dois filhos.	• doys FEEL-yoos
• a baby.	• um bebê.	• oon beh-BAY
• a father.	• um pai.	• oon pahy
• a mother.	• uma mãe.	• OO-mah mahy
• a grandmother.	• uma avó.	• OO-mah ah-VOH-oo
• a grandfather.	• um avô.	• oon ah-VOH
• a grandson.	• um neto.	• oon NEH-too
• a granddaughter.	• uma neta.	• OO-mah NEH-tah
• a cousin (female).	• uma prima.	• OO-mah PREE-mah

English	Portuguese	Pronunciation
• a cousin (male).	• **um primo.**	• oon PREE-moo
• an aunt.	• **uma tia.**	• OO-mah CHEE-ah
• an uncle.	• **um tio.**	• oon CHEE-oo
• a sister.	• **uma irmã.**	• OO-mah eer-MAHN
• a brother.	• **um irmão.**	• oon eer-MOWN
• in-laws.	• **sogros.**	• SOH-groos
• a father-in-law.	• **um sogro.**	• oon SOH-groo
• a mother-in-law.	• **uma sogra.**	• OO-mah SOH-grah
• a sister-in-law.	• **uma cunhada.**	• OO-mah koon-YAH-dah
• a brother-in-law.	• **um cunhado.**	• oon koon-YAH-doo
How old are your children?	**Quantos anos tem os seus filhos?**	KWAHN-toos AH-noos tehn oos SAY-oos FEEL-yoos?
My children are . . .	**Os meus filhos são . . .**	oos MAY-oos FEEL-yoos sown . . .
• very young.	• **muito novos.**	• MWEE-too NOH-voos
• all grown up.	• **crescidos.**	• kray-SEE-doos
Peter is three years old.	**O Pedro tem três anos.**	oo PEH-droo tehn trays AH-noos
He is older than Paul.	**Êle é mais velho do que o Paulo.**	AY-lee eh mahys VEHL-yoo doo keh oo POW-loo
He is my eldest/ youngest son.	**Êle é o meu filho mais velho/ novo.**	AY-lee eh oo MAY-oo FEEL-yoo mahys VEHL-yoo/NOH-voo
She is my eldest/ youngest daughter.	**Ela é a minha filha mais velha/nova.**	EH-lah eh ah MEEN-yah FEEL-yah mahys VEHL-yah/NOH-vah
I am divorced.	**Sou divorciado (-a).**	soh jee-vohr-SYAH-doo(-dah)
I am a widow.	**Sou viúva.**	soh vee-OO-vah
I am a widower.	**Sou viúvo.**	soh vee-OO-voo

JOBS AND PROFESSIONS

English	Portuguese	Pronunciation
Where do you work?	**Onde você trabalha?**	OHN-jee voh-SAY trah-BAHL-yah?
What do you do?	**O que faz?**	oo keh fahz?
What is your profession?	**Qual é a sua profissão?**	kwow eh ah SOO-ah proh-fee-SOWN?

53

I'm* . . .	Sou* . . .	soh . . .
• an artist.	• artista.	• ahr-TEES-tah
• a businessman/ woman.	• empresário(-a).	• ehm-pray-ZAH-ryoo (-ryah)
• a housewife.	• dona de casa.	• DOH-nah jee KAH-zah
• a dentist.	• dentista.	• dehn-TEES-tah
• a doctor.	• médico(-a).	• MEH-jee-koo(-kah)
• a journalist.	• jornalista.	• zhoor-nah-LEES-tah
• a lawyer.	• advogado(-a).	• ah-jee-voh-GAH-doo (-dah)
• a musician.	• músico(-a).	• MOO-zee-koo(-kah)
• a nurse.	• enfermeiro(-a).	• ehn-fehr-MAY-roo (-rah)
• a secretary.	• secretária.	• seh-kray-TAH-ryah
• a teacher.	• professor(-a).	• proh-feh-SOHR(-ah)
I'm retired.	Sou aposentado (-a).	soh ah-poh-zehn-TAH-doo(-dah)
I'm not working.	Não estou tra-balhando.	nown ehs-TOH trah-bahl-YAHN-doo

*For a more complete list of professions, see p.53.

WITH FRIENDS

It's so good to see you.	Prazer em vê-lo(-la).	prah-ZEHR en VAY-loo(-lah)
It's nice to be here.	Prazer estar aqui.	prah-ZEHR ehs-TAHR ah-KEE
Would you like a drink?	Gostaria duma bebida?	gohs-tah-REE-ah DOO-mah beh-BEE-dah?
Yes, please.	Sim, por favor.	seen, poor fah-VOHR
O.K.	Pois não.	poys nown
With pleasure.	Com prazer.	kohn prah-ZEHR
No thanks.	Não, obrigado (-a).	nown, oh-bree-GAH-doo(-dah)
Would you like to go with us . . .	Gostaria de nos acompanhar . . .	gohs-tah-REE-ah jee nohs ah-kohm-pahn-YAHR . . .
• to the theater?	• ao teatro?	• ow chee-AH-troo?
• to the movies?	• ao cinema?	• ow see-NAY-mah?

English	Portuguese	Pronunciation
• to a restaurant?	• a um restaurante?	• ah oon hehs-tow-RAHN-chee?
Gladly.	Com muito prazer.	kohn MWEE-too prah-ZEER
May I bring a friend?	Poderia trazer um(-a) amigo(-a)?	poh-deh-REE-ah trah-ZEHR oon(OO-mah) ah-MEE-goo(-gah)?
Do you mind if I smoke?*	Importar-se se eu fumo?	eem-POHR-tahr-see see AY-oo FOO-moo?
Not at all.	Claro que não.	KLAH-roo keh-nown
It's all right/O.K.	Está bem.	ehs-TAH behn
Can I telephone you?	Posso chamá-lo(-la) por telefone?	POH-soo shah-MAH-loo(-lah) poor teh-lay-FOH-nee?
What is your phone number?	Qual é o número do seu telefone?	kwow eh oo NOO-meh-roo doo SAY-oo teh-lay-FOH-nee?
What is your address?	Qual é o seu endereço?	kwow eh oo SAY-oo ehn-deh-RAY-soo?
Where shall we meet?	Onde vamos nos encontrar?	OHN-jee VAH-mohs nos ehn-kohn-TRAHR?
Meet me at my hotel.	Pode me encontrar no meu hotel.	POH-jee mee ehn-kohn-TRAHR noo MAY-oo oh-TAY-oo.
Are you married?	Você é casado (-a)?	voh-SAY eh kah-ZAH-doo(-dah)?
No, I'm . . .	Não, eu sou . . .	nown, AY-oo soh . . .
• single.	• solteiro(-a).	• sohl-TAY-roo(-rah)
• divorced.	• divorciado(-a).	• jee-vohr-SYAH-doo (-dah)
• widowed.	• viuvo(-a).	• vee-OO-voo(-vah)
My family is with me.	A minha familia está comigo.	ah MEEN-yah fah-MEEL-yah ehs-TAH kohn-MEE-goo
Here are pictures of my family.	Veja estas fotografias da minha familia.	vay-zhah EHS-tahs foh-toh-grah-FEE-ahs dah MEEN-ya fah-MEEL-yah

* Many people smoke in Brazil and Portugal, and smoking is common in public places.

55

It's getting late.	**Já é tarde.**	zhah eh TAHR-jee
It's time to get back.	**E hora de voltar.**	eh OH-rah jee vohl-TAHR
We're leaving tomorrow.	**Nós partimos amanhã.**	nohs pahr-CHEE-moos ah-mahn-YOWN
Many thanks for everything.	**Muito obrigado (-a) por tudo.**	MWEE-too oh-bree-GAH-doo(-dah) poor TOO-doo
I had a very good time.	**Foi ótimo.**	foy OH-chee-moo
I had a very nice time.	**Foi muito agradável.**	foy MWEE-too ah-grah-DAH-vay-oo
We're going to miss you.	**Vamos ter saudades de você.**	VAH-moos tehr sow-DAH-jees jee voh-SAY
It was nice to have met you.	**Prazer em conhecê-lo(-la).**	prah-ZEHR en kohn-yeh-SAY-loo(-lah)
Give my best to your family.	**Dê as minhas lembranças à sua família.**	day ahs MEEN-yahs lehm-BRAHN-sahs ah SOO-ah fah-MEEL-yah
Can I give you a ride?	**Posso levá-lo (-la)?**	POH-soo leh-VAHR-loo(-lah)?
Don't bother, thank you.	**Não se preocupe, obrigado (-a).**	nown see pray-oh-KOO-pee, oh-bree-GAH-doo(-dah)
I can take a taxi.	**Posso tomar um taxi.**	POH-soo toh-MAHR oon TAHK-see
Good-bye.	**Até logo.**	ah-TEH LOH-goo

TALKING ABOUT LANGUAGE

Do you speak[1] . . .	**Você fala . . .**	voh-SAY FAH-lah . . .
• English?	**• inglês?**	• een-GLAYS?
• French?	**• francês?**	• frahn-SAYS?
• German?	**• alemão?**	• ah-lay-MOWN?
I only speak English.	**Falo somente inglês.**	FAH-loo soh-MEHN-chee een-GLAYS

[1]For a more complete list of languages, see Chapter 14.

56

English	Portuguese	Pronunciation
I don't speak Portuguese.	**Não falo português.**	nown FAH-loo pohr-too-GAYS
I speak very little.	**Falo muito pouco.**	FAH-loo MWEE-too POH-koo
I speak a little Portuguese.	**Falo pouco português.**	FAH-loo POH-koo pohr-too-GAYS
I want to learn Portuguese.	**Quero aprender português.**	KEH-roo ah-prehn-DEHR pohr-too-GAYS
I understand.	**Compreendo.**	kohm-pree-EHN-doo
I don't understand.	**Não compreendo.**	nown kohm-pree-EHN-doo
Can you understand me?	**Pode me compreender?**	POH-jee mee kohm-pree-ehn-DEHR?
Please repeat that.	**Por favor, pode repetir isso?**	poor fah-VOHR POH-jee heh-pay-CHEER EE-soo?
Speak slowly.	**Fale devagar.**	FAH-lee jee vah-GAHR
Can you write that?	**Pode escrever isso?**	POH-jee ehs-kray-VEHR EE-soo?
How do you say ___ in . . .	**Como é que se diz ___ em . . .**	KOH-moo eh keh see deez ___ ehn . . .
• Portuguese?	• **português?**	• pohr-too-GAYS?
• English?	• **inglês?**	• een-GLAYS?
Is there anyone here who speaks English?	**Tem alguma pessoa aqui que fala inglês?**	tehn ahl-GOO-mah peh-SOH-ah ah-KEE keh FAH-lah een-GLAYS?
Can you translate this?	**Pode traduzir isto?**	POH-jee trah-doo-ZEER EES-too?
Portuguese is a beautiful language.	**O português é uma língua bonita.**	oo pohr-too-GAYS eh OO-mah LEEN-gwah boh-NEE-tah
I like Portuguese a lot.	**Gosto muito de português.**	GOHS-too MWEE-too jee pohr-too-GAYS

AT HOME

English	Portuguese	Pronunciation
Make yourself at home.	**Sinta-se em casa.**	SEEN-tah-see ehn KAH-zah
You may sit here.	**Pode-se sentar aqui.**	POH-jee see sehn-TAHR ah-KEE

57

English	Portuguese	Pronunciation
What a pretty house!	**Que casa bonita!**	keh KAH-zah boh-NEE-tah!
I really like this neighborhood.	**Gosto muito deste bairro.**	GOHS-too MWEE-too DEHS-chee BAHY-hoo
Here is . . .	**Aqui é . . .**	ah-KEE eh . . .
• the kitchen.	• **a cozinha.**	• ah koh-ZEEN-yah
• the living room.	• **a sala.**	• ah SAH-lah
• the dining room.	• **a sala de jantar.**	• ah SAH-lah jee zhahn-TAHR
• the bedroom.	• **o quarto.**	• oo KWAHR-too
• the bathroom.	• **o banheiro.**	• oo bahn-YAY-roo
• the study.	• **o escritório.**	• oo ehs-kree-TOH-ryoo
• the couch.	• **o sofá.**	• o soh-FAH
• the armchair.	• **a poltrona.**	• ah pohl-TROH-nah
• the table.	• **a mesa.**	• ah MEH-zah
• the chair.	• **a cadeira.**	• ah kah-DAY-rah
• the lamp.	• **a lâmpada.**	• ah LAHM-pah-dah
• the door.	• **a porta.**	• ah POHR-tah
It's . . .	**E . . .**	eh . . .
• a house.	• **uma casa.**	• OO-mah KAH-zah
• an apartment.	• **um apartamento.**	• oon ah-pahr-tah-MEHN-too
• a villa.	• **uma mansão.**	• OO-mah mahn-SOWN
• a farm.	• **uma fazenda.**	• OO-mah fah-ZEHN-dah
Thanks for having invited us.	**Obrigado(-a) por nos ter convidado.**	oh-bree-GAH-doo(-dah) poor nohs tehr kohn-vee-DAH-doo
Please come and visit us sometime.	**Venha nos visitar a qualquer hora.**	VEHN-yah nohs vee-zee-TAHR ah kwow-KEHR OH-rah

6. DINING OUT

RESTAURANTS

Dining out in Brazil or Portugal is likely to be a very pleasurable experience because both countries offer rich and varied cuisines. As the Portuguese spread throughout Brazil during colonial times, aspects of their cuisine were mixed with native foods and African dishes, resulting in many exotic and tasty combinations. Besides restaurants, you will find a variety of places in Brazil and Portugal that serve food and drink:

Café Bar
(kah-FEH bahr)

Here you can find hot and cold drinks and light snacks.

Casa de Fado (P)
(KAH-zah day
FAH-doh)

Typical in Portugal, this type of restaurant serves regional dishes and features guitar players and *fado* (FAH-doh) singers who sometimes double as waiters and waitresses.

Churrasqueira
(shoo-hahs-KAY-rah)

A restaurant specializing in chicken.

Churrascaria
(shoo-hahs-kah-REE-ah)

A restaurant specializing in assorted grilled meats, which are especially common in Brazil.

Confeitaria
(kohn-fay-tah-REE-ah)

A shop serving coffee, tea, and wonderful assortments of pastries.

Estalagem
(ehs-tah-LAH-zhen)

A small, privately owned hotel that serves regional specialties.

Pastelaria
(pahs-teh-lah-REE-ah)

Same as *confeitaria*, above.

Pousada
(poh-ZAH-dah)

An inn specializing in local dishes and usually well maintained and a bit expensive.

Salão de chá
(sah-LOWN jee shah)

A tearoom, serving tea and pastries.

Snack-bar
(SNAH-kee bahr)

Similar to those in the United States.

59

MEALS AND MEALTIMES

Breakfast

The Brazilian breakfast, *o café da manhã* (oo kah-FEH dah mahn-YOWN) or *o pequeno almoço* (oo peh-KAY-noo ahl-MOH-soo), is very light, and commonly served between 7:00 A.M. and 10:00 A.M. at hotels. If breakfast is included in the price of your room, it usually consists of coffee, tea, or hot chocolate, fresh bread, butter, and jam. Warm milk is served on the side so that you can blend to your taste. If breakfast is not included with your hotel room, you will probably find it less expensive and more fun at the corner bar, mingling with Brazilians.

Lunch

Lunch, *o almoço* (oo ahl-MOO-soo), is traditionally the big meal of the day. In recent years, shorter midday breaks have led to quicker lunches for many working people. In general, lunch is served between 12:30 and about 3:00 P.M. Many businesses and most public services close at lunchtime; stores are closed between 12:30 or 1:00 P.M. and 3:00 or 4:00 P.M., depending on the city. At this time you may find that eateries fill up quickly. Those who have the time prefer to go home for a quiet, relaxed lunch.

Dinner

Dinner, *o jantar* (oo zhahn-TAHR), begins later in Brazil (and Portugal) than in the United States. Brazilian families normally serve a lighter meal in the evening, unless there are guests. Restaurants begin serving around 7:30 or 8:00 P.M. Evening dining is a leisurely affair, with people lingering over their food and drinks. The Brazilian dinner provides a very relaxed opportunity to spend some time with your family and friends, discussing things over a sumptuous meal.

DIALOGUE: ORDERING A MEAL (*PEDINDO UMA REFEIÇÃO*)

Garçom:	**Poderia tomar o seu pedido?**	poh-deh-REE-ah toh-MAHR oo SAY-oo peh-JEE-doo?
Cliente:	**Não sei ainda. Qual é a especialidade da casa?**	nown say ah-EEN-dah. kwow eh ah ehs-peh-SYOW-lee dah-jee dah KAH-zah?
Garçom:	**Hoje eu recomendaria a feijoada.**	OH-zhee AY-oo hay-koh-mehn-dah-REE-ah ah fay-ZHWAH-dah.
Cliente:	**Otimo. Traga-me isso, por favor.**	OH chee-moh. TRAH-gah mee EE-soo, poor fah-VOHR.
Garçom:	**Algo para beber?**	AHL-goo PAH-rah beh-BEHR?
Cliente:	**Sim, por favor. Traga-me uma garrafa de água mineral.**	seen, poor fah-VOHR. TRAH-gah mee OO-mah gah-HAH-fah jee AH-gwah mee-neh-ROW.

. . . .

Waiter:	May I take your order?
Customer:	I don't know yet. What's the specialty?
Waiter:	I would recommend the *feijoada* today.
Customer:	Fine. Bring me that, please.
Waiter:	Something to drink?
Customer:	Yes, please. Bring me a bottle of mineral water.

FINDING A RESTAURANT

Can you recommend a good restaurant?	**Pode recomendar um bom restaurante?**	POH-jee hay-koh-mehn-DAHR oon bohn hehs-tow-RAHN-chee?
I want a(n) . . . restaurant.	**Quero um restaurante . . .**	KEH-roo oon hehs-tow-RAHN-chee . . .

61

• typical	• **tipico.**	• CHEE-pee-koo
• international	• **internacional.**	• een-tehr-nah-syoh-NOW
• inexpensive	• **não muito caro.**	• nown MWEE-too KAH-roo
Is that restaurant expensive?	**E caro esse restaurante?**	eh KAH-roo EH-see hehs-tow-RAHN-chee?
What's the name of the restaurant?	**Como é o nome do restaurante?**	KOH-moo eh oo NOH-mee do hehs-tow-RAHN-chee?
Where is it located?	**Onde fica?**	OHN-jee FEE-kah?
What kind of food do they serve?	**Que tipo de comida êles servem?**	keh CHEE-poo jee koh-MEE-dah AY-lees SEHR-vehn?

MAKING RESERVATIONS

Do I need reservations?	**Preciso fazer reservas?**	pray-SEE-zoo fah-ZEHR hay-ZEHR-vahs?
I'd like to reserve a table . . .	**Gostaria de reservar uma mesa . . .**	gohs-tah-REE-ah jee hay-zehr-VAHR OO-mah MAY-zah . . .
• for two people.	• **para duas pessoas.**	• PAH-rah DOO-ahs peh-SOH-ahs
• for this evening.	• **para esta noite.**	• PAH-rah EHS-tah NOY-chee
• for 8:00 P.M.	• **para as oito da noite.**	• PAH-rah ahs OY-too dah NOY-chee
• for tomorrow evening.	• **para amanhã a noite.**	• PAH-rah ah-mahn-YOWN ah NOY-chee
• on the terrace.	• **no terraço.**	• no teh-HAH-soo
• by the window.	• **perto da janela.**	• PEHR-too dah zhah-NEH-lah
• outside.	• **fora.**	• FOH-rah
• inside.	• **dentro.**	• DEHN-troo

AT THE RESTAURANT/ORDERING

We have reservations.	**Nós temos reservas.**	nohs TEH-moos hay-ZEHR-vahs.

English	Portuguese	Pronunciation
Waiter!	**Garçom!**	gahr-SOHN!
Can you bring . . .	**Pode me trazer . . .**	POH-jee mee trah-ZEHR . . .
• the menu?	• **o cardápio?** **a ementa? (P)**	• oo kahr-DAH-pyoo? ah eh-MEHN-tah?
• the wine list?	• **a lista de vinhos?**	• ah LEES-tah jee VEEN-yoos?
• an aperitif?	• **um aperitivo?**	• oon ah-peh-ree-CHEE-voo?
Do you serve local dishes?	**Tem alguns pratos regionais?**	tehn ahl-GOONS PRAH-toos hay-zhyoh-NAHYS?
I'd like . . .	**Gostaria . . .**	gohs-tah-REE-ah . . .
• something light.	• **de algo ligeiro.**	• jee AHL-goo lee-ZHAY-roo
• a full meal.	• **de uma refeição completa.**	• jee OO-mah hay-fay-SOWN kohm-PLEH-tah
• the meal of the day.	• **do prato do dia.**	• doo PRAH-too doo JEE-ah
Do you have children's portions?	**Tem porções para crianças?**	tehm pohr-SOYN-ees PAH-rah kree-AHN-sahs?
I'm ready to order.	**Estou pronto(-a) para pedir.**	ehs-TOH PROHN-too (-tah) PAH-rah peh-JEER
Can I have . . . ?	**Posso pedir . . . ?**	POH-soo peh-JEER . . . ?
To begin . . .	**Para começar . . .**	PAH-rah koh-meh-SAHR . . .
Next . . .	**Depois . . .**	jee-POYS . . .
Finally . . .	**Para terminar . . .**	PAH-rah tehr-mee-NAHR . . .
That's all.	**E tudo.**	eh TOO-doo
Is the dish . . .	**Este prato é . . .**	EHS-chee PRAH-too eh . . .
• baked?	• **assado?**	• ah-SAH-doo?
• boiled?	• **cozido?**	• koh-ZEE-doo?
• stuffed?	• **recheado?**	• hay-SHYAH-doo?
• grilled?	• **grelhado?**	• grehl-YAH-doo?
• fried?	• **frito?**	• FREE-too?

63

I prefer the meat ...	**Prefiro a carne ...**	pray-FEE-roo ah KAHR-nee ...
• well-done.	**• bem passada.**	• behn pah-SAH-dah
• medium.	**• no ponto.**	• noo POHN-too
• rare.	**• mal passada.**	• mow pah-SAH-dah

SPECIAL REQUESTS

More water, please.	**Mais água, por favor.**	mahys AH-gwah, poor fah-VOHR
I'm on a diet.	**Estou de regime.**	ehs-TOH jee heh-ZHEE-mee
I'm on a special diet.	**Estou numa die-ta especial.**	ehs-TOH-NOO-mah JYEH-tah ehs-peh-SYOW
I'm diabetic.	**sou diabético (-a).**	sow jee-ah-BEH-chee-koo(-kah)
I can't eat ...	**Não posso comer ...**	nown POH-soo koh-MEHR ...
• salt.	**• sal.**	• sow
• fat.	**• gordura.**	• gohr-DOO-rah
• sugar.	**• açúcar.**	• ah-SOO-kahr
• flour.	**• farinha.**	• fah-REEN-yah
I don't eat pork.	**Não como porco.**	nown KOH-moo POHR-koo
Where's the rest room?	**Onde fica o ba-nheiro?**	OHN-jee FEE-kah oo bahn-YAY-roo?

RESTAURANT ITEMS

May I have ...	**Poderia ter ...**	poh-deh-REE-ah tehr ...
• some silverware?	**• talheres?**	• tahl-YEH-rees?
• a fork?	**• um garfo?**	• oon GAHR-foo?
• a knife?	**• uma faca?**	• OO-mah FAH-kah?
• a napkin?	**• um guarda-napo?**	• oon gwahr-dah-NAH-poo?
• a cup?	**• uma xícara?**	• OO-mah SHEE-kah-rah?
	uma chávena? (P)	OO-mah SHAH-veh-nah?

• a saucer?	• **um pires?**	• oon PEE-rees?
• a plate?	• **um prato?**	• oon PRAH-too?
• a glass?	• **um copo?**	• oon KOH-poo
• some bread?	• **um pouco de pão?**	• oon POH-koo jee pown?
• some butter?	• **um pouco de manteiga?**	• oon POH-koo jee mahn-CHAY-gah?
• some water?	• **um pouco de água?**	• oon POH-koo jee AH-gwah?
• the salt?	• **o sal?**	• oo sowl?
• the pepper?	• **a pimenta?**	• ah pee-MEHN-tah?
• the mustard?	• **a mostarda?**	• ah mohs-TAHR-dah?
• the mayonnaise?	• **a maionese?**	• ah mah-yoh-NAY-zee?
• some coffee?	• **café?**	• kah-FEH?
• some tea?	• **chá?**	• shah?
• some lemon?	• **um pouco de limão?**	• oon POH-koo jee lee-MOWN?
• the sugar?	• **o açúcar?**	• oo ah-SOO-kahr?
• some sweetener?	• **um pouco de adoçante?**	• oon POH-koo jee ah-doh-SAHN-chee
• a little more?	• **um pouco mais?**	• oon POH-koo mahys?
• an ashtray?	• **um cinzeiro?**	• oon seen-ZAY-roo?
• a toothpick?	• **um palito?**	• oon pah-LEE-too?

PHRASES YOU'LL HEAR

Quantas pessoas são?	KWAHN-tahs peh-SOH-ahs sown?	How many people?
Esta mesa está bem?	EHS-tah MEH-zah ehs-TAH behn?	Is this table all right?
Quer uma cadeira para crianças?	kehr OO-mah kah-DAY-rah PAH-rah kree-AHN-sahs?	Do you want a high chair?
Querem pedir agora?	KEH-rehn peh-JEER ah-GOH-rah?	Do you want to order now?
Querem mais água?	KEH-rehn mahys AH-gwah?	Do you want more water?

65

Desejam mais alguma coisa?	day-ZAY-zhahn mahys ahl-GOO-mah KOY-zah?	Do you want anything else?
Vai tudo bem?	vahy TOO-doo behn?	Is everything O.K.?
Tudo numa só conta?	TOO-doo NOO-mah soh KOHN-tah?	All on one bill?

COMPLAINTS

Something is missing.	**Falta alguma coisa.**	FAHL-tah al-GOO-mah KOY-zah
Please bring us . . .	**Por favor, traga-nos . . .**	poor fah-VOHR, TRAH-gah nohs . . .
• another glass.	• **outro copo.**	• OH-troo KOH-poo
• another set of silverware.	• **outros talheres.**	• OH-troos tahl-YEH-rehs
The tablecloth isn't clean/is dirty.	**A toalha da mesa não está limpa/está suja.**	ah TWAHL-yah dah MEH-zah nown ehs-TAH LEEM-pah/ehs-TAH SOO-zhah
Did you forget the soup/drinks?	**O senhor esqueceu a sopa/as bebidas?**	ooh sehn-YOHR ehs-kay-SAY-oo ah SOH-pah/ahs beh-BEE-dahs?
I think there's a mistake.	**Acho que tem um erro.**	AH-shoo keh tehn oon EH-hoo
I didn't order this.	**Eu não pedi isto.**	AY-oo nown peh-JEE EES-too.
I'd like another dish.	**Gostaria de outro prato.**	gohs-tah-REE-ah jee OH-troo PRAH-too
The soup/food is cold.	**A sopa/comida está fria.**	ah SOH-pah/koh-MEE-dah ehs-TAH FREE-ah
The milk isn't fresh.	**O leite não está fresco.**	oo LAY-chee nown ehs-TAH FREHS-koo

PAYING THE BILL

| The check, please. | **A conta, por favor.** | ah KOHN-tah, poor fah-VOHR |
| Separate checks, please. | **Cheques separados, por favor.** | SHEH-kees seh-pah-RAH-doos, poor fah-VOHR |

Is service included?	**Está incluído o serviço?**	ehs-TAH een-kloo-EE-doo oo sehr-VEE-soo?
Do you accept . . .	**Aceita . . .**	ah-SAY-tah . . .
• traveler's checks?	• **cheques de viagem?**	• SHEH-kees jee VYAH-zhehn?
• credit cards?	• **cartões de crédito?**	• kahr-TOWN-ees jee KREH-jee-too?
The meal was excellent.	**A refeição estava excelente.**	ah hay-fay-SOWN ehs-TAH-vah ehk-seh-LEHN-chee
The service was very good.	**O serviço foi muito bom.**	oo sehr-VEE-soo foy MWEE-too bohn

ABOUT BRAZILIAN FOOD

Indian, African, and Portuguese dietary traditions have simmered for centuries to produce Brazil's savory cuisine. The blend of flavors, spices, and styles of preparation are among the most unusual in the world. Perhaps the most distinctive influence on Brazilian cuisine is from the indigenous and African cultures. Brazil's aboriginal tribes cultivated dozens of varieties of edible plants, many of which have since become world staples: potatoes, corn, manioc, bananas, tomatoes, cocoa, vanilla, pineapple, avocado, pumpkin, and pepper. African slaves brought tropical ingredients and spices, coconut milk, dende oil, cashew nuts, pepper, and other hot spices. Traditional Portuguese recipes were also brought and adapted to New World cuisine, but in general, Brazilian cooking is both sweeter and saltier than its Portuguese counterpart.

Brazilian adaptations of continental Portuguese dishes include the fish stews or *caldeiradas* (kahl-day-RAY-dahs), the beef stews or *cozidos* (koh-ZEE-doos), and dishes based on the ever popular salted cod dishes, or *bacalhau* (bah-kahl-YAH-oo).

The average restaurant in big cities does not usually label its food as "Brazilian." However, typical fare consists of beans, rice, French fries, and beef, chicken, or fish. Vegetables are not common, especially raw ones, and salads must be ordered separately. Inland, regional foods are your best bet.

Brazil's national dish is *feijoada* (fay-ZHWAH-dah), traditionally served on Sundays at lunchtime. Originally a slave dish, *feijoada* has been significantly enriched, and today it commonly consists of black or brown beans, sausage, beef, and pork. It is always served with rice, finely shredded kale, orange slices, and *farofa* (fah-ROH-fah), a manioc flour fried with onions and egg, which is sprinkled on top.

Bahian cuisine offers several well-known dishes, such as *vatapa* (vah-tah-PAH), made with dried shrimp, dende oil, coconut milk, and cashews, and *xinxim de galinha* (sheen-SHEEN jee gah-LEEN-yah) which substitutes lime juice for coconut milk to make a sauce for chicken. Churrasco (shoo-HAHS-koo), or barbecued meats, are more typical of the South. Restaurants specializing in these barbecued meats are called *churrascarias* (shoo-hahs-kah-REE-ahs), serving à la carte and all you can eat. Tables are usually filled with numerous small side dishes of garnishes to accompany the meats, which are continuously served right at your table on large skewers by waiters often dressed like *gaúchos* (gah-OO-shoos), the Brazilian cowboy.

Brazil's national drink is *caipirinha* (kahy-pee-REEN-yah), made of crushed lime, sugar, and *pinga* (PEEN-gah) or *cachaça* (kah-SHAH-sah), a strong liquor made from sugar cane. When whipped with crushed ice and fruit juices and sometimes sweetened condensed milk, *pinga* becomes transformed into the popular *batida* (bah-CHEE-dah). Be sure to try a delicious drink of *guaraná* (gwah-rah-NAH), the Brazilian answer to Coca-Cola. But no drink is more Brazilian than coffee *cafezinho* (kay-fay-ZEEN-yoo). It is served black, strong, and with plenty of sugar in small demi-tasse cups. Coffee is served in larger cups and with milk only at breakfast.

SOUPS (*SOPAS*)

canja (KAHN-zhah)   chicken, ham, and rice soup

sopa de cebola   onion soup
(SOH-pah jee seh-
BOH-lah)

bouquet do mar   Bahian fish soup
(boo-KEH-chee doo
mahr)

POULTRY (AVES)

cuscuz de   molded steamed chicken, corn meal, and
galinha (koos-   vegetables
KOOZ jee gah-
LEEN-yah)

frango assado   roast chicken
(FRAHN-goo ah-SAH-
doo)

MEAT (CARNES)

bife com batatas   steak with fried potatoes
fritas (BEE-fee kohn
bah-TAH-tahs FREE-
tahs)

costoletas   grilled chops
grelhadas
(kohs-toh-LEH-tahs
grehl-YAH-dahs)

cozido à   meat stew Brazilian style
brasileira
(koh-ZEE-doo ah
brah-zee-LAY-rah)

churrasco   barbecued meats
(shoo-HAHS-koo)

feijoada   smoked and fresh meats with black beans
completa
(fay-ZHWAH-dah
kohm-PLEH-tah)

69

SEAFOOD (*MARISCOS*)

bobó (boh-BOH) — shrimp in yucca and tomato sauce

carurú de camarão
(kah-roo-ROO jee kah-mah-ROWN) — shrimp with okra and peanuts

muqueca de camarões
(moo-KEH-kah jee kah-mah-ROYN-ees) — prawn stew

siri recheado
(SEE-ree hay-SHYAH-doo) — stuffed crabs

vatapá
(vah-tah-PAH) — fish and shrimp in ginger-flavored peanut sauce

SAUCES (*MOLHOS*)

molho de pimenta
(MOHL-yoo jee pee-MEHN-tah) — pepper sauce

molho de pimenta e limão
(MOHL-yoo jee pee-MEHN-tah ee lee-MOWN) — pepper and lime sauce

VEGETABLES (*VERDURAS*)

abara (ah-BAH-rah) — steamed black-eyed peas

acarajé (ah-kah-rah-ZHEH) — brown bean fritters

alface com tomate (ahl-FAH-see kohn toh-MAH-chee) — lettuce and tomato salad

arroz brasileiro rice with tomatoes and onions
(ah-HOHZ brah-zee-
LAY-roo)

couve à mineira shredded kale and beans
(KOH-vee ah mee-
NAY-rah)

farofa de toasted manioc meal
manteiga
(fah-ROO-fah jee
mahn-CHAY-gah)

salada de heart of palms salad
palmito
(sah-LAH-dah jee
pahl-MEE-too)

DESSERTS (*SOBREMESAS*)

brasileiras Brazilian coconut cookies
(brah-zee-LAY-rahs)

cocada grated coconut dessert
(koh-KAH-dah)

creme de cream of avocado
abacate (KRAY-mee
jee ah-bah-KAH-chee)

mungunzá hominy and coconut milk pudding
(moon-goon-ZAH)

pirão de arroz rice and coconut milk pudding
com leite de coco
(pee-ROWN jee ah-
HOHZ kohn LAY-chee
jee KOH-koo)

pudim de pumpkin pudding
abóbora (poo-JEEN
jee ah-BOH-boh-rah)

quindins de coconut cupcakes
yayá (KEEN-jeens
jee yah-YAH)

71

DRINKS (*BEBIDAS*)

batida paulista
(bah-CHEE-dah
pow-LEES-tah)

Brazilian rum and *cachaça*, with lemon juice

caipirinha
(kahy-pee-REEN-yah)

cachaça, crushed lime, and sugar

café e Chá
(kah-FAY ee shah)

coffee and tea

ABOUT PORTUGUESE FOOD

Portugal is best known for game and seafood. Vegetables appear early in the season, fruit is abundant, and desserts are a wonder. Meats and fish are usually marinated with wine, olive oil, garlic, or herbs before being cooked, and coriander is particularly popular. Portuguese cuisine relies heavily on olive oil or *azeite* (ah-ZAY-teh), a stronger and less refined variety than that produced in Spain or Italy. If olive oil does not agree with you, however, local dishes cooked in butter or corn oil (*óleo*/ OH-lay-oh) are also available.

The basis of festive and formal meals is soup, made of seasonal vegetables, boiled together and sieved with a spoonful of olive oil added at the end. *Cozido* (koh-ZEE-doh) is a hearty soup that's like a main dish, made with meat, poultry, fat, bacon, smoked sausage, chickpeas, rice, and sage. Another popular and filling soup is *açorda* (ah-SOHR-dah), a kind of porridge based on oiled and garlicked wheat bread, and combined with cod fish, boiled eggs, or other ingredients. The *caldo verde* (KAHL-doh VEHR-deh) is served in a bowl, and consists of green cabbage shredded into a potato broth with slices of smoked sausage. Fish soups are also popular and are made by adding potatoes, rice, onion, tomatoes, and olive oil to a stock in which fish has been cooked.

Crayfish, a classic speciality in Portugal, can be enjoyed boiled, grilled, or steamed and served with a hot sauce. Crabs (*santolas*/sahn-TOH-lahsh) are eaten stuffed or plain, as are shrimp (*camarões*/kah-mah-ROYN-eesh). *Percebes* (pehr-SEHbehsh) are a very special type of seasonal seafood, and oysters (*ostras*/OHS-trahs), mussels (*mexilhões*/meh-sheel-YOYN-eesh), and tiny shellfish (*amêijoas*/ah-MAY-zhoh-ahsh) are also very popular.

In Algarve one must try *cataplana* (kah-tah-PLAH-nah), cockles served with sausages and ham. Excellent fish such as sole, bass, brill, merou, and hake, best eaten grilled or meuniére, are found throughout Portugal. At Setúbal, ask for meillet. Swordfish, smelt, tuna steaks, and conger eel are well worth going a long way to find. Portugal is world famous for sardines. Try fresh sardines grilled over charcoal, accompanied by a salad of tomatoes and green peppers. They are also served as fillets, rolled in oatmeal and fried. Note that sardines and dried salt cod, unlike most other fish dishes, are consumed with red wine. But of all the varieties of fish available, you must be sure to try *bacalhau* (bah-kahl-YOW), Portugal's salted cod, which serves as the basis for so many popular dishes.

The abundance of fish makes up for the relative scarcity of meat in Portugal. Beef, or *carne de vaca* (KAHR-neh deh VAH-kah), is seldom tender enough for the ordinary grill, except in the Azores. Nevertheless you will find *bifes à portuguesa* (BEE-fehsh ah pohr-too-GAY-zah); in Madeira you may try *espetadas* (ehs-pay-TAH-dahsh), a kind of beef kebab marinated in oil, wine, and garlic, then skewered. If you are in a hurry you might enjoy a *prego* (PRAY-goh), a sandwich of hot beefsteak. Kid (*cabrito*/kah-BREE-toh), lamb (*borrego*/boh-rray-goh), and pork (*carne de porco*/KAHR-neh deh POHR-koh) are more tender than veal or mutton in Portugal. Cured meats are also quite special, such as dried ham (*presunto*/pray-ZOON-toh) and smoked loin pork (*salpicão*/sahl-pee-KOWN) often found in taverns. Barbecues (*churrascos*/shoo-rrahs-kohsh) are very popular nowadays.

Almost every dish in Portugal is accompanied by either rice or fried potatoes or both. The best known salads are lettuce (*alface*/ahl-FAH-seh), which is always rather green, watercress (*agrião*/ah-gree-OWN), and tomato and pimiento (*tomate e pimento*/toh-MAH-teh ee pee-MEHN-toh).

73

Portugal also has some very good cheeses, such as *queijo da serra* (KAY-zhoh deh seh-rrah), made of ewe's milk, kneaded by hand and and matured in cool cellars, and *queijo de azeitão* (KAY-zhoh deh ah-zah-TOWN), a robust cheese also made from ewe's milk. White or cottage cheeses *queijinhos de tomar* (kah-ZHEEN-yohs deh toh-MAHR) are occasionally eaten salted, but when consumed fresh, some are silky and feathery. Cheeses are often put on your table in restaurants for you to nibble on between courses.

Sweets are quite popular in Portugal. The one universal dessert is the *flan* (or creme caramelo/KRAY-me Kah-rah-MEH-loh), which appears on the menu of every restaurant. Other famous desserts are *toucinho do céu* (toh-SEEN-yoh doh SAY-oo), or bacon from heaven, and *barrigas de freiras* (bah-RREE-gahsh deh FRAY-rahsh), or nuns' tummies; both are almond-based sweets. One traditional sweet is quince cheese, *marmelada* (mahr-meh-LAH-dah) (from which our word marmalade is derived), perfumed with vanilla, lemon, and bergamot. *Pasteis de nata* (pahs-TAY-eesh deh NAH-tah) are small tartes, made with custard and cinnamon or with cheese (*queijadas*/kay-ZHAH-dahsh). Fruits are excellent, and those popular in Portugal include pears, oranges, plums, figs, almonds, strawberries, peaches, and nectarines.

With the exception of the well-known Port and Madeira wines, most Portuguese wines are still relatively unknown outside of the country. Nonetheless, Portugal is a country where any visitor who likes wine can enjoy an endless variety for little more than the cost of a good beer. Perhaps the best known Portuguese wine is *vinho verde* (VEEN-yoh VEHR-deh). Although the wine is light green, the name, which means "green wine," refers to its delightful youth rather than its color.

SOUPS (*SOPAS*)

caldo verde (KAHL-doh VEHR-deh)	potato and kale soup with smoked sausage
canja (KAHN-zhah)	chicken and rice soup with lemon and mint

sopa alentejana
(SOH-pah ah-lehn-tay-ZHAH-nah)

coriander and garlic soup with poached eggs

sopa da casa
(SOH-pah dah KAH-zah)

garlic soup with chickpeas, mint, and croutons

SEAFOOD (*MARISCOS*)

amêijoas na cataplana
(ah-MAY-zhoh-ahsh nah kah-tah-PLAH-nah)

steamed clams with sausage, ham, tomatoes, and spices

lagosta suada
(lah-GOHSH-tah soo-AH-dah)

steamed crayfish

bacalhau à Gomes da Sá
(bah-kahl-YOW ah GOH-mehsh dah sah)

salted cod with potatoes, onions, and black olives

bacalhau dourado
(bah-kahl-YOW doh-RAH-doh)

cod with eggs and golden fried potatoes

bacalhau à Trás-os-Montes
(bah-kahl-YOW ah traz-oos-MOHN-taysh)

baked cod with ham, tomato, and black olives

caldeirada
(kahl-day-RAH-dah)

seafood stew

escabeche
(ehs-kah-BAY-sheh)

fish pickled with carrots, onions, and bay leaves

meia desfeita de bacalhau (MAY-yah daysh-FAY-tah deh bah-kahl-YOW)

salted cod with chickpeas, hard boiled eggs, and black olives

pasteis de bacalhau
(pahs-TAYSH deh bah-kahl-YOW)

codfish cakes with parsley, coriander, and mint

MEATS (*CARNES*)

bife à portuguesa
(BEE-feh ah pohr-too-GAY-zah)

Portuguese steak with a sweet paprika-and-red-wine sauce served sizzling hot in an earthenware dish; sometimes topped with a fried egg.

carne de porco com amêijoas à alentejana
(KAHR-neh deh POHR-koh kohn ah-MAY-zhoh-ahsh ah ah-lehn-tay-ZHAH-nah)

marinated pork with clams, tomatoes, and coriander

carne de vinho d'alhos (KAHR-neh deh VEEN-yah DAHL-yohsh)

pork braised in white wine with herbs

cordeiro à transmontana
(kohr-DAY-roh ah trahns-mohn-TAH-nah)

rolled leg of lamb, roasted with mint

cozido à portuguesa
(koh-ZEE-doh ah pohr-too-GAY-zah)

boiled meats, chicken, and vegetables

iscas (EES-kahsh)

marinated liver with red wine sauce

lombo de porco com pimentos vermelhos doces
(LOHM-boh deh POHR-koh kohn pee-MEHN-tohsh vehr-MEHL-yohsh DOH-sehsh)

marinated pork loin with sweet red peppers

rojões com cominhos
(rroh-ZHOYN-eesh kon koh-MEEN-yohsh)

braised pork with cumin, coriander, and lemon

tripas à moda do Porto
(TREE-pahsh ah MOH-dah doh POHR-toh)

tripe stew with veal, chicken, sausage, ham, and beans

trouxa de vitela
(TROH-shah deh vee-TEH-lah)

marinated veal roast with red wine

POULTRY (*AVES*)

arroz de pato de Braga (ah-RROHZ deh PAH-toh deh BRAH-gah)

roast duck with sausage-and-ham-flavored rice

VEGETABLES (*VERDURAS*)

batatas à portuguesa
(bah-TAH-tahs ah pohr-too-GAY-zah)

Portuguese fried potatoes

ervilhas guisadas à portuguêsa
(ehr-VEEL-yahsh gee-SAH-dahsh ah pohr-too-GAY-zah)

peas Portuguese style

salada mista
(sah-LAH-dah MEES-tah)

mixed green salad

77

BREADS (*PAOS*)

bôlo rei (BOH-loh RRAY-ee)   candied fruit and nut bread

broa (BROH-ah)   Portuguese corn bread

massa sovada (MAH-sah soh-VAH-dah)   Portuguese sweet bread

DESSERTS (*SOBREMESAS*)

arroz doce (ah-RROHZ DOH-seh)   rice pudding

bôlo de Amêndoa à Algarvia (BOH-loh deh ah-MEHN-doh-ah ah ahl-gahr-VEE-ah)   almond layer cake

bombons de figos (bohn-BOHNSH deh FEE-gohsh)   fig candies with almonds

fatias da China (fah-TEE-ahsh dah SHEE-nah)   egg and almond slices in syrup

figos recheados (FEE-gohsh rray-SHYAH-dohsh)   dried figs stuffed with almonds and chocolate

ovos moles (OH-vohsh MOH-lehsh)   egg yolk icing

papos de anjo (PAH-pohsh deh AHN-zhoh)   sweet egg cakes in syrup

pasteis de nata (pahs-TAY-eesh deh NAH-tah)   custard tartes

78

pudim flan com porto (poo-DEEN flahn kohn POHR-toh)   Portuguese baked caramel custard

queijadas de Évora (kay-ZHAH-dahsh deh EH-voh-rah)   sweet cheese tartes

toucinho do céu (toh-SEEN-yoh doh SAY-oo)   almond cake

WINES AND LIQUORS (*VINHOS E LICORES*)

adamado (ah-dah-MAH-doh)   a medium sweet wine

aguardente (ah-gwahr-DEHN-teh)   brandy

branco (BRAHN-koh)   white

bruto (BROO-toh)   extra-dry, for sparkling wines

doce (DOH-seh)   sweet

espumante (ehs-poo-MAHN-teh)   sparkling wine

garrafeira (gah-rrah-FAY-rah)   fine, matured wine

generoso (zheh-neh-ROH-zoh)   sweet dessert wine

meio seco (MAY-oh SAY-koh)   medium dry

rosé (rroh-ZEH)   rosé

seco (SAY-koh)   dry

tinto (TEEN-toh)   red

velho (VEHL-yoh)   old, matured wine

79

vinho de mesa   table wine
(VEEN-yoh deh
MAY-zah)

vinho da casa   house wine
(VEEN-yoh dah
KAH-zah)

GENERAL FOOD AND DRINK CATEGORIES

MEAT (*CARNE*)

cabrito	kah-BREE-too	goat
carne de vaca	KAHR-nee jee VAH-kah	beef
carneiro	kahr-NAY-roo	lamb
carnes frias (P)	KAHR-nehs FREE-ahsh	cold cuts
cordeiro (P)	kohr-DAY-roo	lamb
costeleta	kohs-teh-LAY-tah	chop
chouriço (P)	shoh-REE-soh	sausage
defumado	jee-foo-MAH-doo	smoked ham
figado	FEE-gah-doo	liver
frios	FREE-oohs	cold cuts
leitão	lay-TOWN	suckling pig
lingua	LEEN-gwah	tongue
presunto (P)	pray-ZOON-toh	smoked ham
porco	POHR-koo	pork
salsicha	sahl-SEE-shah	sausage
toucinho	toh-SEEN-yoo	bacon
vitela	vee-TEH-lah	veal

FOWL AND GAME (*AVES E ANIMAIS DE CAÇA*)

codorna	koh-DOHR-nah	quail
codorniz (P)	koh-dohr-NEEZ	quail
coelho	KWEHL-yoo	rabbit
faisão	fahy-ZOWN	pheasant
frango	FRAHN-goo	chicken
galinha	gah-LEEN-yah	chicken
ganso	GAHN-soo	goose
javali	zhah-vah-LEE	wild boar

lebre	LEH-bree	hare
pato	PAH-too	duck
perdiz	pehr-DEEZ	partridge
peru	pee-ROO	turkey
pombo	POHM-boo	pidgeon
veado	VYAH-doo	venison

FISH AND SEAFOOD (*PESCADO E MARISCOS*)

amêijoas (P)	ah-MAY-zhoh-ahsh	clams
arenque	ah-REHN-kee	herring
atum	ah-TOON	tuna
bacalhau	bah-kahl-YOW	codfish
camarão	kah-mah-ROWN	shrimp
caranquejo	kah-rahn-KAY-zhoo	crab
carapau	kah-rah-POW	smelt/mackerel
cherne	SHEHR-nee	brill
chôco	SHOH-koo	cuttlefish
congro	KOHN-groo	conger
enchovas	ehn-SHOH-vahs	anchovies
enguia	ehn-GEE-ah	eel
esturjão	ehs-toor-ZHOWN	sturgeon
espadarte (P)	ehs-pah-DAHR-teh	swordfish
gambas (P)	GAHM-bahsh	scampi
garoupa	gah-ROH-pah	merou
lagosta	lah-GOHS-tah	crayfish
lagostins	lah-gohs-CHEENS	prawns
lampreia	lahm-PRAY-yah	lamprey
linguado	leen-GAHW-doo	sole
lula	LOO-lah	squid
mexilhões	may-shee-YOYN-ees	mussels
ostras	OHS-trahs	oysters
pargo	PAHR-goo	sea bream
peixe agulha	PAY-shee ah-GOOL-yah	garfish
peixe-espada	PAY-shee eh-SPAH-dah	swordfish
pescada	pehs-KAH-dah	hake
pescadinha	pehs-kah-JEEN-yah	whiting
percebes	pehr-SEH-bees	barnacles

81

polvo	POHL-voo	octopus
robalo	hoh-BAH-loo	sea bass
salmão	sahl-MOWN	salmon
salmonete	sahl-moh-NAY-chee	meillet
santola	sahn-TOH-lah	crab
sardinha	sahr-JEEN-yah	sardine
sável	SAH-vay-oo	shad
sururú	soo-roo-ROO	type of mussel (B)
truta	TROO-tah	trout

VEGETABLES (*VERDURAS*)

abóbora	ah-BOH-boh-rah	pumpkin squash
agriões	ah-gree-OYN-ees	watercress
aipo	AY-poo	celery
alcachofra	ahl-kah-SHOH-frah	artichoke
alface	ahl-FAH-see	lettuce
alho	AHL-yoo	garlic
aspargos	ahs-PAHR-goo	asparagus
batatas	bah-TAH-tahs	potatoes
batata doce	bah-TAH-tah DOH-see	sweet potato
berinjela	beh-reen-ZHEH-lah	eggplant
brócolo	BROH-koh-lee	broccoli
beterraba	beh-teh-HAH-bah	beets
cebolas	seh-BOH-lahs	onions
cenouras	seh-NOH-rahs	carrots
chicória	shee-KOH-ryah	chicory/endive
cogumelos	koh-goo-MEH-loos	mushrooms
couve (P)	KOH-veh	cabbage
couve-flor	KOH-vee flohr	cauliflower
ervilhas	ehr-VEEL-yahs	peas
espinafre	ehs-pee-NAH-free	spinach
favas	FAH-vahs	horse beans
feijão	fay-ZHOWN	beans
feijão verde	fay-ZHOWN VEHR-jee	green beans
funcho	FOON-shoo	fennel
grão-de-bico	grown jee BEE-koo	chickpeas
lentilhas	lehn-TEEL-yahs	lentils
milho doce	MEEL-yoo DOH-see	sweet corn
palmito	pahl-MEE-too	heart of palm
pepino	peh-PEE-noo	cucumber

quiabo	KYAH-boo	okra
rabanetes	hah-bah-NEH-chees	radishes
repolho	heh-POHL-yoo	cabbage
tomates	toh-MAH-chees	tomatoes
vagens	VAH-zhens	string beans
xuxú	shoo-SHOO	rutabaga

CONDIMENTS (*CONDIMENTOS*)

cominhos	koh-MEEN-yoos	cumin
pimenta	pee-MEHN-tah	white/black pepper
sal	sowl	salt

FRUITS (*FRUTAS*)

abacaxi	ah-bah-kah-SHEE	pineapple
alperces (P)	ahl-PEHR-sehs	apricots
ameixas	ah-MAY-shahs	plums
ameixas passas (P)	ah-MAY-shahs PAH-sahs	prunes
ameixas secas	ah-MAY-shahs SEH-kahs	prunes
amêndoas	ah-MAYN-dwahs	almonds
avelãs	ah-veh-LAHNS	hazel nuts
banana	bah-NAH-nah	banana
caqui	KAH-kee	persimmon
castanhas	kahs-TAHN-yahs	chestnuts
cerejas	seh-RAY-zhahs	cherries
damascos	dah-MAHS-koos	apricots
figos	FEE-goos	figs
framboesas	frahm-BWAY-zahs	raspberries
grapefruit	GRAYP-froot	grapefruit
goiaba	goh-YAH-bah	guava
laranja	lah-RAHN-zhah	orange
lima	LEE-mah	lime
limão	lee-MOWN	lemon
limão verde	lee-MOWN VEHR-jee	green lime
maçã	mah-SAHN	apple
maracujá	mah-rah-koo-ZHAH	passion fruit
melancia	meh-lahn-SEE-ah	watermelon

83

melão	meh-LOWN	melon
morangos	moh-RAHN-goos	strawberries
nêsperas	NAYS-peh-rahs	crab apple
nozes	NOH-zees	walnuts
passas de uva (P)	PAH-sahsh deh OO-vah	raisins
pera	PEH-rah	pear
pêssego	PAY-say-goo	peach
tâmaras	TAH-mah-rahs	dates
tangerinas	tahn-zheh-REE-nahs	tangerines
uvas	OO-vahs	grapes
uva passa	OO-vah PAH-sah	raisins
umbú	oom-BOO	a tropical fruit

DRINKS (*BEBIDAS*)

água de côco	AH-gwah jee KOH-koo	coconut milk
aguardente	ah-gwahr-DEHN-chee	brandy
batida	bah-CHEE-dah	fruit juices, ice, and pinga
café	kah-FEH	coffee
café com creme	kah-FEH kohn KRAY-mee	coffee with cream
café com nata (P)	kah-FEH kohn NAH-tah	coffee with cream
café expresso (P)	kah-FEH ehks-PREH-soo	expresso
café gelado	kah-FEH zheh-LAH-doo	iced coffee
café preto	kah-FEH PRAY-too	black coffee
café puro (P)	kah-FEH POO-roh	black coffee
cafezinho	kah-feh-ZEEN-yoo	expresso
caipirinha	kahy-pee-REEN-yah	lime, sugar, and pinga
caldo de cana	KAHL-doo jee KAH-nah	sugar cane juice
cerveja	sehr-VAY-zhah	beer
chocolate	shoh-koh-LAH-chee	chocolate
leite	LAY-chee	milk

limonada	lee-moh-NAH-dah	lemonade
pinga	PEEN-gah	alcoholic beverage
suco de	SOO-koo jee mah-rah-	passion fruit juice
maracujá	koo-ZHAH	
vinho	VEEN-yoo	wine

7. PERSONAL SERVICES

DIALOGUE: GETTING A HAIRCUT (*UM CORTE DE CABELO*)

Barbeiro:	**Quem é o próximo?**	kehn eh oo PROHK-see-moo?
Client	**Eu, obrigada. Desejo um corte de cabelo, por favor.**	AY-oo, oh-bree-GAH-dah. deh-ZAY-zhoo oom KOHR-chee jee kah-BAY-loo, poor fah-VOHR?
Barbeiro:	**Como é que você o quer?**	KOH-moo eh keh voh-SAY oo kehr?
Cliente:	**Comprido atrás, mas mais curto nos lados.**	kohn-PREE-doo ah-TRAHS, mahs mahys KOOR-too nohs LAH-doos.
Barbeiro:	**Pois não! Deseja também lavar a cabeça?**	poys nown! day-ZAY-zha tahm-BEHN lah-VAHR ah kah-BEH-sah?
Cliente:	**Não, obrigada. Somente o corte.**	nown, oh-bree-GAH-dah. soh-MEHN-chee oo KOHR-chee.
Barbeiro:	**Bom.**	bohn.

. . . .

Barber:	Who's next?
Client:	Me. I'd like a haircut, please.
Barber:	How would you like it?
Client:	Long in the back, but shorter on the sides.
Barber:	All right. Do you want a shampoo as well?
Client:	No, thank you. Just the haircut.
Barber:	Fine.

AT THE BARBERSHOP

| I'd like . . . | **Desejo . . .** | day-ZAY-zhoo . . . |
| • a haircut. | **• um corte de cabelo.** | • oon KOHR-chee jee kah-BEH-loo |

• a razor cut.	• um corte a navalha.	• oon KOHR-chee ah nah-VAHL-yah
• a shampoo.	• lavar a cabeça.	• lah-VAHR ah kah-BEH-sah
Cut it short . . .	Deixe-o curto . . .	DAY-shee-oo KOOR-too . . .
• in the front.	• na frente.	• nah FREHN-chee
• on the sides.	• nos lados.	• noos LAH-doos
• in the back.	• atrás.	• ah-TRAHS
• on top.	• em cima.	• ehn SEE-mah
Cut it a little shorter.	Corte-o um pouquinho mais curto.	KOHR-chee-oo oon poh-KEEN-yoo mahys KOOR-too
Leave it long.	Deixe-o longo.	DAY-shee-oo LOHN-goo
Leave it a little longer.	Deixe-o um pouquinho mais longo.	DAY-shee-oo oon poh-KEEN-yoo mahys LOHN-goo
I'd like the part . . .	Quero repartido . . .	KEH-roo hay-pahr-CHEE-doo . . .
• on the right.	• à direita.	• ah jee-RAY-tah
• on the left.	• à esquerda.	• ah ehs-KEHR-dah
• down the middle.	• no meio.	• noo MAY-yoo
Also trim my . . .	Também apare . . .	tahm-BEHN ah-PAH-ree . . .
• beard.	• a barba.	• ah BAHR-bah
• mustache.	• o bigode.	• oo bee-GOH-jee
• sideburns.	• as costeletas.	• ahs kos-teh-LAY-tahs
Cut a bit more here.	Corte um pouco mais aqui.	KOHR-chee oon POH-koo mahys ah-KEE
It's fine like that.	Está bem assim.	ehs-TAH BEHN ah-SEEN

AT THE BEAUTY PARLOR

| Is there a beauty parlor nearby? | Tem um salão de beleza (cabeleireiro/P) por aqui? | tehn oon sah-LOWN jee beh-LEH-zah (kah-beh-lay-RAY-roh) poor ah-Kee? |
| Is there a long wait? | Preciso esperar muito? | pray-SEE-zoo ehs-peh-RAHR MWEE-too? |

87

Do I need an appointment?	**Preciso de hora marcada?**	pray-SEE-zoo jee OH-rah mahr-KAH-dah?
Can I make an appointment for . . .	**Posso marcar para . . .**	POH-soo mahr-KAHR PAH-rah . . .
• later?	• **mais tarde?**	• mahys TAHR-jee?
• this afternoon?	• **esta tarde?**	• EHS-tah TAHR-jee?
• three o'clock?	• **às três?**	• ahs trays?
• tomorrow?	• **amanhã?**	• ah-mahn-YAHN?
I'd like . . .	**Gostaria de . . .**	gohs-tah-REE-ah jee . . .
• a shampoo.	• **lavar a cabeça.**	• lah-VAHR ah kah-BEH-sah
• a set.	• **um penteado.**	• oon pehn-CHYAH-doo
• a permanent.	• **um permanente.**	• oon pehr-mah-NEHN-chee
• a manicure.	• **fazer as unhas.**	• fah-ZEHR ahs OON-yahs
• a touch up.	• **um retoque.**	• oon hay-TOH-kee
• a color rinse.	• **uma rinsagem com cor.**	• OO-mah heen-ZAH-zhen
Can I see a color chart?	**Posso ver uma mostra de cores?**	POH-soo vehr OO-mah MOHS-trah jee KOHR-ees?
I prefer . . .	**Prefiro . . .**	pray-FEE-roo
• auburn.	• **castanho.**	• kahs-TANH-yoo
• light brown.	• **castanho claro.**	• kahs-TAHN-yoo KLAH-roo
• light blond.	• **loiro claro.**	• LOY-roo KLAH-roo
• a darker shade.	• **um tom mais escuro.**	• oon tohn mahys ehs-KOO-roo
• a lighter shade.	• **um tom mais claro.**	• oon tohn mahys KLAH-roo
Please use hairspray.	**Com laquê, por favor.**	kohn lah-KAY, poor fah-VOHR
No hairspray, please.	**Não coloque laquê, por favor.**	nown koh-LOH-kee lah-KAY, poor fah-VOHR

LAUNDRY AND DRY CLEANING

Where is the nearest . . .	**Onde fica a . . . mais próxima?**	OHN-jee FEE-kah ah . . . mahys PROHK-see-mah?

88

• laundry?	• **lavanderia**	• lah-vahn-deh-REE-ah
	• **lavandaria(P)**	• lah-vahn-dah-REE-ah
• dry cleaners?	• **tinturaria**	• teen-too-rah-REE-ah
• laundromat?	• **lavanderia automática**	• lah-vahn-deh-REE-ah ow-toh-MAH-chee-kah
I have some clothes to be . . .	**Tenho roupa para . . .**	TEHN-yoo HOH-pah PAH-rah . . .
• washed.	• **lavar.**	• lah-VAHR
• ironed.	• **passar.**	• pah-SAHR
• dry cleaned.	• **lavar a seco.**	• lah-VAHR ah SEH-koo
• mended.	• **remendar.**	• hay-mehn-DAHR
When will they be ready?	**Quando estarão prontas?**	KWAHN-doo ehs-tah-ROWN PROHN-tahs?
I need them . . .	**Preciso delas para . . .**	pray-SEE-zoo DEH-lahs PAH-rah . . .
• tomorrow.	• **amanhã.**	• ah-mahn-YAWN
• the day after tomorrow.	• **depois-de-amanhã.**	• jee-POYS jee ah-mahn-YAWN
• in a week.	• **dentro de uma semana.**	• DEHN-troo jee OO-mah seh-MAH-nah
• as soon as possible.	• **o mais rápido possível.**	• oo mahys HAH-pee-doo poh-SEE-vay-oo
I'm leaving tomorrow.	**Vou-me embora amanhã.**	VOH-mee ehm-BOH-rah ah-mahn-YAWN
Can you get this stain out?	**Pode tirar esta mancha?**	POH-jee chee-RAHR EHS-tah MAHN-shah?
Can you sew on this button?	**Pode costurar este botão?**	POH-jee kohs-too-RAHR EHS-chee boh-TOWN?
Here is my list.	**Aqui está a minha lista.**	ah-KEE ehs-TAH ah MEEN-yah LEES-tah
This isn't mine.	**Isto não é meu.**	EES-too nown eh MAY-oo
There's an item missing.	**Falta alguma coisa.**	FAHL-tah ahl-GOO-mah KWOY-zah

89

LAUNDRY LIST

I have . . .	Tenho . . .	TEHN-yoo . . .
• two shirts.	• duas camisas.	• DOO-ahs kah-MEE-zahs
• five underpants.	• cinco cuecas.	• SEEN-koo KWAY-kahs
• a suit.	• um terno. um fato. (P)	• oon TEHR-noo oon FAH-toh
• eight pairs of socks.	• oito pares de meias.	• OY-too PAH-rees jee MAY-yahs
• several handkerchiefs.	• alguns lenços.	• ahl-GOONS LEHN-soos
• two ties.	• duas gravatas.	• DOO-ahs grah-VAH-tahs
• a sweater.	• um suéter.	• oon SWEH-tehr
• two pairs of pants.	• duas calças.	• DOO-ahs KAHL-sahs
• pajamas.	• pijama.	• pee-ZHAH-mah
• a raincoat.	• um casaco de chuva. um gabardine. (P)	• oon kah-ZAH-koo jee SHOO-vah oon gah-bahr-DEE-neh
• a jacket.	• um paletó. uma jaqueta. (P)	• oon pah-lay-TOH OO-mah zhah-KEH-tah
• a bathing suit.	• um maiô.	• oon mahy-YOH
• three blouses.	• três blusas.	• trays BLOO-zahs
• a skirt.	• uma saia.	• OO-mah SAH-yah
• a bra.	• um soutien.	• oon soh-CHYEHN
• four panties.	• quatro calcinhas.	• KWAH-troo kahl-SEEN-yahs
• stockings.	• meias.	• MAY-yahs
• sandals.	• sandálias.	• sahn-DAHL-yahs

8. HEALTH CARE

Rio and São Paulo are modern urban centers with good sanitary conditions, but if you plan to travel to rural areas of Brazil, you may be subject to tropical diseases such as yellow fever, dengue, malaria, and hepatitis. Check with your doctor before you go for any special innoculations. Most visitors who stay for a few weeks have no problems, but those that do occur often result from eating unfamiliar foods or trying to tan too fast. It's always safest to eat only peeled fruit and cooked vegetables, and to be selective with street food vendors and stands. In Portugal, there is free medical treatment for visitors whose countries of origin have reciprocal health agreements (such as Great Britain); the United States doesn't have such reciprocal agreements with Brazil.*

It's a good idea to check with your health insurance company to clarify whether accident and illness expenses, which may occur abroad, are covered by your policy. You should be able to locate a British or American hospital in the larger cities of both Portugal and Brazil. Your embassy or consulate can also help you locate appropriate health care.

DIALOGUE: FINDING A DOCTOR (*PROCURANDO UM MÉDICO*)

Turista:	**Não me sinto muito bem.**	nown mee SEEN-too MWEE-too behn.
Recepcionista:	**Precisa de um médico?**	pray-SEE-zeh jee oon MEH-jee-koo?
Turista:	**Acho que sim. Pode recomendar um?**	AH-shoo keh seen. PHO-jee hay-koh-mehn-DAHR oon?

* You might want to contact the International Association for Medical Assistance to Travelers, for more information on insurance and medical treatments, at 736 Center Street, Lewiston, NY 14092; 716-754-4883.

91

Recepcionista:	Sim. Tem um Centro Médico na esquina.	seen. tehn oon SEHN-troo MEH-jee-koo nah ehs-KEE-nah.
Turista:	Tem um médico que fala inglês?	tehn oon MEH-jee-koo keh FAH-lah een-GLAYS?
Recepcionista:	Não, mas a enfermeira fala.	nown, mahs ah ehn-fehr-MAY-rah FAH-lah.

. . . .

Tourist:	I don't feel well.
Hotel Clerk:	Do you need a doctor?
Tourist:	I think so. Can you recommend one?
Hotel Clerk:	Yes. There's a Medical Center on the corner.
Tourist:	Is there a doctor who speaks English?
Hotel Clerk:	No, but the nurse does.

Is there a doctor here?	**Tem médico aqui?**	tehn MEH-jee-koo ah-KEE?
Where can I find a doctor?	**Onde posso encontrar um médico?**	OHN-jee POH-soo ehn-kohn-TRAHR oon MEH-jee-koo?
Can you call me a doctor?	**Pode me chamar um médico?**	POH-jee mee shah-MAHR oon MEH-jee-koo?
Where's the doctor's office?	**Onde fica o consultório do médico?**	OHN-jee FEE-kah oo kohn-sool-TOH-ryoo doo MEH-jee-koo?
I need a doctor who speaks English.	**Preciso de um médico que fale inglês.**	pray-SEE-zoo jee oon MEH-jee-koo kee FAH-lee een-GLAYS
Are you the nurse?	**A senhorita é a enfermeira?**	ah sehn-yoh-REE-tah eh ah ehn-fehr-MAY-rah?

English	Portuguese	Pronunciation
Can I see the doctor?	**Posso ver o médico?**	POH-soo vehr oo MEH-jee-koo?
When can I see the doctor?	**Quando posso ver o médico?**	KWAHN-doo POH-soo vehr oo MEH-jee-koo?
Can the doctor see me now?	**O médico pode-me ver agora?**	oo MEH-jee-koo POH-jee mee vehr ah-GOH-rah?
Do I need an appointment?	**Preciso de uma consulta?**	pray-SEE-zoo jee OO-mah kohn-SOOL-tah?
Can I have an appointment for . . .	**Posso fazer uma consulta para . . .**	POH-soo fah-ZEHR OO-mah kohn-SOOL-tah PAH-rah . . .
• as soon as possible?	• **assim que possível?**	• ah-SEEN keh poh-SEE-vay-oo?
• later?	• **mais tarde?**	• mahys TAHR-jee?
• 2 o'clock?	• **às duas?**	• ahs DOO-ahs?
• today?	• **hoje?**	• OH-zhee?
• tommorrow?	• **amanhã?**	• ah-mahn-YAHN?
What are the office hours?	**Quais são as horas de consulta?**	kwahys sown ahs OH-rahs jee kohn-SOOL-tah?
I need . . .	**Preciso de . . .**	pray-SEE-zoo jee . . .
• a general practitioner.	• **um/uma clinico(-a) geral.**	• oon/oo-mah KLEEN-ee-koo(-kah) zheh-ROW
• a pediatrician.	• **um/uma pediatra.**	• oon/OO-mah peh-jee-AH-trah
• a gynecologist.	• **um/uma ginecologista.**	• oon/OO-mah zhee-nay-koh-loh-ZHEES-tah
• an eye doctor.	• **um/uma oftamologista.**	• oon/OO-mah ohf-tah-moh-loh-ZHEES-tah
• a dentist.	• **um/uma dentista.**	• oon/OO-mah dehn-TEES-tah
It's an emergency.	**E uma emergência.**	eh OO-mah eh-mehr-ZHEHN-syah

TALKING TO THE DOCTOR

I don't feel well.	Não me sinto bem	nown mee SEEN-too behn
I'm sick.	Estou doente.	ehs-TOH DWEHN-chee
I don't know what I have.	Não sei o que tenho.	nown SAY-ee oo keh TEHN-yoo
I feel . . .	Sinto-me . . .	SEEN-too mee . . .
• weak.	• fraco(-a).	• FRAH-koo(-kah)
• dizzy.	• tonto(-a).	• TOHN-too(-tah)
I have a fever.	Tenho febre.	TEHN-yoo FEH-bree
I don't have fever.	Não tenho febre.	nown TEHN-yoo FEH-bree
I'm nauseated.	Estou com náuseas.	ehs-TOH kohn NOW-syahs
I can't sleep.	Não consigo dormir.	nown kohn-SEE-goo dohr-MEER
I threw up.	Vomitei.	voh-mee-TAY
I have diarrhea.	Estou com diarréia.	ehs-TOH kohn jee-ah-HAY-yah
I'm constipated.	Estou com prisão de ventre.	ehs-TOH kohn pree-SOWN jee VEHN-tree
I have . . .	Tenho . . .	TEHN-yoo . . .
• asthma.	• asma.	• AHZ-mah
• a bite.	• uma picada.	• OO-mah pee-KAH-dah
• a bruise.	• uma contusão.	• OO-mah kohn-too-ZOWN
• a burn.	• uma queimadura.	• OO-mah kay-mah-DOO-rah
• something in my eye.	• algo no meu olho.	• AHL-goo noo MAY-oo OHL-yoo
• a cold.	• um resfriado.	• oon hes-FRYAH-doo
• the flu.	• uma gripe.	• OO-mah GREE-pee
• a cough.	• tosse.	• TOH-see
• cramps.	• pontadas.	• pohn-TAH-dahs
• a cut.	• um corte.	• oon KOHR-chee
• a headache.	• dor de cabeça.	• dohr jee kah-BAY-sah
• a lump.	• um calombo.	• oon kah-LOHM-boo

• rheumatism.	• **reumatismo.**	• hay-oo-mah-CHEEZ-moo
• a sore throat.	• **dor de garganta.**	• dohr jee gahr-GAHN-tah
• a stomachache.	• **dor de estômago.**	• dohr jee ehs-TOH-mah-goo
• a sunstroke.	• **insolação.**	• een-soh-lah-SOWN
• a swelling.	• **uma inchaço.**	• OO-mah een-SHAH-soo
• an upset stomach.	• **malestar do estômago.**	• mahl-ehs-TAHR doo ehs-TOH-mah-goo
• a rash.	• **errupção na pele.**	• eh-HOOP-sown nah PEH-lee
I'm allergic to . . .	**Sou alérgico (-a) . . .**	soh ah-LEHR-zhee-koo (-kah) . . .
• penicillin.	• **àpenicilina.**	• ah peh-nee-see-LEE-nah
• sulfa.	• **à sulfamidas.**	• ah sool-fah-MEE-dahs
• certain medicines.	• **a certos remédios.**	• ah SEHR-toos hay-MEH-joos
Here is the medicine I take.	**Aqui está o remédio que eu tomo.**	ah-KEE ehs-TAH oo hay-MEH-joo keh AY-oo TOH-moo
I've had this pain for two days.	**tinha tido esta dor há dois dias.**	CHEEN-yah CHEE-doo EHS-tah dohr ah doys JEE-ahs
I had a heart attack four years ago.	**Tive um enfarto há quatro anos.**	CHEE-vee oon ehn-FAHR-too ah KWAH-troo AH-noos
I'm four months pregnant.	**Estou grávida de quatro meses.**	ehs-TOH GRAH-vee-dah jee KWAH-troo MAY-zees
I have menstrual pains.	**Tenho cólicas menstruais.**	TEHN-yoo KOH-lee-kahs mehns-troo AHYS

PARTS OF THE BODY

appendix	**o apêndice**	oo ah-PEHN-jee-see
arm	**o braço**	oo BRAH-soo
ankle	**o tornozelo**	oo tohr-noh-ZAY-loo

back	as costas	ahs KOHS-tahs
bladder	a bexiga	ah beh-ZEE-gah
breast	o seio	oo SAY-yoo
chest	o peito	oo PAY-too
ear	a orelha	ah oh-REHL-yah
elbow	o cotovelo	oo koh-toh-VEH-loo
eye	o olho	oo OHL-yoo
face	o rosto	oo HOS-too
foot	o pé	oo peh
glands	as glândulas	ahs GLAHN-doo-lahs
hand	a mão	ah mown
head	a cabeça	ah kah-BAY-sah
heart	o coração	oo koh-rah-SOWN
hip	o quadril	oo kwah-DREE-oo
knee	o joelho	oo zhoh-EHL-yoo
leg	a perna	ah PEHR-nah
liver	o fígado	oo FEE-gah-doo
lungs	os pulmões	oos pool-MOYN-ees
mouth	a boca	ah BOH-kah
neck	o pescoço	oo pehs-KOO-soo
nose	o nariz	oo nah-REEZ
shoulder	o ombro	oo OHM-broo
stomach	o estômago	oo ehs-TOH-mah-goo
throat	a garganta	ah gahr-GAHN-tah
tongue	a língua	ah LEEN-gwah
tooth	o dente	oo DEHN-chee
torso	o tronco	oo TROHN-koo
waist	a cintura	ah seen-TOO-rah
wrist	o pulso	oo POOL-soo

WHAT THE DOCTOR SAYS

Onde é que dói?	OHN-jee eh keh doy?	Where does it hurt?
O qué sintomas tem?	oo keh seen-TOH-mahs tehn?	What symptoms do you have?
Dispa-se.	DEES-pah-see	Get undressed.
Dispa-se até a cintura.	DEES-pah-see ah-TEH ah seen-TOO-rah	Undress to the waist.
Deite-se aqui.	DAY-chee-see ah-KEE.	Lie down here.
Abra a boca.	AH-brah ah BOH-kah	Open your mouth.
Tussa!	TOO-sah!	Cough!

Portuguese	Pronunciation	English
Respire fundo.	hehs-PEE-ree FOON-doo	Breathe deeply.
Mostre-me onde é que dói.	MOHS-tree-mee OHN-jee eh keh doy	Show me where it hurts.
Ponha a lingua para fora.	POHN-yah ah LEEN-gwah PAH-rah FOH-rah	Stick your tongue out.
Vista-se.	VEES-tah-see	Get dressed.
Vou-lhe tirar a sua . . .	voh yee chee-RAHR ah SOO-ah . . .	I'm going to take your . . .
• **temperatura.**	• tehm-peh-rah-TOO-rah	• temperature.
• **pressão.**	• pray-SOWN	• blood pressure.
Preciso de uma mostra . . .	pray-SEE-soo jee OO-mah MOHS-trah . . .	I need a sample of . . .
• **de sangue.**	• jee SAHN-gee	• your blood.
• **de fezes.**	• jee FAY-zees	• your stool.
• **de urina.**	• jee oo-REE-nah	• your urine.
Vou-lhe dar um calmante.	voh yee dahr oon kahl-MAHN-chee	I'm going to give you a painkiller.
O senhor (a senhora) precisa . . .	oo sehn-YOHR (ah sehn-YOH-rah) pray-SEE-zah . . .	You'll need . . .
• **de um raio-X.**	• jee oon HAH-yoo shees	• an x-ray.
• **de uma inje-ção.**	• OO-mah een-zheh-SOWN	• an injection.
• **ir ao hospital.**	• eer ow ohs-pee-TOW	• to go to the hospital.
• **ver um especialista.**	• vehr oon ehs-peh-syah-LEES-tah	• to see a specialist.
Não é sério./ Não é grave.	nown eh SEH-ryoo/ nown eh GRAH-vee	It's not serious.
E . . .	eh . . .	It's . . .
• **sério.**	• SEH-ryoo	• serious.
• **um pouco sério.**	• oon POH-koo SEH-ryoo	• somewhat serious.
Está . . .	ehs-TAH . . .	It's . . .
• **deslocado.**	• dehs-loh-KAH-doo	• dislocated.
• **quebrado.**	• kay-BRAH-doo	• broken.
• **torcido.**	• tohr-SEE-doo	• sprained.

• **infeccionado.**	• een-fehk-syo-NAH-doo	• infected.
Tem . . .	tehn . . .	You have . . .
• **apendicite.**	• ah-pehn-jee-SEE-chee	• apendicitis.
• **um resfriado.**	• oon hays-FRYAH-doo	• a cold.
• **uma fractura.**	• OO-mah frahk-TOO-rah	• a fracture.
• **un osso quebrado.**	• oon OH-soo kay-BRAH-doo	• a broken bone.
• **gastrite.**	• gahs-TREE-chee	• gastritis.
• **gripe.**	• GREE-pee	• the flu.
• **uma intoxica-ção.**	• OO-mah een-tohk-see-kah-SOWN	• food poisoning.
• **pneumónia.**	• nay-oo-MOHN-yah	• pneumonia.
• **sarampo.**	• sah-RAHM-poo	• the measles.

PATIENT'S QUESTIONS

Is it serious?	**E grave?**	eh GRAH-vee?
Is it contagious?	**E contagioso?**	eh kohn-tah-ZHOH-zoo?
How long should I stay in bed?	**Quanto tempo devo ficar de cama?**	KWAHN-too TEHM-poo DEH-voo fee-KAHR jee KAH-mah?
What exactly is wrong with me?	**O que é que tenho exata-mente?**	oo keh eh keh TEHN-yoo eh-zah-tah-MEHN-chee?
How frequently do I take the medica-tion?	**Com que fre-qüência tomo o remédio?**	kohn keh fray-KWEHN-syah TOH-moh oo hay-MEH-joo?
Do I need to see you again?	**Devo vê-lo outra vez?**	DEH-voo VAY-loo OH-trah vehz?
Do I need a pre-scription?	**Preciso uma re-ceita?**	pray-SEE-zoo OO-mah hay-SAY-tah?
When can I start traveling again?	**Quando posso começar a via-jar de novo?**	KWAHN-doo POH-soo koh-may-SAHR ah vee-ah-ZHAHR jee NOH-voo?
Can you give me a prescription for . . .	**Pode me receitar . . .**	POH-jee mee hay-say-TAHR . . .
• a painkiller?	• **um calmante?**	• oon kahl-MAHN-chee?

98

English	Portuguese	Pronunciation
• a tranquilizer?	• **um tranquilizante?**	• oon trahn-kee-lee-ZAHN-chee?
• a sleeping pill?	• **um comprimido para dormir?**	• oon kohn-pree-MEE-doo PAH-rah dohr-MEER?
Can I have a bill for my insurance?	**Posso ter um recibo para o seguro?**	POH-soo tehr oon hay-SEE-boo PAH-rah oo say-GOO-roo?
Can you fill out this medical form?	**Pode preencher este formulário médico?**	POH-jee pray-ehn-SHEHR EHS-chee fohr-moo-LAH-ryoo MEH-jee-koo?

AT THE HOSPITAL

English	Portuguese	Pronunciation
Is there a hospital nearby?	**Tem um hospital por aqui?**	tehn oon ohs-pee-TOW poor ah-KEE?
Call an ambulance!	**Chame uma ambulância!**	SHAH-mee OO-mah ahm-boo-LAHN-syah!
Help!	**Socorro!**	soh-KOH-hoo!
Get me to the hospital!	**Leve-me ao hospital!**	LAY-vee mee ow ohs-pee-TOW!
I need first aid fast!	**Preciso de primeiros socorros rápido.**	pray-SEE-zoo jee pree-MAY-roos soh-KOH-hoos HAH-pee-doo!
I was in an accident!	**Tive um acidente!**	CHEE-vee oon ah-see-DEHN-chee.
I cut my . . .	**Cortei . . .**	kohr-TAY . . .
• hand.	• **a mão.**	• ah mown
• leg.	• **a perna.**	• ah PEHR-nah
• face.	• **o rosto.**	• oo HOHS-too
• finger.	• **o dedo.**	• oo DAY-doo
• leg.	• **a perna.**	• ah PEHR-nah
• neck.	• **o pescoço.**	• oo pays-KOH-soo
I can't move.	**Não posso me mexer.**	nown POH-soo mee meh-ZHEHR
He/She hurt his/her head.	**Machucou a cabeça.**	mah-shoo-KOH ah kah-BAY-sah
His/Her ankle is . . .	**Tem o tornozelo . . .**	tehn oo tohr-noh-ZEH-loo . . .

99

• broken.	• **quebrado.**	• kay-BRAH-doo
• twisted.	• **torcido.**	• tohr-SEE-doo
• swollen.	• **inchado.**	• een-SHAH-doo
He's/She's bleeding heavily.	**Está sangrando muito.**	ehs-TAH sahn-GRAHN-doo MWEE-too
He's/She's unconscious.	**Está inconsciente.**	ehs-TAH een-kohn-SYEHN-chee
I burned myself.	**Queimei-me.**	kay-MAY-mee
I ate something poisonous.	**Comi algo venenoso.**	koh-MEE AHL-goo veh-neh-NOH-zoo
When will the doctor come?	**Quando vai chegar o médico?**	KWAHN-doo vahy shay-GAHR oo MEH-jee-koo?
Where is the nurse?	**Onde está a enfermeira?**	OHN-jee ehs-TAH ah ehn-fehr-MAY-rah?
I can't . . .	**Não consigo . . .**	nown kohn-SEE-goo . . .
• eat.	• **comer.**	• koh-MEHR
• drink.	• **beber.**	• beh-BEHR
• sleep.	• **dormir.**	• dohr-MEER
What are the visiting hours?	**Quais são as horas de visita?**	kwahys sown ahs OH-rahs jee vee-ZEE-tah?
When can I leave?	**Quando posso sair?**	KWAHN-doo POH-soo sah-EER?

THE DENTIST

Can you recommend a dentist?	**Pode recomendar um dentista?**	POH-jee heh-koh-mehn-DAHR oon dehn-TEES-tah?
It's an emergency.	**E uma emergência.**	eh OO-mah eh-mehr-ZHAYN-syah.
I'm in a lot of pain.	**Estou com muita dor.**	ehs-TOH kohn MWEE-tah dohr
I've lost a filling.	**Perdi a obturação.**	pehr-JEE ah oh-bee-toor-ah-SOWN
I broke a tooth.	**Quebrei um dente.**	kay-BRAY-ee oon DEHN-chee.
This tooth hurts.	**Este dente dói.**	EHS-chee DEHN-chee doy
I don't want to have it extracted.	**Não quero que o extraia.**	nown KEH-roo keh oo ehks-TRAH-yah

Can you fill it . . .	**Pode tapá-lo . . .**	POH-jee tah-PAH-loo . . .
• with gold?	• **com ouro?**	• kohn OH-roo?
• with silver?	• **com prata?**	• kohn PRAH-tah?
• temporarily?	• **temporária-mente?**	• tehm-poh-rah-ryah-MEHN-chee?
I want a local anesthetic.	**Quero anestesia local.**	KEH-roh ah-nehs-TEH-zyah loh-KOW
My denture is broken.	**A minha dentadura está quebrada.**	ah MEEN-yah dehn-tah-DOO-rah ehs-TAH kay-BRAH-dah
Can you fix . . .	**Pode consertar . . .**	POH-jee kohn-sehr-TAHR . . .
• the denture?	• **a dentadura?**	• ah dehn-tah-DOO-rah?
• this bridge?	• **esta ponte?**	• EHS-tah POHN-chee?
• this crown?	• **esta coroa?**	• EHS-tah koh-ROH-ah?
How much do I owe?	**Quanto lhe devo?**	KWAHN-too yee DEH-voo?

WHAT THE DENTIST SAYS

O senhor (a senhora) tem . . .	oo sehn-YOHR (ah sehn-YOH-rah) tehn . . .	You have . . .
• **uma infecção.**	• OO-mah een-fehk-SOWN	• an infection.
• **uma cárie.**	• OO-mah KAH-ree	• a cavity.
• **um abcesso.**	• oon ahb-SAY-soo	• an abcess.
Isto dói?	EES-too doy?	Does this hurt?
Devo lhe estrair este dente.	DAY-voo yee ehks-trah-EER EHS-chee DEHN-chee	This tooth must come out.
Deve voltar . . .	DEH-vee vohl-TAHR . . .	You'll need to come back . . .
• **amanhã.**	• ah-mahn-YAHN	• tomorrow.
• **dentro de alguns dias.**	• DEHN-troo jee ahl-GOONS JEE-ahs	• in a few days.
• **a próxima semana.**	• ah PROHK-see-mah seh-MAH-nah.	• next week.

THE OPTICIAN

I broke . . .	Quebrei . . .	kay-BRAY-ee . . .
• a lens.	• uma lente.	• OO-mah LEHN-chee.
• the frame.	• a armação.	• ah ahr-mah-SOWN.
• my eyeglasses.	• os óculos.	• oos OH-koo-loos
I lost a contact lens.	Perdi uma lente de contato.	pehr-JEE OO-mah LEHN-chee jee kohn-TAH-too
Can you repair them right away?	Pode consertá-los agora mesmo?	POH-jee kohn-sehr-TAH-loos ah-GOH-rah MEHZ-moo?
When will they be ready?	Quando estarão prontos?	KWAHN-doo ehs-tah-ROWN PROHN-toos?
Do you have sunglasses?	Tem óculos de sol?	tehn OH-koo-loos jee sohl?

AT THE PHARMACY

Usually identified by a prescription symbol outside, pharmacies in Brazil and Portugal are easy to find. When a pharmacy is closed, a sign in the door may indicate another which is "on duty" (*de plantão*/ jee-plahn-TOWN). You can also check a local newspaper to see which pharmacies are open after regular hours.

You may be surprised to see that most pharmacies sell many medicines, including antibiotics, without a prescription. Pharmacies in Portugal tend to sell primarily medicinal products, whereas in Brazil the *farmácias* (fahr-MAH-syahs) usually sell other items as well, such as beauty products, baby food, toilet paper, etc.

Is there a pharmacy nearby?	Tem uma farmácia por aqui?	tehn OO-mah fahr-MAH-syah poor ah-KEE?
When does the pharmacy open/close?	Quando abre/fecha a farmácia?	KWAHN-doo AH-bree/FAY-shah ah fahr-MAH-syah?
What pharmacy is open now?	Qual é a farmácia de plantão?	kwow eh ah fahr-MAH-syah jee plahn-TOWN?

102

It's urgent!	E urgente!	eh oor-ZHEHN-chee!
I need something for . . .	Preciso de algo para . . .	pray-SEE-zoo jee AHL-goh PAH-rah . . .
• a cold.	• o resfriado.	• oo hays-FRYAH-doo
• constipation.	• a prisão de ventre.	• ah pree-ZOWN jee VEHN-tree
• a cough.	• a tosse.	• ah TOH-see
• diarrhea.	• a diarréia.	• ah jee-ah-HAY-ah
• fever.	• a febre.	• ah FEH-bree
• hay fever.	• alergia.	• ah-lehr-ZHEE-ah
• headache.	• a dor de cabeça.	• ah dohr jee kah-BAY-sah
• an insect bite.	• uma picada.	• OO-mah pee-KAH-dah
• motion sickness.	• enjôo de viagem.	• ehn-ZHOH-oo jee vee-AH-zhehn
• sunburn.	• a queimadura de sol.	• ah kay-mah-DOO-rah jee sohl
• an upset stomach.	• a indisposição de estômago.	• ah een-dees-poh-zee-SOWN jee ehs-TOH-mah-goo

OTHER ITEMS*

alcohol	álcool	AHL-kohl
analgesic	analgésico	ah-nahl-ZHEH-see-koo
antiseptic	antiséptico	ahn-chee-SEHP-chee-koo
aspirin	aspirina	ahs-pee-REE-nah
bandages	atadura	ah-tah-DOO-rah
Band-Aids	Band-Aids	bahn-DAHY-jees
contraceptives	contraconceptivos	kohn-trah-kohn-sehp-CHEE-voos
cotton	algodão	ahl-goh-DOWN
cough drops	gotas para a tosse	GOH-tahs PAH-rah ah toh-see
disinfectant	desinfectante	deh-seen-fehk-TAHN-chee

* See "Toiletries," p. 153 for any items not listed here.

103

ear drops	**gotas para os ouvidos**	GOH-tahs PAH-rah oos oh-VEE-doos
gauze	**gaze**	GAH-zee
insect repellent	**repelente**	hay-pay-LEHN-chee
iodine	**iodo**	YOH-doo
laxative	**laxante**	lahk-SAHN-chee
nose drops	**gotas para o nariz**	GOH-tahs PAH-rah oo nah-REEZ
sanitary napkins	**toalhas higiénicas**	TWAHL-yahs ee-ZHAYN-ee-kahs
sleeping pills	**tranquilizantes**	trahn-kee-lee-ZAHN-chees
suppositories	**supositórios**	soo-poh-zee-TOH-ryoos
tablets	**tabletes**	tah-BLAY-chees
tampons	**tampões sanitários**	tahm-POYN-ees sah-nee-TAH-ryoos
thermometer	**termômetro**	tehr-MOH-meh-troo
vitamins	**vitaminas**	vee-tah-MEE-nahs

9. ON THE ROAD

CAR RENTALS

Because Brazil is enormous (roughly the size of Europe), you may decide that traveling by car is the best way to see much of the country. Highways between major cities are excellent, and other roads are paved and in good condition. Car rental agencies have offices in larger cities like São Paulo and Rio. If you wish to have a car upon arrival, consider making arrangements before leaving home, because many well-known U.S. agencies have branches abroad. Your hotel can also help you locate an agency after you arrive. Prices in Rio start about $20.00 a day for a small car, plus 5% tax, mileage charges, and insurances fees. Major credit cards are accepted.

Portugal, by contrast, is a small country with few highways. The posted speed limit on highways is 120 KPH (74 miles), and 90 KPH on other roads. In populated areas, limits are usually only 50–60 KPH. Roads are good but narrow, with many curves and an incredible variety of surfaces. Traffic is normally light. On country roads, look out for people, often women, walking on the roads carrying loads on their heads.

The whole of Portugal can be explored easily by car, from north to south, entering from Spain across the Minho, and leaving through the Algarve across the Guadiana into Spain, or vice-versa.

Accidents can result in complicated legal problems. The laws of Brazil and Portugal are based on the Napoleonic Code, which means that one is guilty until proven innocent. If you rent a car, be sure to take out adequate insurance coverage.

DIALOGUE: RENTING A CAR (*ALUGANDO UM CARRO*)

| Turista: | **Preciso alugar um carro.** | pray-SEE-zoo ah-loo-GAHR oon KAH-hoo |
| Empleado: | **Por quanto tempo vai precisar?** | poor KWAHN-too TEHM-poo vahy pray-see-ZAHR? |

105

Turista:	**Qual é a tarifa por dia?**	kwaw eh ah tah-REE-fah poor JEE-ah?
Empleado:	**Custa CR$30.000 por dia, mais a quilometragem.**	KOOS-tah TREEN-tah MEE-oo kroo-ZAY-roos poor JEE-ah, mahys ah kee-loh-MEH-trah-zhehn
Turista:	**E mais barato por semana?**	eh mahys bah-RAH-too poor say-MAH-nah?
Empleado:	**Claro que sim! Quer levá-lo hoje?**	KLAH-roo keh seen! kehr lay-VAH-loh OH-zhee?
Turista:	**Sim, por favor. Vou levá-lo por uma semana.**	seen, poor fah-VOHR. voh lay-VAH-loh poor OO-mah say-MAH-nah

. . . .

Tourist:	I need to rent a car.
Clerk:	For how long do you want it?
Tourist:	What's the rate per day?
Clerk:	It's 30,000 cruzeiros per day plus mileage.
Tourist:	Is it cheaper by the week?
Clerk:	Of course! Do you want it today?
Tourist:	Yes, please. I'd like it for a week.

I need to rent . . .	**Preciso alugar . . .**	pray-SEE-zoo ah-loo-GAHR . . .
• a compact car.	• **um carro pequeno.**	• oon KAH-hoo peh-KEH-noo
• an automatic car.	• **um carro automático.**	• oon KAH-hoo ow-toh-MAH-chee-koo
• a car with standard shift.	• **um carro com standard.**	• oon KAH-hoo kohn STAHN-dahrd
How much is it . . .	**Quanto é . . .**	KWAHN-too eh . . .
• per hour?	• **por hora?**	• poor OH-rah?
• per day?	• **por dia?**	• poor JEE-ah?
• per week?	• **por semana?**	• poor say-MAH-nah?
• per month?	• **por mês?**	• poor mays?

106

per kilometer?	**por quilô-metro?**	poor kee-LOH-meh-troo?
How much is the insurance?	**Quanto custa o seguro?**	KWAHN-too KOOS-tah oo say-GOO-roo?
Do you need a deposit?	**Precisa um de-pósito?**	pray-SEE-zah oon deh-POH-see-too?
Do you accept credit cards?	**Aceita cartões de crédito?**	ah-SAY-tah kahr-TOWN-ees jee KREH-jee-too?
Can I turn in the car in another city?	**Posso entregar o carro em outra cidade?**	POH-soo ehn-tray-GAHR oo KAH-hoo ehn OH-trah see-DAH-jee?

AT THE SERVICE STATION

Where's the nearest service station?	**Onde fica o posto de gaso-lina mais pró-ximo?**	OHN-jee FEE-kah oo POHS-too jee gah-zoh-LEE-nah mahys PROHK-see moo?
	Onde fica a bomba de gasolina mais próxima? (P)	OHN-deh FEE-kah ah BOHM-bah deh gah-zoh-LEE-nah mahys PROHK-see-mah?
Fill it with . . .	**Encha-o com . . .**	EHN-shah-oo kohn . . .
• regular.	**• normal.**	• nohr-MOW
• super.	**• super.**	• SOO-pehr
• diesel.	**• diesel.**	• DEE-say-oo
	• gasóleo (P).	
Give me 40 liters of regular gasoline.	**Dê-me 40 litros de gasolina normal.**	DAY-mee kwah-REHN-tah LEE-troos jee gah-zoh-LEE-nah nohr-MOW
Please check the . . .	**Por favor, veri-fique . . .**	poor fah-VOHR, veh-ree-FEE-kee . . .
• battery.	**• a bateria.**	• ah bah-teh-REE-ah
• carburetor.	**• o carburador.**	• oo kahr-boo-rah-DOHR
• brake fluid.	**• o líquido de freios.**	• oo LEE-kee-doo jee FRAY-yoos
	o líquido dos travões. (P)	oh LEE-kee-doh deh trah-VOYN-eesh

107

• spark plugs.	• **as velas de ig-nição.**	• ahs VEH-lahs jee eeg-nee-SOWN
• tires.	• **os pneus.**	• os pee-NAY-oos
• water.	• **a água.**	• ah AH-gwah
• oil.	• **o óleo.**	• oo OO-lee-oo
Change the oil.	**Troque o óleo.**	TROH-kee oo OO-lee-oo

DRIVING AROUND

Before taking off on a car trip, ask for a map of the country at a tourist office. Tourist offices are usually found in airports as well as in central locations in major cities. They often provide excellent road maps and may be helpful in advising you on car travel and sites of interest.

Main highways are called *carreteras* (kah-hay-TEH-rahs) and *autopistas* (ow-toh-PEES-tahs); *estradas* (ehs-TRAH-dahsh) in Portugal. These should be clearly indicated on the country's road map, showing toll roads and freeways. If you're driving far from major centers, service stations may not be easy to find, so plan accordingly.

In Brazil and Portugal, drivers tend not to pay much attention to speed limits. However, radar control is common and if you are found exceeding the speed limit, you may receive a ticket. If you are unfamiliar with the roads, it is probably a good idea to let others pass. Driving in large cities can also be quite challenging. So if you're planning to drive, plot your route before you set out.

Is this the way to . . .	**E esta a estrada para . . .**	eh EHS-tah ah ehs-TRAH-dah PAH-rah . . .
• Santos?	• **Santos?**	• SAHN-toos?
• Estoril? (P)	• **Estoril? (P)**	• ehs-toh-REE-oo?
Is there a better road?	**Tem outra es-trada melhor?**	tehn OH-trah ehs-TRAH-dah mehl-YOHR?
Is there a less congested road?	**Tem uma es-trada menos congestionada?**	tehn OO-mah ehs-TRAH-dah MAY-noos kohn-zhehs-tyoh-NAH-dah?

108

English	Portuguese	Pronunciation
Is there a shortcut?	**Tem uma estrada mais direta?**	tehn OO-mah ehs-TRAH-dah mahys jee-RAY-tah?
I think we are . . .	**Acho que estamos . . .**	AH-shoo keh ehs-TAH-moos . . .
• lost.	• **perdidos.**	• pehr-DEE-doosa
• in the outskirts.	• **nos subúrbios.**	• noos soo-BOOR-byoos
• in the wrong lane.	• **na pista errada.**	• nah PEES-tah eh-HAH-dah
• in the wrong exit.	• **na saida errada.**	• nah sah-EE-dah eh-HAH-dah
• in the center of town.	• **no centro da cidade.**	• noo SEHN-troo dah see-DAH-jee
• arriving at the next town.	• **chegando na próxima cidade.**	• shay-GAHN-doo nah PROK-see-mah see-DAH-jee
• very far from town.	• **muito longe da cidade.**	• MWEE-too LOHN-zhee dah see-DAH-jee
• close to the city.	• **perto da cidade.**	• PEHR-too dah see-DAH-jee
How do I get to . . .	**Como posso ir . . .**	KOH-moo POH-soo eer . . .
• the hotel?	• **ao hotel?**	• ow oh-TAY-oo?
• the next town?	• **à próxima cidade?**	• ah PROHK-see-mah see-DAH-jee?
• the main highway?	• **à estrada principal?**	• ah ehs-TRAH-dah preen-see-POW?
• the center of town?	• **ao centro da cidade?**	• ow SEHN-troo dah see-DAH-jee?
Do I go . . .	**Vou . . .**	voh . . .
• straight ahead?	• **em frente?**	• ehn FREHN-chee?
• to the right?	• **à direita?**	• ah jee-RAY-tah?
• to the left?	• **à esquerda?**	• ah ehs-KEHR-dah?
• two (three, etc.) more blocks?	• **dois (três, etc.) quarteirões mais?**	• doys (trays, etc.) kwahr-tay-ROYN-ees mahys?
Is it . . .	**Fica . . .**	FEE-kah . . .
• nearby?	• **perto?**	• PEHR-too?
• far from here?	• **longe daqui?**	• LOHN-zhee dah-KEE?

109

• far from the center?	• **longe do centro?**	• LOHN-zhee doo SEHN-troo?
• near the center?	• **perto do centro?**	• PEHR-too doo SEHN-troo?
Are there any tourist services?	**Tem serviços turísticos?**	tehn sehr-VEE-soos too-REES-chee-koos?

DISTANCES AND LIQUID MEASURES

Distances in Brazil and Portugal are expressed in kilometers, and liquid measures (for gas and oil), in liters. Unless you are a whiz at mental calculations, converting one system to another can be hard to get used to. The following conversion formulas and charts will help:

DISTANCE CONVERSIONS

1 kilometer (km.) = .62 miles
1 mile = 1.61 km.

Kilómetros	Miles
1	0.62
5	3.1
8	5.0
10	6.2
15	9.3
20	12.4
50	31.0
75	46.5
100	62.0

LIQUID MEASURE CONVERSION

1 liter (l) = .26 gallons
1 gallon = 3.75 liters

Liters	Gallons
10	2.6
15	3.9
20	5.2
30	7.8
40	10.4
50	13.0
60	15.6
70	18.2

EMERGENCIES AND CAR PROBLEMS

If you drive in Brazil or Portugal, make sure your car is in good condition and that you take along tools for small repairs. When renting a car, ask for a list of authorized agencies and repair shops. You should also obtain a list of authorized insurance agents.

English	Portuguese	Pronunciation
My car won't start.	**O carro não arranca.**	oo KAH-hoo nown ah-HAHN-kah
Something must be wrong.	**Tem algum problema.**	tehn ahl-GOON proh-BLEH-mah
I don't know what's wrong.	**Não sei o que tem.**	nown say oo keh tehn
I have a flat tire.	**O pneu está furado.**	oo pee-NAY-oo ehs-TAH foo-RAH-doo
I'm out of gas.	**Acabou-se a gasolina.**	ah-kah-BOH-see ah gah-zoh-LEE-nah
The battery's dead.	**A bateria não funciona.**	ah bah-teh-REE-ah nown foon-SYOH-nah
It's overheating.	**Está esquentando muito.**	eh-STAH ah ah-kay-SEHR MWEE-toh
	Está a aquecer muito. (P)	eh-STAH ehs-kehn-TAHN-doh MWEE-too
I left the keys inside the car.	**Esqueci as chaves dentro.**	ehs-kay-SEE ahs SHAH-vees DEHN-troo
I don't have an extra key.	**Não tenho uma chave extra.**	nown TEHN-yoo OO-mah-SHAH-vee EHKS-trah
I don't have any tools.	**Não tenho ferramentas.**	nown TEHN-yoo feh-hah-MEHN-tahs
I need . . .	**Preciso de . . .**	pray-SEE-zoo jee . . .
• a flashlight.	• **uma lanterna.**	• OO-mah lahn-TEHR-nah
• a hammer.	• **um martelo.**	• oon mahr-TEH-loo
• a jack.	• **um macaco.**	• oon mah-KAH-koo
• pliers.	• **uns alicates.**	• oons ah-lee-KAH-chees
• a bolt.	• **um ferrolho.**	• oon feh-HOHL-yoo
• a nut.	• **uma porca.**	• OO-mah POHR-kah
• a screwdriver.	• **uma chave-de-fenda.**	• OO-mah SHAH-vee jee FEHN-dah
Can you open the . . .	**Pode abrir . . .**	POH-jee ah-BREER . . .
• hood?	• **o capô?**	• oo kah-POH?

111

• trunk?	• o porta-malas? (P) a bagageira?	oo POHR-tah-MAH-lahs? ah bah-gah-ZHAY-rah?
• gas tank?	• o tanque da gasolina?	o TAHN-kee dah gah-zoh-LEE-nah?
Can you . . .	Pode . . .	POH-jee . . .
• charge the battery?	• carregar a bateria?	kah-hay-GAHR ah bah-teh-REE-ah?
• change the tire?	• trocar o pneu?	troh-KAHR oo pee-NAY-oo?
• tow the car to a garage?	• levar o carro até uma garagem?	lay-VAHR oo KAH-hoo ah-TEH OO-mah gah-RAH-zhehn?
There's something wrong with the . . .	Algo está errado com . . .	AHL-goo ehs-TAH eh-HAH-doo kohn . . .
• car.	• o carro.	oo KAH-hoo
• brakes.	• os freios.	ohs FRAY-oos
• tires.	• os pneus.	oos pee-NAY-oos
• spark plugs.	• as velas de ignição.	ahs VEH-lahs jee eeg-nee-SOWN
• air conditioner.	• o ar-condicionado.	oo ahr kohn-dee-syoh-NAH-doo
• motor.	• o motor.	oo moh-TOHR
Please check the . . .	Por favor, cheque . . .	poor fah-VOHR SHEH-kee . . .
• oil.	• o óleo.	oo OH-lay-oo
• water.	• a água.	ah AH-gwah
• carburetor.	• o carburador.	oo kahr-boo-rah-DOHR
• battery.	• a bateria.	ah bah-teh-REE-ah
• radiator.	• o radiador.	oo hah-jyah-DOHR
• brake fluid.	• o líquido para os freios.	oo LEE-kee-doo PAH-rah ohs FRAY-yoos
• tire pressure.	• a pressão dos pneus.	ah pray-SOWN doos pee-NAY-oos
I have a problem with the . . .	Tenho problema com . . .	TEHN-yoo proh-BLEH-mah kohn . . .
• gears.	• as marchas. as velocidades. (P)	ahs MAHR-shahs ahs veh-loh-see-DAH-dehsh

112

• headlights.	• **os faróis.**	• ohs fah-ROYS
• high beams.	• **os faróis altos.**	• oos fah-ROYS AHL-toos
• directional signals.	• **os sinais.**	• oos see-NAHYS
• ignition.	• **a ignição.**	• ah eeg-nee-SOWN
• radiator.	• **o radiador.**	• oo hah-jyah-DOHR
• transmission	• **a transmissão.**	• ah trahns-mee-SOWN
• windshield wipers.	• **os limpadores-de-parabrisas.**	• ohs leem-pah-DOH-rees jee PAH-rah-BREE-zahs
	o limpa-vidros (P)	oh LEEM-pah VEE-drohsh
Can you repair the . . .	**Pode con-sertar . . .**	POH-jee kohn-sehr-TAHR . . .
• brakes?	• **os freios?** **os travões (P)**	• ohs FRAY-yoos? oh trah-VOYN-ees?
• horn?	• **a buzina?**	• ah-boo-ZEE-nah?
• radio?	• **o rádio?**	• oo HAH-dyoo?
• steering wheel?	• **o volante?**	• o voh-LAHN-chee?
• electrical system?	• **o sistema eléc-trico?**	• oo sees-TAY-mah eh-LEH-tree-koo?
• door?	• **a porta?**	• ah POHR-tah?
• speedometer?	• **o marcador de quilometra-gem?**	• oo mahr-kah-DOHR jee kee-loh-meh-TRAH-zhehn?
How long will this take?	**Quanto de-morará isto?**	KWAHN-too jee-moh-rah-RAH EES-too?
How much will this cost?	**Quanto vai custar?**	KWAHN-too vahy koos-TAHR?

PARTS OF THE CAR

the brakes	**os freios** **os travões (P)**	oo FRAY-yoos oh trah-VOYN-ees
directional signals	**os sinais**	oos see-NAHYS
the distributor	**o distribuidor**	oo dees-tree-bwee-DOHR
the fan	**o ventilador** **a ventoinha (P)**	oo vehn-chee-lah-DOHR ah vehn-too-EEN-yah
the fan belt	**a correia do ven-tilador**	ah koh-HAY-yah doo vehn-chee-lah-DOHR

113

the filter	**o filtro**	oo FEEL-troo
the fuel pump	**a bomba de gasolina**	ah BOHM-bah jee gah-zoh-LEE-nah
the fuel tank	**o tanque de gasolina**	oo TAHN-kee jee gah-zoh-LEE-nah
the gear shift	**o câmbio de velocidade**	oo KAHM-byoo jee veh-loh-see-DAH-jee
the headlights	**os faróis dianteiros**	ohs fah-ROYS jyahn-TAY-roos
the motor	**o motor**	oo moh-TOHR
the radiator	**o radiador**	oo hah-jyah-DOHR
the spark plugs	**as velas de ignição**	ahs VEH-lahs jee eeg-nee-SOWN
the taillights	**as luzes traseiras**	ahs LOO-zees trah-SAY-rahs
the tires	**os pneus**	oos pee-NAY-oos
the transmission	**a transmissão**	ah trahns-mee-SOWN
the valve	**a vávula**	ah VAHL-voo-lah
the water pump	**a bomba de água**	ah BOHM-bah jee AH-gwah
the wheels	**as rodas**	ahs HOH-dahs

ROAD SIGNS

auto estrada	highway
ceda o passo	yield
cruzamento	crossroads
curva perigosa	dangerous curve
descida ingreme	steep hill
desvio	detour
encruzilhada	crossroads
estacionamento	parking
estacionamento proibido	no parking allowed
gasolina a 10 kms	gasoline at 10 kms
guie com cuidado	drive with care
homens trabalhando	men working
mão unica	one way
não ultrapasse	no passing
em obras	construction
pare	stop
passagem proibida	no entrance

pedagio	toll
portágem (p)	
pedestres	pedestrians
peões (p)	
perigo	danger
ponto de ōnibus	bus stop
posto de socorros	first aid
proibida a entrada	no entrance
saida de caminhões	trucks exiting
sem saida	no through road
siga pela direita	keep right
siga pela esquerda	keep left
stop	stop
tránsito proibido	road closed
veiculos pesados	alternate for heavy vehicles
velocidade máxima	maximum speed
velocidade minima	minimum speed

ONE WAY

MAIN ROAD

PARKING

SUPERHIGHWAY

YIELD

GAS
(10 km ahead)

DANGER AHEAD

DANGEROUS DESCENT

BUMPS

ROAD NARROWS

LEVEL (RAILROAD) CROSSING

TWO-WAY TRAFFIC

SLIPPERY ROAD

CAUTION—SHARP CURVES

PEDESTRIAN CROSSING

NO ENTRY FOR MOTOR VEHICLES

DANGEROUS INTERSECTION AHEAD

STOP

NO ENTRY

MINIMUM SPEED (km/hr)

SPEED LIMIT (km/hr)

DIRECTION TO BE FOLLOWED

OVERHEAD CLEARANCE (meters)

ROTARY

NO PASSING

END OF NO PASSING ZONE

END OF RESTRICTION

NO LEFT TURN

NO U-TURN

NO PARKING

10. COMMUNICATIONS

TELEPHONE

Telephones are easy to find in most public places, such as stations, parks, main streets, post offices, and department stores. In Brazil, the national telephone company, Embratel (ehm-brah-TAY-oo), connects all points of the country. Public phones, called *orelhões* (oh-rehl-YOWN-ees) or "big ears," are everywhere. They are normally yellow with the blue phone company logo for local calls, or solid blue for calls between cities (*interurbanal*/een-tehr-oor-BAH-nah).

To use a public phone, buy tokens, or *fichas* (FEE-shahs), at newspaper stands or at special telephone stations, where you can make long distance calls. Unused *fichas* are returned when you hang up. For international telephone calls through an operator, dial 000111. For information on international calls, dial 000333. Operators who assist from these numbers speak English. To make an automated collect intercity phone call within Brazil, dial 9 plus the area code and number. Telephone numbers in Brazil do not always have an equal number of digits, nor do area codes. The area code for Rio is 021, and for São Paulo, 011.

In Portugal, public telephone booths are painted red, blue, or green. You can use public phones for local calls, long distance, and international calls. It makes sense to call collect or to use a telephone credit card for international calls, if possible. Hotels often add a surcharge to these calls. You will find dialing codes listed in the directory (*lista telefónica* / LEES-tah teh-lay-FOO-nee-kah). At the time of this writing, telephone numbers throughout the country are being changed. If you cannot get through, ask a hotel attendant to verify the number for you.

DIALOGUE: USING THE TELEPHONE (*USANDO O TELEFONE*)

Turista:	**Uma ligação para os Estados Unidos, por favor.**	OO-mah lee-gah-SOWN PAH-rahoos ehs-TAH-doos oo-NEE-doos, poor fah-VOHR.
Operadora:	**Que lugar deseja chamar?**	keh loo-GAHR day-ZAY-zhah shah-MAHR?
Turista:	**A Brattleboro, Vermont.**	ah Brattleboro, Vermont.
Operadora:	**Pode repetir isso, por favor?**	POH-jee hay-peh-CHEER EE-soo, poor fah-VOHR.
Turista:	**Brattleboro, Vermont.**	Brattleboro, Vermont.
Operadora:	**Tem o número?**	tehn oh NOO-meh-roo?
Turista:	**Sim, é 802-555-1212.**	seen, eh 802-555-1212.
Operadora:	**Com quem deseja falar?**	kohn kehn day-ZAY-zhah fah-LAHR?
Turista:	**Qualquer pessoa.**	kwahl-KEHR peh-SOH-ah.

. . . .

Tourist:	I'd like to make a call to the United States, please.
Operator:	Where would you like to call?
Tourist:	Brattleboro, Vermont.
Operator:	Can you repeat that, please?
Tourist:	Brattleboro, Vermont.
Operator:	Do you have the number?
Tourist:	Yes, it's 802-555-1212.
Operator:	With whom do you wish to speak?
Tourist:	Anyone.

COMMUNICATIONS

119

MAKING A TELEPHONE CALL

Is there a . . .
- public telephone?

- telephone booth?

- telephone directory?

Operator
I'd like to call . . .

- this number.

- information.

- the international operator.

I'd like to use my credit card.

I'd like to make a(n) . . .
- international call.

- person-to-person call.
- local call.
- collect call.
- conference call.

- call with time and charges.

Hello!
This is . . .
- Mr. . . .
- Mrs. . . .
- Miss/Ms. . . .

Tem . . .
- um telefone público?
- uma cabine telefônica?
- uma lista telefônica?

Telefonista
Desejo ligar para . . .

- este número.

- informações

- a telefonista internacional.

Quero usar o meu cartão de crédito.

Quero uma ligação . . .
- internacional.

- pessoa a pessoa.
- local.
- a cobrar.
- por conferência.

- com tempo e preço.

Alô!
E . . .
- o senhor . . .
- a senhora . . .
- a senhorita . . .

a menina (P)

tehn . . .
- oon teh-lay-FOH-nee POOB-lee-koo?
- OO-mah kah-BEE-nee teh-lay-FOHN-ee-kah?
- OO-mah LEES-tah teh-lay-FOHN-ee-kah?

teh-lay-foh-NEES-tah
day-ZAY-zhoo lee-GAHR PAH-rah . . .

- EHS-chee NOO-meh-roo

- een-fohr-mah-SOYN-ees

- ah teh-lay-foh-NEES-tah een-tehr-nah-syo-NOW

KEH-roo oo-ZAHR oo MAY-oo kahr-TOWN jee KREH-jee-too

KEH-roo OO-mah lee-gah-SOWN . . .
- EEN-tehr-nah-syoh-now

- peh-SOH-ah ah peh-SOH-ah
- loh-KOW
- ah koh-BRAHR
- poor kohn-feh-REHN-syah
- kohn TEHM-poo ee PRAY-soo

ah-LOH
eh . . .
- oo sehn-YOHR . . .
- ah sehn-YOH-rah . . .
- ah sehn-YOH-ree-tah . . .

ah meh-NEE-nah . . .

English	Portuguese	Pronunciation
• John.	• João.	• zhown
May I speak to . . . ?	Poderia falar com . . . ?	poh-deh-REE-ah fah-LAHR kohn . . . ?
Can you repeat, please?	Pode repetir, por favor?	POH-jee heh-peh-CHEER, poor fah-VOHR?
I can't hear very well.	Não ouço muito bem.	nown OH-soo MWEE-too behn
It's a bad connection.	E uma má ligação.	eh OO-mah mah lee-gah-SOWN
Speak louder, please.	Fale mais alto, por favor.	FAH-lee mahys AHL-too, poor fah-VOHR
I'd like to leave a message.	Gostaria de deixar um recado.	gohs-tah-REE-ah jee day-SHAHR oon hay-KAH-doo.
My number is . . .	O meu número é . . .	oo MAY-oo NOO-meh-roh eh . . .

WHAT THE OPERATOR SAYS

Portuguese	Pronunciation	English
A linha está ocupada.	ah LEEN-yah eh-STAH oh-koo-PAH-dah	The line is busy.
Não respondem.	nown hays-POHN-dehn	They don't answer.
Quer que continue tentando?	kehr keh kohn-chee-NOO-ay tehn-TAHN-doo?	Do you want me to keep trying?
Pode tentar mais tarde?	POH-jee tehn-TAHR mahys TAHR-jee?	Can you try later?
Não desligue.	nown dehs-LEE-gee	Don't hang up.
Por favor, espere um momento.	poor fah-VOHR, ehs-PEH-ree oon moh-MEHN-too	Please wait a moment.
Sua chamada foi desligada.	SOO-ah shah-MAH-dah foy dehs-lee-GAH-dah	Your call was disconnected.
Com quem deseja falar?	kohn kehn day-ZAY-zhah fah-LAHR?	With whom do you wish to speak?
Quer deixar um recado?	kehr day-SHAHR oon hay-KAH-doo?	Do you want to leave a message?
Tem outro número?	tehn OH-troo NOO-meh-roo?	Do you have another number?

121

POSTAL SERVICES

In Brazil, post offices (*correios*/koh-HAY-yoos) are open from 8 A.M. to 5 P.M. weekdays, and until noon on Saturdays. Stamps can be purchased at the post office and at newstands. Some hotels and stores which sell postcards occasionally also carry limited supplies of stamps.

Letters usually take about five days to one week from Brazil to the U.S., and vice-versa. Brazil has both national and international rapid mail service, the price of which varies according to the weight of the package and the destination.

Do not use general delivery to receive mail; have it forwarded to American Express. Major hotels will also hold mail for arriving guests.

In Portugal, post office branches are open from 9 A.M. to 12:30 P.M. and from 2:30 P.M. to 6:00 P.M. on weekdays. Main offices stay open at lunchtime as well.

AT THE POST OFFICE

Where is the post office?	**Onde é o correio?**	OHN-jee eh oo koh-HAY-yoo?
I would like to send . . .	**Quero enviar . . .**	KEH-roo ehn-VYAHR . . .
• a letter.	• **uma carta.**	• OO-mah KAHR-tah
• a postcard.	• **um cartão postal.**	• oon kahr-TOWN pohs-TOW
• a registered letter.	• **uma carta registrada.**	• OO-mah KAHR-tah hay-jees-TRAH-dah
• a special delivery letter.	• **uma carta com entrega especial.**	• OO-mah KAHR-tah kohn ehn-TREH-gah ehs-peh-SYOW
• a package.	• **um pacote.**	• oon pah-KOH-chee
• a money order.	• **uma ordem postal.**	• OO-mah OHR-dehn pohs-TOW
How many stamps do I need for . . .	**Quantos selos preciso para . . .**	KWAHN-toos SEH-loos pray-ZEE-soo PAH-rah . . .
• surface mail?	• **via terrestre?**	• VEE-ah teh-HEHS-tree?

122

English	Portuguese	Pronunciation
• airmail?	• **via aérea?**	• VEE-ah ah-EH-ryah?
• a postcard?	• **um cartão postal?**	• oon kahr-TOWN pohs-TOW?
• a letter?	• **uma carta?**	• OO-mah KAHR-tah?
• the United States?	• **para os Estados Unidos?**	• PAH-rah oos ehs-TAH-doos oo-NEE-doos?
• Central America?	• **a América Central?**	• ah ah-MEH-ree-kah sehn-TROW?
• South America?	• **a América do Sul?**	• ah ah-MEH-ree-kah doo sool?
• North America?	• **a América do Norte?**	• ah ah-MEH-ree-kah doo NOHR-chee?
• Europe?	• **a Europa?**	• ah ay-oo-ROH-pah?
• the Middle East?	• **o Médio Oriente?**	• oo MEH-joo oh-RYEHN-chee?
• the Far East?	• **o Extremo Oriente?**	• oo ehks-TRAY-moo oh-RYEHN-chee?
• Africa?	• **a África?**	• ah AH-free-kah?
• Australia?	• **a Austrália?**	• ah ows-TRAH-lyah?
I'd (also) like . . .	**(Também) quero . . .**	(tahm-BEHN) KEH-roo. . .
• airmail envelopes.	• **envelopes aéreos**	• ehn-veh-LOH-pees ah-AY-ryoos
• aerograms.	• **aerogramas.**	• ah-eh-roh-GRAH-mahs
• airmail paper.	• **papel aéreo.**	• pah-PAY-oo ah-EH-ryoo
• a collection of stamps.	• **uma coleção de selos.**	• OO-mah koh-leh-SOWN jee SAY-loos
Where is the . . .	**Onde está . . .**	OHN-jee ehs-TAH . . .
• letterbox?	• **a caixa de correio?**	• ah KAY-shah jee koh-HAY-yoo?
• window for registered mail?	• **o balcão para correio registrado?**	• oo bahl-KOWN PAH-rah koh-HAY-yoo heh-jees-TRAH-doo?

TELEGRAMS AND FAXES

Telegraph offices are usually located in the same building as the post office. Some hotels conveniently provide telegram service as well. ''Night letters'' are generally less expensive than

123

overseas cables. Sending telegrams within the same country can sometimes be more effective than writing a letter. Most large hotels have fax machines for your convenience.

How late are you open?	**Até que horas fica aberto?**	ah-TEH keh OH-rahs FEE-kah ah-BEHR-too?
I would like to send a . . .	**Gostaria de enviar um . . .**	gohs-tah-REE-ah jee ehn-VYAHR oon . . .
• telegram.	• **telegrama.**	• teh-lay-GRAH-mah
• telex.	• **telex.**	• TAY-lehks
• cable.	• **cable.**	• KAH-blee
• fax.	• **fax.**	• fahks
How much is it per word?	• **Quanto custa por palavra?**	KWAHN-too KOOS-tah poor pah-LAH-vrah?
When will it arrive?	**Quando chegará?**	KWAHN-doo shay-gah-RAH?

THE MEDIA

You should be able to find English-language newspapers and magazines in all major Brazilian cities. Various bookstores specialize in English-language magazines and books. With timely jet schedules to Brazil, there is little delay receiving airmail editions of New York and Miami newspapers. International editions of news magazines are also on sale in leading hotels.

Rio's leading Portuguese newspapers are the *Jornal do Brasil* (zhohr-NOW doo brah-ZEE-oo) and *O Globo* (oo GLOH-boo). In São Paulo, there are several major newspapers in Portuguese: *Folha de São Paulo* (FOHL-yah jee sown POW-loo), *Folha da Tarde* (FOHL-yah da TAHR-jee), *Jornal de Tarde* (zhohr-NOW dah TAHR-jee), *O Estado de São Paulo* (oo ehs-TAH-doo jee sown POW-loo), and *Gazeta Mercantil* (gah-ZEH-tah mehr-kahn-CHEE-oo). Nightly news reports are broadcast in Portuguese on all major television networks.

In Lisbon you can get newspapers and magazines from all over the world. Among the English-language newspapers, look for the *London Times* and the *New York Times* (international editions), the *Herald Tribune,* the *Wall Street Journal,* and, in some cases, the *Christian Science Monitor*. You can also find the *Anglo-Portuguese News,* a British-Portuguese weekly covering local and general news. In addition, Lisbon has several daily and weekly newspapers. A leading Portuguese-language publication is the *Diário de Noticias* (dee-AH-ryoh deh noh-TEE-syahss), which is the most comprehensive daily newspaper in the city.

In Brazil, CBS affiliates feature syndicated news programs on a regular basis and there is also an English-speaking radio station. Thanks to *Cablevisão* (kah-blay-vee-ZOWN) you can now see TV programs directly from the United States. In Portugal you can listen to the London BBC. Portugal also carries various foreign programs from other parts of Europe via satellite.

Books and Newspapers

Do you have . . . in English?	**O senhor/a senhora tem . . . em inglês?**	oo sehn-YOHR/ah sehn-YOH-rah tehn . . . ehn een-GLAYS?
• newspapers	• **jornais**	• zhohr-NAHYS
• magazines	• **revistas**	• hay-VEES-tahs
• books	• **livros**	• LEEV-roos
• publications	• **publicações**	• poo-blee-kah-SOWN-ees
• *Newsweek* or *Time*	• **as revistas Newsweek ou Time**	• ahs hay-VEES-tahs NOOS-week OH-oo taym

Radio and Television

Is there . . .	**Tem uma . . .**	tehn OO-mah . . .
• an English-speaking station?	• **estação em inglês?**	• ehs-tah-SOWN ehn een-GLAYS?
• a music station?	• **estação com música?**	• ehs-tah-SOWN kohn MOO-zee-kah?
• a news station?	• **estação de noticias?**	• ehs-tah-SOWN jee noh-CHEE-syahs?
• a weather station?	• **estação que dê o tempo?**	• ehs-tah-SOWN kee day oo TEHM-poo?

125

What station is it?	**O que estação é?**	oo keh ehs-tah-SOWN eh?
Do you have a TV guide?	**Tem um guia de televisão?**	tehn oon GEE-ah jee teh-lay-vee-ZOWN?
Is there an English-speaking channel?	**Tem um canal em inglês?**	tehn oon kah-NOW ehn een-GLAYS?
What time is the program?	**A que horas é o programa?**	ah keh OH-rahs eh oo proh-GRAH-mah?
At what time is the news?	**A que horas são as notícias?**	ah keh OH-rahs sown ahs noh-CHEE-syahs?
Do they have international news?	**Tem notícias internacionais?**	tehn noh-CHEE-syahs een-tehr-nah-syoh NAHYS?
When is the weather forecast?	**Quando dão a previsão do tempo?**	KWAHN-doo down ah pray-vee-ZOWN doo TEHM-poo?

11. SIGHT-SEEING

TRAVELING AROUND

Ask at your hotel for a guide to the city and activities of the week. You may also be able to obtain information about bus tours and other events. If you prefer to get a native's view of the city, however, use local transportation whenever possible.

IN BRAZIL

São Paulo

No matter how familiar you are with Latin America, São Paulo will come as a startling surprise. There is nothing like it anywhere else in South America; no other place comes close! It is the richest.

Nothing important happens in Brazil that does not begin in São Paulo. Brasília may be the capital, but politically, economically, and culturally, São Paulo is the number one city in the country, and the largest, wealthiest, fastest-growing metropolis in the entire continent and the pride of all Brazilians. São Paulo is very different from Rio: Rio is often described as beautiful, relaxed, and laid-back, whereas São Paulo is characterized as brilliant, dynamic, productive, and propelled by the work ethic.

The best place to "feel" the pulse of São Paulo is right at its heart, at the Viaduto do Chá (vee-ah-DOO-too doo shah) or the Viaduct of Tea, named for the crop once grown in this valley. The viaduct leads over the vast Avenida Anhangabaú, into the Praça do Patriarca, the Times Square of Brazil. Edifício Itália, South America's tallest building, is situated at the highest point in São Paulo. A visit to one of its rooftop bars or restaurants on a clear day or night will allow you to see a most spectacular view.

Rio de Janeiro

Rio de Janeiro is considered the most beautiful city in the world by many experienced travelers. With a natural setting surpassing even Hong Kong and San Francisco, Rio has long stretches

127

of soft sandy beaches and lines of tall palm trees. There are great fleecy clouds floating lazily over the ocean, which push in cool breezes and occasional rainstorms. The days are warm and the nights cool, with starlit skies and huge full moons. Music and sound are everywhere, from the honking of automobile horns to soft singing voices. There is an excitement in the air, curiously mixed with a tropical languor. Rio is especially known for the section called Copacabana, a word that evokes romantic images of sunny beaches, including the world-famous Ipanema.

IN PORTUGAL

Lisbon

Lisbon is one of Europe's smallest capitals. It is a peculiarly beautiful city, descending from many hills to the great River Tagus. The city is a port, less busy now that international shipping has declined, but wharves, dockyards, and warehouses still line the banks for some 16 kilometers from Xabregas to Belém. Terreiro do Paço or Palace Square is the usual name for the Praça do Comércio. Surrounded on three sides by color-washed buildings above arcaded walks, Terreiro do Paço is one of the most noble squares in Europe.

The architecture of central Lisbon dates back to the 18th century, since much of it was rebuilt after the great earthquake of 1755. Streets are lined with rows of elegantly proportioned and uniform housefronts with windows and doorframes made of stone. Most streets are wide and straight with others crossing at right angles, a perfect example of early and very successful town planning. The *Rossio* (rroh-SEE-oh), surrounded by austere 18th-century facades, is the center of the city, full of cafés, restaurants, flower vendors, and a diminishing number of shops. Bright yellow trams still run in the less busy parts of town, adding to the color and animation of the scene. Public transport in the Baixa and up the Avenida da Liberdade, however, is confined to motorbuses and taxis, which can be instantly recognized by their green tops.

The Avenida da Liberdade, like the Champs Elysées in Paris, has been marred by commercial development. But even so, examples of Victorian and art noveau architecture can still be found scattered around the city on either side of the Parque Eduardo VII at the top of the Avenida da Liberdade.

DIALOGUE: SIGHT-SEEING IN TOWN (*VISITANDO OS LUGARES NOTAVEIS EM CIDADE*)

Turista:	**Que lugares podemos visitar?**	keh loo-GAHR-ees poh-JEE-moos vee-zee-TAHR?
Empregado do hotel:	**Há muitas coisas interessantes nesta cidade.**	ah MWEE-tahs KOY-zahs een-teh-ray-SAHN-chees NEHS-tah see-DAH-jee
Turista:	**E fácil ir ao bairro histórico?**	eh FAH-see-oo eer AH-oo BAHY-hoo ees-TOH-ree-koo?
Empregado:	**Sim, pode pegar um ônibus (auto-carro/P) na esquina. Vai até a parte velha da cidade.**	seen, POH-deh peh-GAHR oon OH-nee-boos nah ehs-KEE-nah. vay ah-TEH ah PAHR-chee VEL-yah dah see-DAH-jee
Turista:	**Tem muitas igrejas ali?**	tehn MWEE-tahs ee-GRAY-zhahs ah-LEE?
Empregado:	**Sim, e também há vários museus.**	seen, eh tahm-BEHN ah VAH-ryoos moo-ZAY-oos
Turista:	**Obrigado pela informação.**	oh-bree-GAH-doo PEH-lah een-fohr-mah-SOWN

. . . .

Tourist:	What are some places we can visit?
Hotel clerk:	There are many interesting things to see in this city.

Tourist:	Is it easy to get to the historic district?
Hotel clerk:	Yes, you can take a bus.
	It goes right to the old part of town.
Tourist:	Are there many churches there?
Hotel clerk:	Yes, and also several museums.
Tourist:	Thanks for the information.

GENERAL SIGHT-SEEING EXPRESSIONS

Where is the bus stop?	**Onde é o ponto de ônibus?**	OHN-jee eh oo POHN-too jee OH-nee-boos?
I want to visit the . . .	**Quero visitar . . .**	KEH-roo vee-zee-TAHR . . .
• art museum.	• **o museu de arte.**	• oo moo-ZAY-oo jee AHR-chee
• botanical garden.	• **o jardim botânico.**	• oo jahr-JEEN boh-TAH-nee-koo
• business district.	• **o setor comercial.**	• oo seh-TOHR koh-mehr-SYOW
• cathedral.	• **a catedral.**	• ah kah-tay-DROW
• folk art museum.	• **o museu de arte folclórica.**	• oo moo-ZAY-oo jee AHR-chee fohlk-LOH-ree-kah
• government palace.	• **o palácio do governo.**	• oo pah-LAH-syoo doo goh-VEHR-noo
• library.	• **a biblioteca.**	• ah bee-blyoh-TAY-kah
• main market.	• **o mercado central.**	• oo mehr-KAH-doo sehn-TROW
• national theater.	• **o teatro nacional.**	• oo chee-AH-troo nah-syoh-NOW
• natural science museum.	• **o museu de ciências naturais.**	• oo moo-ZAY-oo jee SYAYN-syahs nah-too-RAY-ees
• old part of town.	• **a parte velha da cidade.**	• ah PAHR-chee VEL-yah dah see-DAH-jee
• zoo.	• **o zoológico.**	• oo zoh-LOH-zhee-koo
At what time do they open?	**A que horas abrem?**	ah keh OH-rahs AH-brehn?

130

At what time do they close?	**A que horas fecham?**	ah keh OH-rahs fay-SHAHN?
Are they open today?	**Está aberto hoje?**	ehs-TAH ah-BEHR-too OY-zhee?
How much is the admission?	**Quanto é a entrada?**	KWAHN-too eh ah ehn-TRAH-dah?
How much is it for children?	**Quanto pagam os meninos?**	KWAHN-too PAH-gah oos may-NEE-noos?
How much is it for students?	**Quanto pagam os estudantes?**	KWAHN-too PAH-gahn oos ehs-too-DAHN-chees?
How much is it for a group?	**Quanto é por um grupo?**	KWAHN-too eh poor GROO-poo?

AT THE MUSEUM

Museums in Brazil

In São Paulo, three museums should be on your list of musts. The first is the Museu de Arte de São Paulo (MASP), containing the only collection in South America that shows a panorama of Western art, from the Gothic Age to the present. This museum houses Raphael's famed "Resurrection," painted when the artist was only 17 years old. Along with this are other masterpieces by Rembrandt, Renoir, Toulouse-Lautrec, and many others. The second important museum is the Museu de Arte Contemporânea (MAC), containing over 1,650 works by modern masters. The third is the Museum of Brazilian Art, housing copies of all the monuments and statues in the parks and buildings of Brazil.

The Museu Nacional de Belas Artes is probably the largest museum in Rio. The Museu Chácara do Ceu, located in the residential area of Santa Teresa, exhibits works by great European artists such as Degas, Dali, Matisse, Miró, Monet, and Picasso. Many Brazilian artists also have their works here.

Museums in Portugal

The Gulbenkian and the Coach Museums in Lisbon are world famous. Other museums also contain fine and unusual exhibits

131

such as the 15th-century polyptych panels of St. Vincent by Nuno Gonçalves. Oporto has several delightful collections, as have all major towns, and there is an unusually large number of small, personal collections throughout the country.

Museums usually open at 10:00 A.M. and close at 5:00 P.M. They are normally closed on Mondays and holidays.

Where can I get a guide?	**Onde há um guia?**	OHN-jee ah oon GEE-ah?
How long does a tour take?	**Quanto demora um "tour"?**	KWAHN-too day-MOR-rah oon toor?
Where is the gift shop?	**Onde fica a loja do museu?**	OHN-jee FEE-kah ah LOH-zhah doo moo-ZAY-oo?
Do they sell prints?	**Têm reprodu-ções?**	tayn hay-proh-doo-SOYN-ees?
Do they sell postcards?	**Têm cartões?**	tayn kahr-TOYN-ees?
Is there a restaurant here?	**Tem um restaurante aqui?**	tehn oon hehs-tow-RAHN-chee ah-KEE?
Do you tip the guide?	**Se da gorjeta ao guia?**	see dah gohr-ZHEH-tah ow GEE-ah?

IN THE OLD PART OF TOWN

Which are the historic sites?	**Quais são os lugares históri-cos?**	kwahys sown oos loo-GAH-rees ees-TOH-ree-koos?
What is the name of this church?	**Qual é o nome desta igreja?**	kwow eh oo NOH-mee DAYS-tah ee-GRAY-zhah?
Is that church old?	**Esta igreja é an-tiga?**	EHS-tah ee-GRAY-zhah eh ahn-CHEE-gah?
What religion is it?	**Que religião que é?**	keh hay-lee-ZHOWN keh eh?
Can you tell me about the history of that theater?	**Qual é a história desse teatro?**	kwow eh ah ees-TOH-ryah DEH-see chee-AH-troo?
Which are the important monuments?	**Quais são os monumentos importantes?**	kwahys sown oos moh-noo-MEHN-toos eem-pohr-TAHN-chees?

What does that commemorate?	**Isso comemora o que?**	EE-soo koh-may-MOH-rah oo keh?
When was that built?	**Quando que isto foi construido?**	KWAHN-doo keh EES-too foy kohn-stroo-EE-doo?
How old is that building?	**Quantos anos tem aquele prédio?**	KWAHN-toos AH-noos tehn ah-KEH-lee PREH-joo?
Whose statue is that?	**De quem é essa estátua?**	jee kehn eh AY-sah ehs-TAH-too-ah?
Who was he/she?	**Quem foi êle/ela?**	kehn foi AY-lee/EH-lah?

IN THE BUSINESS DISTRICT

At what time are businesses open?	**Qual é o horário comercial?**	kwow eh oo oh-RAH-ryoo koh-mehr-SYOW?
Where are the department stores?	**Onde ficam as lojas de departamentos?**	OHN-jee FEE-kahn ahs LOO-zhahs jee deh-pahr-tah-MEHN-toos?
Are they open on weekends?	**Abrem no fim de semana?**	AH-brehn noo feen jee say-MAH-nah?
Where is there . . .	**Onde tem . . .**	OHN-jee tehn . . .
• a souvenir shop?	• **uma loja de lembranças?**	• OO-mah LOH-zhah jee lehm-BRAHN-sahs?
• a bank?	• **um banco?**	• oon BAHN-koo?
• a money exchange?	• **um câmbio?**	• oon KAHM-byoo?

IN THE COUNTRY

| What is the best way to get to the country? | **Qual é a melhor maneira de ir ao campo?** | kwow eh ah mehl-YOHR mah-NAY-rah jee eer ow KAHM-poo? |
| Can I take a bus from here? | **Posso pegar um ônibus daqui?** | POH-soo peh-GAHR oon OH-nee-boos dah-KEE? |

133

English	Portuguese	Pronunciation
How long does it take?	**Quanto tempo demora?**	KWAHN-too TEHM-poo jee-MOH-rah?
Is there any place to eat there?	**Tem algum lugar para comer lá?**	tehn ahl-GOON loo-GAHR PAH-rah koh-MEHR lah?
Should we take some food?	**Devemos levar comida?**	day-VAY-moos lay-VAHR koh-MEE-dah?
I like . . .	**Eu gosto . . .**	AY-oo GOOS-too . . .
• birds.	• **dos pássaros.**	• doos PAH-sah-roos
• cottages.	• **das cabanas.**	• dahs kah-BAH-nahs
• fields.	• **dos campos.**	• doos KAHM-poos
• flowers.	• **das flores.**	• dahs FLOH-rees
• houses.	• **das casas.**	• dahs KAH-zahs
• mountains.	• **das montanhas.**	• dahs mohn-TAH-nyahs
• plants.	• **das plantas.**	• dahs PLAHN-tahs
• villages.	• **das vilas.**	• dahs VEE-lahs
• wild animals.	• **dos animais selvagens.**	• doos ah-nee-MAHYS sehl-VAH-zhehns
• woods.	• **dos bosques.**	• doos BOHS-kees
Look! There's a . . .	**Olha! lá tem . . .**	OHL-yah! lah tehn . . .
• barn.	• **um celeiro.**	• oon seh-LAY-roo
• beach.	• **uma praia.**	• OO-mah PRAHY-yah
• bridge.	• **uma ponte.**	• OO-mah POHN-chee
• farm.	• **uma fazenda.**	• OO-mah fah-ZEHN-dah
	uma quinta. (P)	OO-mah KEEN-tah
• lake.	• **um lago.**	• oon LAH-goo
• river.	• **um rio.**	• oon HEE-oo
• stream.	• **um riacho.**	• oon hee-AH-shoo
	um ribeiro. (P)	oon rree-BAY-roh
• tree.	• **uma árvore.**	• OO-mah AHR-voh-ree
• valley.	• **um vale.**	• oon VAH-lee
• waterfall.	• **uma cachoeira d'água.**	• OO-mah kah-shoh-AY-rah DAH-gwah
The view is . . .	**A vista é . . .**	ah VEES-tah eh . . .
• fantastic.	• **fantástica.**	• fahn-TAHS-chee-kah
• incredible.	• **incrível.**	• een-KREE-vay-oo
• breathtaking.	• **impressionante.**	• eem-preh-syoh-NAHN-chee
This place is . . .	**Este lugar é . . .**	EHS-chee loo-GAHR eh
• beautiful.	• **bonito.**	• boh-NEE-too

English	Portuguese	Pronunciation
• very pretty.	• **muito bonito.**	• MWEE-too boh-NEE-too
• very touristy.	• **de muito turismo.**	• jee MWEE-too too-REEZ-moo
Is there a beach nearby?	**Tem uma praia perto daqui?**	tehn OO-mah PRAHY-yah PEHR-too dah-KEE?
Are there rest rooms?	**Tem toaletes?**	tehn twah-LEH-chees?
What is a typical souvenir from here?	**Qual é uma lembrança tipica daqui?**	kwow eh OO-mah lehm-BRAHN-sah CHEE-pee-kah dah-KEE?

PLACES TO SEE IN BRAZIL

São Paulo

Brazil offers many attractions for tourists. Below are a variety of sight-seeing suggestions for São Paulo and Rio.

Instituto Butantã
(een-stee-TOO-too boo-tahn-TAHN)

The largest snake farm in Latin America, with more than 70,000 snakes in its collection, as well as thousands of spiders, scorpions, and lizards. Open daily. Be sure to see them milk the snakes (for serum) between 10:00 A.M. and 4:00 P.M.

The Exotiquarium

Here you can see the pink freshwater dolphins of the Amazon, in captivity for the first time in South America. Open from Tuesday through Sunday, 10 A.M. to 10 P.M.

Casa do Bandeirante
(KAH-zah doo bahn-day-RAHN-chee)

The House of the Flagbearer is an old ranch house that dates back to the 18th century. The building was restored in 1954 and decorated with priceless 18th-century furniture and pottery.

Ibirapuera Park
(ee-bee-rah-PWEH-rah)

Covering two million square meters, this park is perhaps the biggest one of its kind in the world. It contains natural lakes,

135

rolling lawns, and ten modern exhibition halls. There are museums of science, aeronautics, and contemporary Latin American art, a planetarium, a Japanese pavillion, and more.

Anhembi Park
(ahn-YEHM-bee)

The exposition hall here is the world's largest aluminum structure.

The Zoological Park

The largest zoo in South America, with 400 animals and 600 birds.

Simba Safari
(SEEM-bah sah-FAH-ree)

Here, lions, camels, monkeys, and cheetahs roam free in their own wilderness and only visitors are caged.

Rio de Janeiro

Museu do indio
(moo-ZAY-oo doo EEN-jyoo)

Located in the Botafogo area of the city, this museum is in an old home containing a storehouse of Indian work (feathers, ceramics, stone, and weaving), as well as a growing archive of films and recordings of the indigenous peoples' music and ways of life. The collection gives a taste of the enormous contributions of indigenous tribes to Brazilian culture.

Casa Rui Barbosa (KAH-zah HOO-ee bahr-BOO-zah)

This is the house of one of Brazil's leading citizens of the 19th century. Barbosa was a diplomat and politician who wrote the country's first constitution.

Pão de Açúcar
(pown jee ah-SOO-kahr)

Impressive Sugar Loaf Mountain, located in the middle of Rio, is one of the city's favorite tourist spots. A cable car gets you to the top, where you can enjoy a panoramic view of the city.

Corcovado Christ Statue

After visiting Sugar Loaf, you will want to visit the statue of Corcovado, an impressive statue of Christ that can be seen from many places in Rio.

Igreja da Glória
(ee-GRAY-zhah dah GLOH-ryah)

Built in the 18th century, Glory Church was the favorite spot of the imperial family. It contains many fine examples of art from both the old and new worlds.

Jardim Botánico
(zhahr-JEEN boh-TAH-nee-koo)

One of the best botanical gardens in the world. It covers an area of 5,657,000 square meters, and contains over 135,000 plants and trees.

Tijuca Forest
(tee-ZHOO-kah)

Once part of a private estate belonging to the Baron de Taunay, this forest is studded with exotic trees, thick jungle vines, and a delightful waterfall.

PLACES TO SEE IN PORTUGAL

Lisbon

Port Wine Institute

An excellent place for a pre-dinner drink of dry white port wine. Despite its formidable name, this is an attractive spot, open daily from 6:00 P.M. to midnight.

Adega Tipica
(ah-DEH-gah TEE-pee-kah)

This is the name for places where you can enjoy both Portuguese food and listen to *fado* (FAH-doh) music. You are not required to dine and can spend a whole evening sipping wine, and enjoying small talk. Singing seldom starts before 10:00 P.M.

Basilica da Estrela
(bah-ZEE-lee-kah da ehs-TREH-lah)

A very important monument which offers splendid views of Lisbon and the Tagus River from its dome.

Fundação Ricardo Espirito Santo
(foon-dah-SOWN rree-KAHR-doh ehs-PEE-ree-toh SAHN-toh)

Well worth a visit: part museum, part training center for craftsmen. Here you can see some of the best rugs, silver, furniture, and lamps made in Portugal.

137

| **Igreja de Madre de Deus** (ee-GRAY-zhah deh MAH-dreh deh DAY-oosh) | A masterpiece of Portuguese baroque architecture, with fine tiles and gilded woodwork. |

Fátima and Other Cities and Sites

From Lisbon, you can easily visit other sites and nearby towns, such as Estoril, Cascais, Sintra, Paço da Vila, the Palácio da Pena, and Colares. But one of the most famous places to visit is Fátima. From May until October, pilgrimages to the sanctuary at Fátima occur on the 13th of each month, the date of the apparition of the Virgin to the three shepherd children. The biggest celebration takes place May 12–13; the second most important is that of October 12–13. This sanctuary is visited not only by Catholics, but by people of every faith. Cities like Oporto, Madeira, Algarve, and Alentejo are also worth a trip.

RELIGIOUS SERVICES

Brazil is basically a Catholic country, and you can find churches in every part of town no matter where you are. Most of the old churches are found in the old part of the city, and many are beautiful examples of colonial architecture and art. In cosmopolitan centers like São Paulo and Rio, you can also find temples, synagogues, and churches of other faiths. In Portugal, also a Catholic country, it is more difficult to find churches of other denominations. In Brazil and Portugal, look in the yellow pages to find churches of other faiths.

Where is there . . .	**Onde tem . . .**	OHN-jee tehn . . .
• a Catholic church?	• **uma igreja católica?**	• OO-mah ee-GRAY-zhah kah-TOH-lee-kah?
• a Protestant church?	• **uma igreja protestante?**	• OO-mah ee-GRAY-zhah proh-tehs-TAHN-chee?
• a synagogue?	• **uma sinagoga?**	• OO-mah see-nah-GOH-gah?

138

When does the mass/service begin?	**Quando começa a messa/o serviço?**	KWAHN-doo koh-MAY-sah ah MAY-sah/oo sehr-VEE-soo?
Is there a mass in English?	**Tem messa em inglês?**	tehn MAY-sah ehn een-GLAYS?
I'm looking for a . . . who speaks English.	**Estou procurando um . . . que fala inglês.**	ehs-TOW proh-koo-RAHN-doo oon . . . keh FAH-lah een-GLAYS
• minister	• **ministro**	• mee-NEES-troo
• priest	• **padre**	• PAH-dree
• rabbi	• **rabino**	• hah-BEE-noo

12. SHOPPING

SHOPPING IN BRAZIL

Shopping in Brazil is a special treat for tourists—you'll find clothing, precious stones, leather goods, all sorts of handicrafts, and much more. And to make shopping easier, most stores accept traveler's checks and dollars at close to black market rates. Also, you can often bargain for items at outdoor stands.

As the largest commercial center of South America, São Paulo offers just about anything you can think of. Four major shopping malls in the Zona Sul—Iguatemi, Ibirapuera, Morumbi, and Eldorado—are open from 9:00 A.M. to 10:00 P.M. There are also a number of special streets throughout the city lined with great shops. The area known as the Quadrilátero dos Jardins, encompassing 28 streets, has the finest shops; whether you are looking for a great sandwich, French baguettes, or party clothes, you'll find it in this area.

To capture the flavor of Rio, wander up and down Avenida Copacabana or Visconde de Pirajá and their cross streets, which constitute the main shopping drag. If you want to buy gems, the top gem seller is H. Sterns, who in the last 30 years has built an international organization with branches in other principal cities and around the world.

SHOPPING IN PORTUGAL

Portugal is most famous for its handicrafts. Some specialty items are baskets, hand-embroidered table linens, blouses, and dresses (especially those made in Madeira). In Castelo Branco you will find traditionally embroidered bedspreads and in Vila do Conde, near Oporto, you'll find exquisite lace. The porcelain of Vista Alegre is also famous, as are the traditional and brightly colored roosters, made in Barcelos. The artisans of Alentejo make products of natural cork, in addition to items of tin, brass, and copper. Fine leather shoes, handbags, and belts can be found all the country.

DIALOGUE: AT THE SOUVENIR SHOP (À *LOJA DE LEMBRANÇAS*)

Turista:	**Tem coisas típicas do país?**	tehn KOY-zahs CHEE-pee-koos doo pah-EES?
Vendedor:	**Sim, temos muitos objetos típicos.**	seen, TEH-moos MWEE-toos oh-bee-ZHEH-toos CHEE-pee-koos.
Turista:	**Posso ver alguma coisa feito de couro?**	POH-soo vehr ahl-GOO-mah KOY-sah jee KOH-roo?
Vendedor:	**Claro que sim. Te-mos bolsas, cartei-ras e muitas outras coisas.**	KLAH-roo keh seen. TEH-mohs BOHL-sahs, kahr-TAY-rahs ee MWEE-tahs OH-trahs KOY-zahs.
Turista:	**Bem. Posso ver uma bolsa?**	behn. POH-soo vehr OO-mah BOHL-sah?
Vendedor:	**Sim. De que cor deseja?**	seen. jee keh kohr deh-ZAY-zhah?
Turista:	**Preta, acho.**	PRAY-tah, AH-shoo.
Vendedor:	**Um momento, por favor.**	oon moh-MEHN-too, poor fah-VOHR.
Turista:	**Obrigada.**	oo-bree-GAH-doo.

. . . .

Tourist:	Do you have handicrafts from the country?
Vendor:	Yes, we have many typical items.
Tourist:	May I see something in leather?
Vendor:	Of course. We have bags, billfolds, and many other things.
Tourist:	Fine. Can I see a bag?
Vendor:	Yes. What color would you like?
Tourist:	Black.
Vendor:	One moment, please.
Tourist:	Thank you.

141

TYPES OF STORES

English	Portuguese	Pronunciation
Where can I find a . . .	Onde posso encontrar uma . . .	OHN-jee POH-soo ehn-kohn-TRAHR OO-mah . . .
• bakery?	• padaria?	• pah-dah-REE-ah?
• bookstore?	• livraria?	• leev-rah-REE-ah?
• camera shop?	• loja de artigos fotográficos? loja de fotografia (P)?	• LOH-zhah jee ahr-CHEE-goos foh-toh-GRAH-fee-koos? LOH-zhah jee foh-toh-grah-FEE-ah?
• candy store?	• confeitaria?	• kohn-fay-tah-REE-ah?
• clothes store?	• loja de roupa?	• LOH-zhah jee HOH-pah?
• flower shop?	• floricultura?	• floh-ree-kool-TOO-rah?
• fruit stand?	• banca de frutas?	• BAHN-kah jee FROO-tahs?
• grocery store?	• armazém?	• ahr-mah-ZEHN?
• jewelry store?	• joalharia?	• zhoh-ahl-yah-REE-ah?
• shoe store?	• loja de sapatos?	• LOH-zhah jee sah-PAH-toos?
Is there a . . . nearby?	Tem uma . . . perto daqui?	tehn OO-mah . . . PEHR-too dah-KEE?
• grocery store	• mercearia (P)	• mehr-say-ah-REE-ah
• hardware store	• ferragem	• feh-HAH-zhehn
• liquor store	• loja de bebidas	• LOH-zhah jee beh-BEE-dahs
• record store	• loja de discos	• LOH-zhah jee DEES-koos
• souvenir shop	• loja de lembranças	• LOH-zhah jee lehm-BRAHN-sahs
• tobacco shop	• tabacaria	• tah-bah-kah-REE-ah
Where is there a . . .	Onde há um(a) . . .	OHN-jee ah oon (OO-mah) . . .
• butcher shop?	• açougue? talho? (P)	• ah-SOH-gee? TAHL-yoh?
• department store?	• loja de departamento? armazém? (P)	• LOH-zhah jee deh-pahr-tah-MEHN-too? ahr-mah-ZEHN?

142

• market?	• **mercado?**	• mehr-KAH-doo?
• newsstand?	• **barraca?**	• bah-HAH-kah?
• supermarket?	• **supermercado?**	• soo-pehr-mehr-KAH-doo?

GENERAL SHOPPING EXPRESSIONS

Excuse me.	**Desculpe-me.**	dehs-KOOL-pee mee
I would like to buy . . .	**Gostaria de comprar . . .**	gohs-tah-REE-ah jee kohm-PRAHR . . .
• some books.	• **alguns livros.**	• ahl-GOONS LEEV-roos
• some candy.	• **bombons. rebuçados. (P)**	• bohn-BOHNS rray-boo-SAH-dohsh
• cigarettes.	• **cigarros.**	• see-GAH-hoos
• clothes.	• **roupas.**	• HOH-pahs
• film.	• **um filme.**	• oon FEEL-mee
• some food.	• **comida.**	• koh-MEE-dah
• gifts.	• **presentes.**	• pray-ZEHN-chees
• jewelry.	• **jóias.**	• ZHOY-ahs
• medicine.	• **remédios.**	• heh-MEH-jyoos
• postcards.	• **cartões postais.**	• kahr-TOYN-ees pohs-TAH-ees
• shoes.	• **sapatos.**	• sah-PAH-toos
• souvenirs.	• **lembranças.**	• lehm-BRAHN-sahs
I'm just looking.	**Só estou olhando.**	soh ehs-TOW ohl-YAHN-doo.
How much is this?	**Quanto custa isto?**	KWAHN-too KOOS-tah EES-too?
It's rather expensive!	**E um pouco caro!**	eh oon POH-koo KAH-roo!
Do you have a cheaper one?	**Tem outro mais barato?**	tehn OW-troo mahys bah-RAH-too?
What is the lowest price?	**Qual é o preço minimo?**	kwow eh oo PRAY-soo MEE-nee-moo?
Is that the final price?	**E o preço final?**	eh oo PRAY-soo fee-NOW?
Can you give me a discount?	**Pode me dar um desconto?**	POH-jee mee dahr oon dehs-KOHN-too?
I'll give you . . .	**Ofereço . . .**	oh feh-RAY-soo . . .

143

I won't pay more than . . .	**Não pago mais que . . .**	nown PAH-goo mahys keh . . .
Can I have it for . . .	**Posso levar por . . .**	POH-soo lay-VAHR poor . . .
This is damaged.	**Esta estragado.**	ehs-TAH ehs-trah-GAH-doo
Do you have another?	**Tem outro?**	tehn OH-troo?
Can you order this for me?	**Pode-me encomendar isto?**	POH-jee mee heh-kohn-mehn-DAHR EES-too?
I'll look somewhere else.	**Vou ver em outro lugar.**	voh vehr ehn OH-troo loo-GAHR
No, thank you.	**Não, obrigado (-a).**	nown, oh-bree-GAH-doo(-dah)

WHAT THE VENDOR SAYS

Poderia ajudá-lo(-la)?	poh-deh-REE-ah ah-zhoo-DAH-loo(-lah)?	May I help you?
O que deseja?	oo keh deh-ZAY-zhah?	What would you like?
Lamento, mas não temos.	lah-MEHN-too, mahs nown TAY-moos	I'm sorry we don't have any.
O artigo está esgotado.	oo ahr-CHEE-goo ehs-TAH ehs-goh-TAH-doo	We're out of stock.
Mais alguma coisa?	mahys ahl-GOO-mah KOY-zah?	Anything else?
O caixa está ali.	oo KAY-shah ehs-TAH ah-LEE	The cashier's over there.
A caixa é ali. (P)	ah KAY-shah eh ah-LEE	
O que quer levar?	oo keh kehr lay-VAHR?	What are you going to buy?
Compre!	KOHM-pree!	Buy something!
Vendo por . . .	VEHN-doo poor . . .	I'll sell it for . . .
E o mínimo.	eh oo MEE-nee-moo	That's the lowest price.
Não é possível.	nown eh poh-SEE-vay-oo	It's not possible.

| **Quer comprá-lo?** | kehr kohm-PRAH-loo? | Will you buy it? |
| **Obrigado(-a).** | oh-bree-GAH-doo (-dah). | Thank you. |

THE CLOTHING STORE

I want to buy . . .	**Quero comprar . . .**	KEHR-oo kohm-PRAHR . . .
• a blouse.	• **uma blusa.**	• oo-mah BLOO-zah
• a belt.	• **um cinto.**	• oon SEEN-too
• a dress.	• **um vestido.**	• oon vehs-CHEE-doo
• an evening gown.	• **um vestido de noite.**	• oon vehs-CHEE-doo jee NOY-chee
• handkerchiefs.	• **lenços.**	• LEHN-soos
• a hat.	• **um chapéu.**	• oon shah-PAY-oo
• an overcoat.	• **um casaco.** **um casacão. (P)**	• oon kah-ZAH-koo oon kah-zah-KOWN
• a raincoat.	• **uma capa de chuva.** **um impermeável. (P)**	• OO-mah KAH-pah jee SHOO-vah oon eem-pehr-may-AH-vay-oo
• a robe.	• **um robe.**	• oon HOH-bee
• a shirt.	• **uma camisa.**	• OO-mah kah-MEE-zah
• a skirt.	• **uma saia.**	• OO-mah SAH-yah
• stockings.	• **meias.**	• MAY-yahs
• a sweater.	• **uma malha.**	• OO-mah MAHL-yah
• a tie.	• **uma gravata.**	• OO-mah grah-VAH-tah
My size is . . .	**O meu tamanho é . . .**	oo MAY-oo tah-MAHN-yoo eh . . .
• small.	• **pequeno.**	• peh-KEH-noo
• medium.	• **médio.**	• MEH-joo
• large.	• **grande.**	• GRAHN-jee
• extra-large.	• **extra-grande.**	• EHKS-trah GRAHN-jee
• 10.	• **dez.**	• days
• 12.	• **doze.**	• DOH-zee

145

• 14.	• catorze.	• kah-TOHR-zee
It does not fit me well.	Não me fica bem.	nown mee FEE-kah behn
It seems . . .	Parece . . .	pah-RAY-see . . .
• tight.	• apertado.	• ah-pehr-TAH-doo
• loose.	• solto.	• SOHL-too
• long.	• comprido.	• kohm-PREE-doo
• short.	• curto.	• KOOR-too
• big.	• grande.	• GRAHN-jee
• just right.	• certo.	• SEHR-too
• fine.	• bom.	• bohn
It fits well.	Me cai bem.	mee kahy behn
I'll take it.	Vou comprar.	voh kohm-PRAHR

See pages 147 for a complete chart of size equivalents.

COLORS AND FABRICS

Do you have this in . . .	Você tem isto em . . .	voh-SAY tehn EES-too ehn . . .
• black?	• preto?	• PRAY-too?
• blue?	• azul?	• ah-ZOOL?
• brown?	• marrom? castanho? (P)	• mah-HOHN? kahs-TAHN-yoh?
• gray?	• cinza?	• SEEN-zah?
• green?	• verde?	• VEHR-jee?
• orange?	• cor de laranja?	• kohr jee lah-RAHN-zhah?
• red?	• vermelho? encarnado? (P)	• vehr-MEHL-yoo? ehn-kahr-NAH-doh?
• white?	• branco?	• BRAHN-koo?
• yellow?	• amarelo?	• ah-mah-REH-loo?
Do you have this in . . .	Você tem isto em . . .	voh-SAY tehn EES-too ehn . . .
• acrylic?	• acrilico?	• ah-KREE-lee-koo?
• cotton?	• algodão?	• ahl-goh-DOWN?
• corduroy?	• veludo? bombazine? (P)	• veh-LOO-doo? bohm-bah-ZEE-neh?
• gabardine?	• gabardine?	• gah-bahr-DEE-nee?
• lace?	• renda?	• HEHN-dah?

• leather?	• **couro?**	• KOH-roo?
	cabedal? (P)	kah-beh-DOWN?
• linen?	• **linho?**	• LEEN-yoo?
• nylon?	• **nailon?**	• NAHY-lohn?
• satin?	• **cetim?**	• seh-CHEEN?
• silk?	• **seda?**	• SAY-dah?
• suede?	• **camurça?**	• kah-MOOR-sah?
• taffeta?	• **tafetá?**	• tah-fay-TAH?
• terrycloth?	• **turco?**	• TOOR-koo?
• velvet?	• **veludo?**	• veh-LOO-doo?
• wool?	• **lã?**	• lahn?
• worsted?	• **estambre?**	• ehs-TAHM-bree?

CLOTHING SIZES

We recommend trying on all clothing before buying because sizes vary and do not always correlate exactly with U.S. sizes. Also, it's less customary in Latin America and Portugal to return purchased clothing, except at large department stores.

WOMEN'S CLOTHES

Dresses/Suits						
American	8	10	12	14	16	18	20
Brazilian	38	40	42	44	46	48	50
Portuguese	36	38	40	42	44	46	48

Stockings			
American	8–8½	9–9½	10–10½
Brazilian	36–38	38–40	40–42
Portuguese	36–38	38–40	40–42

Shoes					
American	5	6	7	8	9
Brazilian	35	36	37	38	39
Portuguese	35	36	37	38	39

MEN'S CLOTHES

Suits/Overcoats						
American	36	38	40	42	44	46
Brazilian	46	48	50	52	54	56
Portuguese	46	48	50	52	54	56
Shirts						
American	15	16	17	18		
Brazilian	38	41	43	45		
Portuguese	38	41	43	45		
Shoes						
American	5	6	7	8	8½	9
Brazilian	38	39	41	42	43	43
Portuguese	38	39	41	42	43	43

THE JEWELRY STORE

I'd like to see . . .	**Gostaria de ver . . .**	gohs-tah-REE-ah jee vehr . . .
• a bracelet.	• **uma pulseira.**	• OO-mah pool-SAY-rah
• a brooch.	• **um broche.**	• oon BROH-shee
• a chain.	• **uma corrente.**	• OO-mah koh-HEHN-chee
• some earrings.	• **ums brincos.**	• oons BREEN-koos
• a necklace.	• **uma colar.**	• OO-mah koh-LAHR
• a pin.	• **um alfinete.**	• oon ow-fee-NAY-chee
• a ring.	• **un anel.**	• oon ah-NAY-oo
• a wrist watch.	• **um relógio de pulso.**	• oon hay-LOH-zhoo jee POOL-soo
Do you have this in . . .	**Tem isto em . . .**	tehn EES-too ehn . . .
• gold?	• **ouro?**	• OH-roo?
• white gold?	• **ouro branco?**	• OH-roo BRAHN-koo?
• silver?	• **prata?**	• PRAH-tah?
• stainless steel?	• **aço inoxidável?**	• AH-soo een-ohk-see-DAH-vay-oo?

• platinum?	• **platina?**	• plah-CHEE-nah?
I prefer it with . . .	**Prefiro com . . .**	pray-FEE-roo . . .
• amber.	• **âmbar.**	• AHM-bahr
• an amethyst.	• **uma ametista.**	• OO-mah ah-may-CHEES-tah
• an aquamarine.	• **uma áqua-marinha.**	• OO-mah ah-gwah-mah-REEN-yah
• coral.	• **coral.**	• koh-ROW
• crystal.	• **cristal.**	• krees-TOW
• cut glass.	• **cristal talhado.**	• krees-TOW tahl-YAH-doo
• a diamond.	• **um diamante.**	• oon jee-ah-MAHN-chee
• ebony.	• **ébano.**	• EH-bah-noo
• an emerald.	• **uma esmer-alda.**	• OO-mah ehs-mehr-AHL-dah
• ivory.	• **marfim.**	• mahr-FEEN
• jade.	• **jade.**	• ZHAH-jee
• onyx.	• **ônix.**	• OH-neeks
• a pearl.	• **uma pérola.**	• OO-mah PEH-roh-lah
• ruby.	• **um rubi.**	• oon hoo-BEE
• sapphire.	• **safira.**	• sah-FEE-rah
• topaz.	• **topázio.**	• toh-PAH-zyoo
• turquoise.	• **turquesa.**	• toor-KAY-zah

THE CAMERA SHOP

I would like a roll of film.	**Desejo um filme.**	day-ZAY-zhoo oon FEEL-mee
Do you have . . .	**Tem . . .**	tehn . . .
• film for prints?	• **filme para fo-tografias?**	• FEEL-mee PAH-rah foh-toh-grah-FEE-ahs?
• film for slides?	• **filme para slides?**	• FEEL-mee PAH-rah SLAHY-jees?
• movie film?	• **filme para fil-magem?**	• FEEL-mee PAH-rah feel-mah-ZHEHN?
• color film?	• **filme em cores?**	• FEEL-mee ehn KOH-rees?

149

• video film?*	• **filme para video?***	• FEEL-mee PAH-rah vee-DAY-oo
Do you develop film here?	**Vocês revelam filmes aqui?**	voh-SAYS hay-VAY-lahn FEEL-mee ah-KEE?
How much does it cost?	**Quanto custa?**	KWAHN-too KOOS-tah?
How long does it take?	**Quanto tempo demora?**	KWAHN-too TEHM-poo day-MOR-rah?
When should I pick up the pictures?	**Quando devo voltar para pegar as fotografias?**	KWAHN-doo DAY-voo vohl-TAHR PAH-rah peh-GAHR as foh-toh-grah-FEE-ahs?

*The *film* you buy in Brazil will work fine on a VCR at home as long as the *video recording equipment* is the kind you use at home, and not one bought abroad.

THE BOOKSTORE

In both São Paulo and Rio you will find stores that sell books, magazines, and newspapers in different languages from all over the world. The same is true of major cities in Portugal.

Where is there a bookstore?	**Onde há uma livraria?**	OHN-jee ah OO-mah leev-rah-REE-ah?
Is there a bookstore that carries English books?	**Há uma livraria que vende livros em inglês?**	ah OO-mah leev-rah-REE-ah keh VEHN-jee LEEV-roos ehn een-GLAYS?
Do you have the book . . . ?	**Tem o livro . . . ?**	tehn oo LEEV-roo . . . ?
Do you have this book in English?	**Tem este livro em inglês?**	tehn EHS-chee LEEV-roo ehn een-GLAYS?
Do you have an English-Portuguese dictionary?	**Tem um dicionário inglês-português?**	tehn oon dee-syoh-NAH-ryoo een-GLAYS pohr-too-GAYS?
Do you have . . .	**Tem . . .**	tehn . . .
• books?	• **livros?**	• LEEV-roos?

150

• a guide book?	• **um guia?**	• oon GEE-ah?
• magazines?	• **revistas?**	• hay-VEES-tahs?
• a map of the city?	• **um mapa ro-doviário?**	• oon MAH-pah hoh-doh-VYAH-ryoo?
• novels?	• **romances?**	• hoh-MAHN-sees?
• a pocket dictionary?	• **um dicionário de bolso?**	• oon dee-syoh-NAH-ryoo jee BOHL-soo?

THE STATIONERY SHOP

I would like . . .	**Desejo . . .**	day-ZAY-zhoo . . .
• envelopes.	• **envelopes.**	• ehn-veh-LOH-pees
• a notebook.	• **um caderno.**	• oon kah-DEHR-noo
• a pen.	• **uma caneta.**	• OO-mah kah-NAY-tah
• posters.	• **cartaz. posters. (P)**	• kahr-TAHZ POHS-tehrs
• ribbon.	• **fita.**	• FEE-tah
• Scotch tape.	• **fita-durex.**	• FEE-tah DOO-rehks
• stamps.	• **selos.**	• SAY-loos
• stationery.	• **papel de carta.**	• pah-PAY-oo jee KAHR-tah
• string.	• **barbante.**	• bahr-BAHN-chee
• wrapping paper.	• **papel de em-brulhar.**	• pah-PAY-oo jee ehm-brool-YAHR
• a writing pad.	• **um bloco.**	• oon BLOH-koo

ELECTRICAL APPLIANCES

Most Brazilian hotels have transformers for the electrical current and adapters for plugs so that foreign guests may use their own electric razors, hair dryers, etc. However, it is always wise to take along an extra adapter plug just in case. In Rio and São Paulo, 110 or 120 volts, 60-cycle AC is usually used. In Portugal, the voltage is 220 AC, and in a few remote areas, 110 volts.

| What's the voltage? | **Qual é a volta-gem?** | kwow eh ah vohl-TAH-zhehn? |
| Can you show me how it works? | **Pode me mostrar como é que funciona?** | POH-jee mee mohs-TRAHR KOH-moo eh keh foon-SYOH-nah? |

151

Do you have batteries for this?	**Tem pilhas para isto?**	tehn PEEL-yahs PAH-rah EES-too?
It's broken.	**Está quebrado.**	ehs-TAH kay-BRAH-doo
Can you fix this?	**Pode consertar isto?**	POH-jee kohn-sehr-TAHR EES-too?
I need . . .	**Preciso de . . .**	pray-SEE-zoo jee . . .
• an adapter plug.	• **um adaptador.**	• oon ah-dahp-tah-DOHR
• batteries.	• **pilhas.**	• PEEL-yahs
• a bulb.	• **uma lâmpada.**	• OO-mah LAHM-pah-dah
• a cassette recorder.	• **um gravador.**	• oon grah-vah-DOHR
• a clock radio.	• **um rádio relógio.**	• oon HAH-jyoo hay-LOH-jyoo
• an extension cord.	• **uma extensão.**	• OO-mah ehks-tehn-ZOWN
• a hair dryer.	• **um secador de cabelo.**	• oon seh-kah-DOHR jee kah-BAY-loo
• a plug.	• **uma tomada.**	• OO-mah toh-MAH-dah
	uma ficha. (P)	OO-mah FEE-shah
• a shaver.	• **um barbeador.**	• oo bahr-byah-DOHR
• a transformer.	• **um transformador.**	• oon trahs-fohr-mah-DOHR
• a travel iron.	• **um ferro de viagem.**	• oon feh-HOO jee vee-AH-zhehn

THE MUSIC STORE

Do you have . . .	**Tem . . .**	tehn . . .
• cassettes?	• **fita cassete?**	• FEE-tah kah-SEH-chee?
	cassete para gravador-audio? (P)	kah-SEH-teh PAH-rah grah-vah DOHR OW-dyoh?
• records?	• **discos?**	• JEES-koos?
• tapes?	• **fitas?**	• FEE-tahs?
• compact discs?	• **discos compactos?**	• JEES-koos kohm-PAHK-toos?

152

Where is the . . . music?	**Onde fica a música . . .**	OHN-jee FEE-kah ah MOO-zee-kah . . .
• Brazilian	• **brasileira?**	• bray-zee-LAY-rah?
• classical	• **clássica?**	• KLAH-see-kah?
• folk	• **folclórica?**	• fohlk-LOH-ree-kah?
• instrumental	• **instrumental?**	• een-stroo-mehn-TOW?
• Latin	• **latina?**	• lah-CHEE-nah?
• popular	• **popular?**	• poh-poo-LAHR?
• Portuguese	• **portuguesa?**	• pohr-too-GAY-zah?
• rock 'n' roll	• **rock?**	• hohk?
Do you sell . . .	**Vende . . .**	VEHN-jee . . .
• maracas?	• **maracas?**	• mah-RAH-kahs?
• musical instruments?	• **instrumentos musicais?**	• een-stroo-MEHN-toos moo-zee-KAHYS?

TOILETRIES

Toiletry items can be found in pharmacies, drugstores, or sometimes in department stores. Hotels often have small drugstores that carry most basic items.

a brush	**uma escova**	OO-mah ehs-KOH-vah
cologne	**água de colônia**	AH-gwah jee koh-LOH-nyah
a comb	**um pente**	oon PEHN-chee
deodorant	**um desodorante**	oon deh-zoh-doh-RAHN-chee
	um desodorizante (P)	oon deh-zoh-doh ree-ZAHN-teh
disposable diapers	**fraldas descartáveis**	FRAHL-dahs dehz-kahr-TAH-vay-ees
hairspray	**laquê**	lah-KAY
	laca (P)	LAH-kah
a mirror	**um espelho**	oon ehs-PEHL-yoo
nail clippers	**um alicate de unhas**	oon ah-lee-KAH-chee jee OON-yahs
nail polish	**esmalte de unhas**	ehs-MAHL-chee jee OON-yahs
	um verniz de unhas (P)	oon vehr-NEEZ deh OON-yahsh

153

nail polish remover	**removedor de esmalte**	hay-moh-veh-DOHR jee ehs-MAHL-chee
	acetona (P)	ah-say-TOH-nah
perfume	**perfume**	pehr-FOO-mee
sanitary napkins	**toalhas higiênicas**	TWAHL-yahs ee-ZHAY-nee-kahs
shampoo	**um xampu**	oon SHAHM-poo
	um champô (P)	oon shahm-POH
shaving cream	**loção de barbear**	loh-SOWN jee bahr-BYAHR
	um creme para a barba (P)	oon KRAY-meh PAH-rah ah BAHR-bah
soap	**sabonete**	sah-boh-NEH-chee
	sabão (P)	sah-BOWN
a sponge	**uma esponja**	OO-mah ehs-POHN-zhah
tampons	**tampões**	tahm-POYN-ees
tissues	**lenços de papel (P)**	LEHN-soos jee pah-PAY-oo
toilet paper	**papel higiênico**	pah-PAY-oo ee-ZHAY-nee-koo
a toothbrush	**uma escova de dentes**	OO-mah ehs-KOH-vah jee DEHN-chees
toothpaste	**pasta de dentes**	PAHS-tah jee DEHN-chees
tweezers	**uma pinça**	OO-mah PEEN-sah

See page 102, ''At the Pharmacy: Other Items,'' for products not listed here.

THE GROCERY STORE

I would like a . . .	**Gostaria de . . .**	gohs-tah-REE-ah-jee . . .
• bottle of juice.	• **uma garrafa de suco.**	• OO-mah gah-HAH-fah jee SOO-koo
• bottle of milk.	• **uma garrafa de leite.**	• OO-mah gah-HAH-fah jee LAY-chee
• box of cereal.	• **uma caixa de flocos.**	• OO-mah KAHY-shah jee FLOH-koos
• box of cookies.	• **uma caixa de biscoitos.**	• OO-mah KAHY-shah jee bees-KOY-toos

154

• can of tomato sauce.	• **uma jarra de suco de to-mate.**	• OO-mah JAH-hah jee SOO-koo jee toh-MAH-chee
• dozen eggs.	• **uma dúzia de ovos.**	• OO-mah DOO-zyah jee OH-voos
• package of candies.	• **um pacote de doces.**	• oon pah-KOH-chee jee DOH-sees
Do you have . . .	**Tem . . .**	tehn . . .
• cheese?	• **queijo?**	• KAY-zhoo?
• cold cuts?	• **frios?**	• FREE-oos?
• soft drinks?	• **refrigerantes?**	• hay-free-zheh-RAHN-chees?

WEIGHTS AND MEASURES

Metric Weight	**U.S.**
1 grama (g)	0.035 ounce
454 gramas	1 pound
1 quilograma (quilo)	2.2 pounds

Metric Distance	**U.S.**
1 centímetro (cm)	0.3937 inch
2.54 centímetros	1 inch
1 metro (m)	3.280 feet
1609.3 metros	1 mile

Liquids	**U.S.**
1 litro (1)	2.113 pints
1 litro	1.056 quarts
3.785 litros	1 gallon

Dry Measures	**U.S.**
1 litro	0.908 quart
1 decalitro	1.135 pecks
1 hectalitro	2.837 bushels

155

one inch = 2.54 centimeters.
One centimeter = .39 inch.

	in.	feet	yards
1 mm.	0.039	0.003	0.001
1 cm.	0.39	0.03	0.01
1 dm	3.94	0.32	0.10
1 m.	39.40	3.28	1.09

.39 (# of centimeters) = (# of inches)
2.54 (# of inches) = (# of centimeters)

	mm.	cm.	m.
1 in.	25.4	2.54	0.025
1 ft.	304.8	30.48	0.304
1 yd.	914.4	91.44	0.914

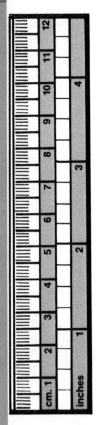

13. SPORTS AND ENTERTAINMENT

In Brazil and Portugal, you will surely see many people sitting in parks or cafés, enjoying a cup of coffee, reading a magazine or newspaper, talking, or just relaxing. Since both countries have long coastlines with wonderful beaches, swimming is also popular, as is soccer, the national sport of both Brazil and Portugal. For cultural entertainment there are also movies, shows, operas, and concerts. Bullfighting is an additional tourist attraction in Portugal.

DIALOGUE: ON THE BEACH (*NA PRAIA*)

João:	**Está muito quente!**	ehs-TAH MWEE-too KEHN-chee!
Mary:	**Sim, gostaria de ir nadar?**	seen, gohs-tah-REE-ah jee eer nah-DAHR?
João:	**Otima idéia. Adoro o mar!**	OH-chee-moo ee-DAY-ah! ah-DOH-roo oo mahr!
Mary:	**Mais não é perigoso por aqui?**	mahys nown eh peh-ree-GOH-zoo poor ah-KEE?
João:	**Não acho. O mar aqui geralmente é muito calmo.**	nown AH-shoo. oh mahr ah-KEE zheh-row-MEHN-chee eh MWEE-too KAHL-moo.
Mary:	**Que bom! Então, lhe vejo na praia em cinco minutos.**	keh bohn! ehn-TOWN, yee veh-zhoo nah PRAHY-yah ehn SEEN-koo mee-NOO-toos.
João:	**Certo! Não esqueça o bronzeador.**	SEHR-too! nown ehs-KAY-sah ao brohn-zeh-ah-DOHR.

. . . .

John:	It's so hot out!
Mary:	Yes. Would you like to go swimming?
John:	Good idea! I love the sea!
Mary:	But isn't it dangerous around here?

157

John: No! The sea here is usually pretty calm.

Mary: Good. Then I'll see you on the beach in five minutes.

John: Right. And don't forget the suntan lotion!

At the Beach

Where are the best beaches?	**Onde ficam as melhores praias?**	OHN-jee FEE-kahn ahs mehl-YOH-rees PRAHY-yahs?
How do I get there?	**Como posso ir lá?**	KOH-moo POH-soo eer lah?
Is it a private or public beach?	**E uma praia particular ou pública?**	eh OO-mah PRAHY-yah pahr-chee-koo-LAHR oh POOB-lee-kah?
Is there a life guard?	**Tem salvavida?**	tehn sahl-vah-VEE-dah?
Is it dangerous for children?	**E perigoso para crianças?**	eh peh-ree-GOH-zoo PAH-rah kree-AHN-sahs?
Are there dangerous currents?	**Têm correntes perigosas?**	tayn koh-HEHN-chees peh-ree-GOH-zahs?
When is . . .	**Quando é a . . .**	KWAHN-doo eh ah . . .
• high tide?	• **maré alta?**	• mah-REH AHL-tah?
• low tide?	• **maré baixa?**	• mah-REH BAHY-shah?
Where can I get . . .	**Onde posso obter . . .**	OHN-jee POH-soo oh-bee-TEHR . . .
• a beach chair?	• **uma cadeira de praia?**	• OO-mah kah-DAY-rah jee PRAHY-yah?
• a beach mat?	• **uma esteira?**	• OO-mah ehs-TAY-rah?
• an umbrella?	• **um guarda-sol?**	• oon gwahr-dah-SOHL?
• skin diving equipment?	• **equipamento para mergulho?**	• eh-kee-pah-MEHN-too PAH-rah mehr-GOOL-yoo?

158

• water skis?	• **esquis aquáti-cos?**	• ehs-KEES ah-KWAH-chee-koos?
• a rowboat?	• **um barco a re-mos?**	• oon BAHR-koo ah HAY-moos?
• a sailboat?	• **um veleiro?**	• oon veh-LAY-roo?

At the Swimming Pool

Where's the pool?	**Onde fica a pis-cina?**	OHN-jee FEE-kah ah pee-SEE-nah?
Is the pool . . .	**A piscina é . . .**	ah pee-SEE-nah eh . . .
• outdoors?	• **ao ar livre?**	• ow ahr LEEV-ree?
• indoors?	• **coberta?**	• KOH-behr-tah?
• heated?	• **aquecida?**	• ah-keh-SEE-dah?
When does the pool open?	**A que horas abre a piscina?**	ah keh OH-rahs AH-bree ah pee-SEE-nah?
When does the pool close?	**A que horas fecha a pis-cina?**	ah keh OH-rahs FAY-shah ah pee-SEE-nah?

CAMPING

While not common in Brazil, camping in Portugal has been on the upswing over the past few years, and more than 100 good camping sites are available throughout the country. One of the largest is the Monsanto Parque Florestal site, managed by the Lisbon Municipality. Not far from city center, this campsite is located along the Estoril *autostrada* (ow-toh-STRAH-dah), and offers tennis, a swimming pool, a restaurant, cafés, a chapel, a library, a game room, a mini-market, and a bank. More camping grounds can be found in Cascais, Castelo Branco, Coimbra, Viana do Castelo, Vila Real, Ericeira, and Algarve. Check with Turismo or the Federação Portuguesa de Campismo for a complete list of campsites.

Where is the campsite?	**Onde fica a área de 'camping'?**	OHN-jee FEE-kah ah AH-ryah jee KAHM-peen?
Can we camp here?	**Podemos acampar aqui?**	poh-DAY-moos ah-kahm-PAHR ah-KEE?

159

Is there room for a trailer?	**Tem lugar para um 'trailer'?**	tehn loo-GHAR PAH-rah oon TRAHY-lehr?
What does it cost per day?	**Quanto custa por dia?**	KWAHN-too KOOS-tah poor JEE-ah?
Is/are there . . .	**Tem . . .**	tehn . . .
• drinking water?	• **água potável?**	• AH-gwah poh-TAH-vay-oo?
• electricity?	• **electricidade?**	• eh-lehk-tree-see-DAH-jee?
• a market?	• **um mercado?**	• oon mehr-KAH-doo?
• a playground?	• **um play-ground?**	• oon plahy-GROWN?
• a pool?	• **uma piscina?**	• OO-mah pee-SEE-nah?
• showers?	• **chuveiros? duches? (P)**	• shoo-VAY-roos? DOO-shahs?
• butane gas?	• **gás?**	• gahs?

SPORTS

Soccer is by far the most popular sport in both Brazil and Portugal. Rio is world famous for its teams and players. In recent years, however, São Paulo has supplanted Rio as the most soccer-mad city in this soccer-mad country. Other sports played are tennis, volleyball, and handball; few hotels have courts, but sometimes permission can be obtained from private clubs. Squash has also gained popularity in recent years. In Lisbon, squash courts can be found near Campo Grande or at Cruz Quebrada. Also the Libson Sports Club offers facilities for tennis, swimming, and 9-hole golf.

In Brazil, and specifically in São Paulo, people have begun to take up jogging. Ibiripuera Park is a favorite spot for this, offering jogging as well as bicycle paths. On the beaches of Copacabana, more and more people are into surfing, especially at Ipanema's Arproador and Práia dos Bandeirantes. The same is true of beaches near Estoril in Portugal. Also, if you enjoy fishing, you can rent boats in Portugal, specially equipped for deep-sea fishing. There is also fresh water fishing for trout, rainbow trout, and large-mouthed bass, which were imported a few years ago from America.

160

I'd like to see a soccer match.	**Gostaria de ver uma partida de futebol.**	gohs-tah-REE-ah jee vehr OO-mah pahr-CHEE-dah jee foo-chee-BOHL
Who's playing?	**Quem está jogando?**	kehn ehs-TAH zhoh-GAHN-doo?
Which is the best team?	**Qual é o melhor time?**	kwow eh oo mehl-YOHR CHEE-mee?
	Qual é a melhor equipa? (P)	kwow eh ah mehl-YOHR eh-KEE-pah?
Where's the stadium?	**Onde fica o estádio?**	OHN-jee FEE-kah oo ehs-TAH-jyoo?
How much are the tickets?	**Quanto custam as entradas?**	KWAHN-too KOOS-tahn ahs ehn-TRAH-dahs?
Are there better seats?	**Têm melhores? assentos?**	tehn mehl-YOH-rees? ah-SEHN-toos?
What's the score?	**Quanto está?**	KWAHN-too ehs-TAH?
Who's winning?	**Quem está ganhando?**	kehn ehs-TAH gahn-YAHN-doo?

CULTURAL DIVERSIONS

Carnival

Brazil is almost synonymous with Carnival. The official season is actually the Saturday night before and the days leading up to Ash Wednesday, but in practice the action starts Friday at 11:00 P.M. While this period usually falls in February (and sometimes in March), the visitor can see preparations for Carnival as early as January. And though Carnival is celebrated throughout Brazil, it is in Rio that tourists will find its most fantastic expression. Canival is a fast-moving, mad, unbelievable, music-filled, sleepless time, when the entire nation rockets off into orbit and doesn't come back to earth for four days and five nights. This celebration affects not only the young—children start parading on the streets of Copacabana, beating tambourines, tin cans, or the hoods of parked cars—but also older people, who are active participants. While many of the celebrants are poor, Carnival—with its continuous display of pageantry—provides people with a chance to "act rich."

Dance troupes, known as "schools of samba" (*escolas de samba*/ehs-KOH-lahs jee SAHM-bah), start rehearsing about a year in advance. Most schools come from slum neighborhoods, or *favelas* (fah-VEH-lahs), and most dancers are black or mulattoes. A samba school can consist of as many as 3,000 people. Costumes are costly, sometimes as much as $500 each, a considerable sum for people who often earn under $100 a month. Besides the samba school parades, balls are held in private and social clubs, homes, or public places in Rio, São Paulo, and other Brazilian cities.

Movies

Check the entertainment page of local newspapers to find out what's playing at the movies. American movie titles are sometimes changed so you may not always recognize films from their original titles, but the actors' names will help identify many well-known movies. Many English-speaking films are dubbed into Portuguese, but occasionally English is left and subtitles are added. On the other hand, you may find it a valuable experience to see some locally produced movies even if you don't understand everything. Moviegoing is often a weekend activity for the entire family so movie theaters may be crowded. It is not uncommon to purchase numbered tickets in advance to be sure you will have a seat.

Let's go to the movies.	**Vamos ao cinema.**	VAH-moos ow see-NAY-mah
What's playing?	**O que está passando?**	oo keh ehs-TAH pah-SAHN-doo?
Is it in English or Portuguese?	**E em inglês ou português?**	eh ehn een-GLAYS ow pohr-too-GAYS?
Is it dubbed?	**E dublado?**	eh doo-BLAH-doo?
	E dobrado? (P)	eh doh-BRAH-doh?
Are there subtitles?	**O filme tem legenda?**	oo FEEL-mee tehn lay-ZHEHN-dah?
What kind of film is it?	**Que tipo de filme é?**	keh CHEE-poo jee FEEL-mee eh?

It's . . .	E . . .	eh . . .
• a comedy.	• **uma comédia.**	• OO-mah koh-MEH-jyah
• science fiction.	• **ficção cientí-fica.**	• feek-SOWN syehn-CHEE-fee-kah
• a musical.	• **um musical.**	• oon moo-zee-KOW
• a drama.	• **um drama.**	• oon DRAH-mah
• a political film.	• **um filme polit-ico.**	• oon FEEL-mee poh-LEE-chee-koo
• a war film.	• **um filme de guerra.**	• oon FEEL-mee jee GEH-hah
• a love story.	• **uma história de amor.**	• OO-mah ees-TOH-ryah jee ah-MOHR
• a horror movie.	• **um filme de terror.**	• oon FEEL-mee jee teh-HOHR
• a family movie.	• **um filme para toda a família.**	• oon FEEL-mee PAH-rah TOH-dah ah fah-MEEL-yah
When does the show start?	**Quando começa o espetáculo?**	KWAHN-doo koh-MAY-sah oo ehs-pay-TAH-koo-loo?
How much are the tickets?	**Quanto custam as entradas?**	KWAHN-too KOOS-tahn ahs ehn-TRAH-dahs?
Which theatre is showing the film . . . with . . . ?	**Em que cinema está o filme . . . com . . . ?**	ehn keh see-NAY-mah ehs-TAH oo FEEL-mee . . . kohn . . . ?

Art, Theater, Concerts, and Ballet

Brazil has a lively art scene. The many openings are listed in the newspaper entertainment section under *Artes Plásticas* (AHR-chees PLAHS-chee-kahs) and in Rio's *Monthly Rio Guide*, especially during the cultural season (beginning in April and extending through the Brazilian autumn and winter). Galleries and antiques stores are concentrated in the shopping Center de Gávea, the Shopping Cassino Atlântico, and the Rio Design Center. Rio and São Paulo have rich resources in the area of musical entertainment. There are concerts by visiting performers as well as resident artists. The Teatro Municipal

163

houses the city's opera and ballet companies and is the favored performance space for touring orchestras and dance troupes. For classical music, try the Sala Cecília Meireles, and for jazz and Brazilian popular music try the Sala Sidney Miller. In São Paulo's São Carlos and São Luiz Theatres, concerts, recitals, and ballet are performed from October through June.

I'd like to go to . . .	**Gostaria de ir a . . .**	gohs-tah-REE-ah jee eer ah . . .
• a play.	• **uma peça.**	• OO-mah PAY-sah
• an opera.	• **uma ópera.**	• OO-mah OH-peh-rah
• a ballet.	• **um balé.**	• oon bah-LEH
• a musical.	• **um musical.**	• oon moo-zee-KOW
• a concert.	• **um concerto.**	• oon kohn-SEHR-too
What type of play is it?	**Que tipo de peça é?**	keh CHEE-poo jee PAY-sah eh?
Who wrote it?	**Quem a escreveu?**	kehn ah ehs-kreh-VAY-oo?
Are there tickets for today?	**Tem entradas para hoje?**	tehn ehn-TRAH-dahs PAH-rah OH-zhee?
How much are the tickets?	**Quanto custam as entradas?**	KWAHN-too KOOS-tahn ahs ehn-TRAH-dahs?
Do we need a reservation?	**Precisamos fazer reserva?**	pray-see-ZAH-moos fah-ZEHR hay-ZEHR-vah?
Please give me two tickets.	**Por favor, me dê dois ingressos.**	poor fah-VOHR, mee day doys een-GRAY-soos
I'd like . . .	**Gostaria de . . .**	gohs-tah-REE-ah jee . . .
• an orchestra seat.	• **um lugar na platéia.**	• oon loo-GAHR nah plah-TAY-yah
• seats in the balcony.	• **assentos no balcão.**	• ah-SEHN-toos noo bahl-KOWN
• a place up front.	• **um lugar na frente.**	• oon loo-GAHR nah FREHN-chee
• a place in back.	• **um lugar atrás.**	• oon loo-GAHR ah-TRAHS
• a place on the side.	• **un lugar nos lados.**	• oon loo-GAHR noos LAH-doos
• good seats.	• **bons lugares.**	• bohns loo-GAH-rees

164

• inexpensive tickets.	• **entradas baratas.**	• ehn-TRAH-dahs bah-RAH-tahs
• tickets for the matinee.	• **entradas para a matinê.**	• ehn-TRAH-dahs PAH-rah ah mah-chee-NAY
• tickets for the evening.	• **entradas para a noite.**	• ehn-TRAH-dahs PAH-rah ah NOY-chee
A program, please.	**Um programa, por favor.**	oon proh-GRAH-mah, poor fah-VOHR
Who's . . .	**Quem é que . . .**	kehn eh keh
• playing?	• **atua?**	• ah-TOO-ah?
• singing?	• **canta?**	• KAHN-tah?
• dancing?	• **dança?**	• DAHN-sah?
• directing?	• **dirige?**	• jee-REE-zhee?
• speaking?	• **fala?**	• FAH-lah?
• announcing?	• **anuncia?**	• ah-NOON-syah?

NIGHTLIFE

Music, food, and friends are the key ingredients of Rio's varied nightlife. There is always music playing, whether it's a bunch of guys at the corner bar singing samba a capella and using anything available as percussion instruments, or a star-studded show staged with the latest audio technology and visual effects. Rio's nightlife gets started late, around 10 or 11 P.M., and goes until 4 to 5 in the morning, or until the last customer leaves. Shows, concerts, and club performances begin around 9 or 9:30 P.M.; sometimes later. However, there are probably better clubs and bars in São Paulo than in Rio. The Paulista enjoys going out after a day in the office and seems to have more money to spend on entertainment. Like New York, São Paulo has sophisticated nightlife, revolving around food and music. The functions of restaurants, nightclubs, and bars frequently overlap. There are ample bars, nightclubs, shows, and discotheques (*dancerias*/dahn-seh-REE-ahs) to choose from in both Rio and São Paulo.

There is not much in terms of similar nightlife in Portugal, although Lisbon has its share of discos. However, if you are after a more typical evening, seek out one of the *Adegas Típicas*

165

(ah-DAY-gahsh TEE-pee-kahsh), which are usually inexpensive and offer a chance to enjoy the *fado* (FAH-doh), Portugal's most characteristic type of music. The *fado* dates back to medieval times and is said to best reflect the soul of the Portuguese people. It has been described as sentimental, melancholy, dramatic, gay, heroic, and pungent. The *fado* experience is something all Portuguese share. The singer, or *fadista* (fah-DEESH-tah), is usually accompanied by a guitar and viola. A person does not have to have an extraordinary voice to sing the *fado* (although many do), but you must feel it. That's essential!

Why don't we go dancing tonight?	**Porque não vamos dançar esta noite?**	poor keh nown VAH-mohs dahn-SAHR EHS-tah NOY-chee?
Do we need reservations?	**Precisamos fazer reservas?**	pray-see-ZAH-moos fah-ZEHR hay-ZEHR-vahs?
Can you suggest a good nightclub?	**Pode recomendar um bom clube noturno?**	POH-jee hay-koh-mehn-DAHR oon bohn KLOO-bee noh-TOOR-noo?
Do they serve dinner?	**Servem o jantar?**	SEHR-vehn oo zhahn-TAHR?
Do they have a show?	**Têm show?**	tayn shoh?
What kind of show is it?	**Que tipo de show é?**	keh CHEE-poo jee shoh eh?
Is it expensive?	**E muito caro?**	eh MWEE-too KAH-roo?
Is there an entrance fee?	**Cobram entrada?**	KOH-brahn ehn-TRAH-dah?
Is there a cover charge?	**Se cobra couvert?**	see KOH-brah koo-VEHRT?
What kind of dress is needed?	**Como devo me vestir?**	KOH-moo DAY-voo mee vehs-CHEER?
Is there a place to go after dinner?	**Tem algum lugar para onde ir depois do jantar?**	tehn ahl-GOON loo-GAHR PAH-rah OHN-jee eer jee-POYS doo zhahn-TAHR?

166

SPORTS AND ENTERTAINMENT

English	Portuguese	Pronunciation
We would like a table . . .	Desejamos uma mesa . . .	day-zay-ZHAH-moos OO-mah MAY-zah . . .
• near the stage.	• perto do palco.	• PEHR-too doo PAHL-koo
• near the dance floor.	• perto da pista.	• PEHR-too dah PEES-tah
Is there a minimum charge?	Tem consumo mínimo?	tehn kohn-SOO-moo MEE-nee-moo?
How much are drinks?	Quanto custam as bebidas?	KWAHN-too KOOS-tahn ahs beh-BEE-dahs?
Are there any special drinks?	Têm algumas bebidas especiais?	tehn ahl-GOO-mahs beh-BEE-dahs ehs-peh-SYAH-ees?
Can we see the menu?	Podemos ver o cardápio?	poh-DAY-moos vehr oo kahr-DAH-pyoo?
	Podemos ver o menú? (P)	poh-DAY-mohs vehr oh meh-NOO?
At what time is the show?	A que horas é o espetáculo?	ah keh OH-rahs eh oo ehs-peh-TAH-koo-loo?
How many shows are there?	Quantos shows tem?	KWAHN-toos shohs tehn?

BULLFIGHTS IN PORTUGAL

Portuguese-style bullfighting combines elegance, daring, and skill. The combat is waged between the bull and the *toureiro* (toh-RAY-roh), or bullfighter, the latter on superbly trained horses. Unlike in Spanish bullfighting, the bull is not killed. The bullfighting season lasts from Easter Sunday through October, with fights on Sundays and sometimes also Thursdays. Portugal boasts over 30 bullrings, the main one being Campo Pequeno in Lisbon. The biggest names in the bullfighting world usually appear at Santarém in June, and in Vila Franca de Xira in July.

| Is there a bullfight today? | Tem uma corrida hoje? | tehn OO-mah koh-RREE-dah oy-zheh? |

167

Where is the bull-ring?	**Onde fica a praça dos touros?**	OHN-jee FEE-kah ah PRAH-sah dohsh TOH-rohsh?
Who is the main bullfighter?	**Quem é o toureiro principal?**	kehn eh oo toh-RAY-roh preen-see-POW?
Do you have seats in the . . .	**Tem lugares . . .**	tehn loo-GAH-rehsh . . .
• shade?	**• na sombra?**	• nah SOHM-brah?
• sun?	**• no sol?**	• noh sowl?
Bravo!	**Olé!**	oh-LEH!

14. GENERAL EXPRESSIONS

DAYS, MONTHS, AND SEASONS

Days of the Week

What day is it?	**Que dia é hoje?**	keh JEE-ah eh OH-zhee?
Today is . . .	**Hoje é . . .**	OH-zhee eh . . .
• Monday.	• **segunda-feira.**	• say-GOON-dah FAY-rah
• Tuesday.	• **terça-feira.**	• TEHR-sah FAY-rah
• Wednesday.	• **quarta-feira.**	• KWAHR-tah FAY-rah
• Thursday.	• **quinta-feira.**	• KEEN-tah FAY-rah
• Friday.	• **sexta-feira.**	• SEHKS-tah FAY-rah
• Saturday.	• **sábado.**	• SAH-bah-doo
• Sunday.	• **domingo.**	• doh-MEEN-goo

Months of the Year

January	**janeiro**	zhah-NAY-roo
February	**fevereiro**	feh-veh-RAY-roo
March	**março**	MAHR-soo
April	**abril**	ah-BREE-oo
May	**maio**	MAY-yoo
June	**junho**	ZHOON-yoo
July	**julho**	ZHOOL-yoo
August	**agosto**	ah-GOHS-too
September	**setembro**	seh-TEHM-broo
October	**outubro**	oh-TOO-broo
November	**novembro**	noh-VEHM-broo
December	**dezembro**	jee-ZEHM-broo

Seasons

spring	**primavera**	pree-mah-VEHR-ah
summer	**verão**	veh-ROWN
autumn/fall	**outono**	oh-TOH-noo
winter	**inverno**	een-VEHR-noo
in spring	**na primavera**	nah pree-mah-VEHR-ah
during the summer	**durante o verão**	doo-rahn-CHEE oo veh-ROWN

169

in autumn	**no outono**	noo oh-TOH-noo
during the winter	**durante o inverno**	doo-rahn-CHEE oo een-VEHR-noo

THE DATE

What is today's date?	**Qual é a data de hoje?**	kwow eh ah DAH-tah jee OH-zhee?
What day is today?	**Que dia é hoje?**	oo keh JEE-ah eh OH-zhee?
Today is Friday, June 11.	**Hoje é sexta-feira, onze de junho.**	OH-zhee eh SEHKS-tah FAY-rah, OHN-zee jee ZHOON-yoo
It's Wednesday, August 1, 1993.	**E quarta-feira, primeiro de agosto, mil novecentos e noventa e três.**	eh KWAHR-tah FAY-rah, pree-MAY-roo jee ah-GOHS-too, MEE-oo noh-vay-SEHN-toos ee noh-VEHN-tah ee trays.

AGE

How old are you?	**Quantos anos você tem?**	KWAHN-toos AH-noos voh-SAY tehn?
I am forty years old.	**Tenho quarenta anos.**	TEHN-yoo kwah-REHN-tah AH-noos.
How old is he/she?	**Quantos anos ele/ela tem?**	KWAHN-toos AH-noos AY-lee/EH-lah tehn?
She is twenty.	**Ela tem vinte anos.**	EH-lah tehn VEEN-chee AH-noos
I'm older/younger than he is.	**Eu sou mais velho(a)/ novo(-a) que ele.**	AY-oo soh mahys VEHL-yoo(-yah)/ NOH-voo(-vah) keh AY-lee
I was born in 1940.	**Eu nasci em mil novecentos e quarenta.**	AY-oo NAH-see ehn MEE-oo noh-vay-SEHN-toos ee kwah-REHN-tah
When is your birthday?	**Quando é o seu aniversário?**	KWAHN-doo eh oo SAY-oo ah-nee-vehr-SARH-ryoo?

My birthday is April 30.	**O meu aniversá-rio é no dia trinta de abril.**	oo MAY-oo ah-nee-vehr-SAH-ryoo eh noo JEE-ah TREEN-tah jee ah-BREE-oo

TIME EXPRESSIONS

now	**agora**	ah-GOH-rah
on time	**na hora**	nah OH-rah
earlier	**mais cedo**	mahys SEH-doo
later	**mais tarde**	mahys TAHR-jee
before 10:30	**antes das dez e meia**	AHN-chees dahs dehs ee MAY-yah
after 8:00	**depois das oito**	jee-POYS dahs OY-too
since 9:00	**desde as nove**	DEHS-jee ahs NOH-vee
soon	**logo**	LOH-goo
five minutes ago	**há cinco minutos**	ah SEEN-koo mee-NOO-toos
in five seconds	**em cinco segun-dos**	ehn SEEN-koo say-GOON-doos
morning	**manhã**	mahn-YOWN
noon	**meio-dia**	MAY-yoo-JEE-ah
afternoon	**tarde**	TAHR-jee
night	**noite**	NOY-chee
midnight	**meia-noite**	meh-yah-NOY-chee
this morning	**esta manhã**	EHS-tah mahn-YAHN
tomorrow	**amanhã**	ah-mahn-YAHN
tomorrow morning	**amanhã de manhã**	ah-mahn-YAHN jee mahn-YAHN
the day after tomor-row	**depois de amanhã**	jee-POYS jee ah-mahn-YAHN
yesterday	**ontem**	OHN-tehn
yesterday morning	**ontem de manhã**	OHN-tehn jee mahn-YOWN
the day before yes-terday	**anteontem**	ahn-chee-OHN-tehn
in a week	**numa semana**	NOO-mah say-MAH-nah
next week	**na semana que vem**	nah say-MAH-nah keh vehn

171

last week	**a semana pas-sada**	ah say-MAH-nah pah-SAH-dah
next month	**o mês que vem**	oo mays keh vehn
last month	**o mês passado**	oo mays pah-SAH-doo
all year	**o ano todo**	oo AH-noo TOH-doo
last year	**no ano passado**	noo AH-noo pah-SAH-doo

PUBLIC HOLIDAYS

Some holidays in Brazil and Portugal—like Christmas, New Year's, and Mother's Day—are the same as those celebrated in many other parts of the world. However, there are also many holidays specific to each country. Public holidays are often religious or national in origin, and, in Brazil, dates are often "moved" to Monday or Friday to permit a longer weekend. In addition, small towns have local celebrations, often to honor a patron saint or the namesake of the town (e.g., São José, São Luiz, and so on). Keep this in mind when traveling about because most public offices and buildings will be closed on these dates.

Brazil

January 1	**Ano Novo**	New Year's Day
Usually in February	**Carnaval**	Carnival
Contingent on Easter	**Sexta-Feira Santa**	Good Friday
Date varies	**Páscoa**	Easter
April 21	**Tiradentes**	National Holiday
Date varies in June	**Corpus Christi**	Religious Holiday
September 7	**Dia da Independência**	Independence Day
October 12	**Nossa Senhora de Aparecida**	Religious Holiday
November 1	**Dia dos Mortos**	All Soul's Day
December 25	**Natal**	Christmas

172

Portugal

January 1	**Ano Novo**	New Year's Day
January 6	**Dia de Reis**	Epiphany
Contingent on Easter	**Sexta-Feira Santa**	Good Friday
Date varies	**Páscoa**	Easter
April 25	**Vinte e cinco de Abril**	April 25th (Revolution Day)
May 1	**Dia dos Trabalhadores**	Labor Day
Date varies, often in May	**Pentecostes**	Pentecostal Sunday
Date varies, often in June	**Corpo de Deus**	Corpus Christi
June 10	**Dia de Portugal**	Portugal National Day
August 15	**Assunção**	Assumption Day
October 5	**Dia da República**	Proclamation of the Portuguese Republic
November 1	**Todos os Santos**	All Saints' Day
December 8	**Imaculada Conceição**	Immaculate Conception
December 25	**Natal**	Christmas

THE WEATHER

Weather varies in different areas of Brazil and Portugal. During the summer, the coast of Portugal is hot and humid, especially in the south. Along coastal areas of Brazil where Rio is located, weather is warm to hot all year round, with a great deal of humidity. The equator also runs across Brazil, and the Amazon jungles cover a very large area of the country. In interior cities located in mountainous areas, however, the weather is mild and pleasant, whereas in the north and northeast, the weather is often hot and dry.

What lovely weather!	**Que tempo lindo!**	keh TEHM-poo LEEN-doo!
What a nice day!	**Que dia lindo!**	keh JEE-ah LEEN-doo!

English	Portuguese	Pronunciation
What terrible weather!	Que tempo horrível!	keh TEHM-poo oh-HEE-vay-oo!
What's the weather going to be like?	Qual é a previsão do tempo?	kwow eh ah pre-vee-ZOWN doo TEHM-poo?
Is it going to . . .	Vai . . .	vahy . . .
• be sunny?	• fazer sol?	• fah-ZEHR sohl?
• be nice?	• estar bom?	• ehs-TAHR bohn?
• rain?	• chover?	• shoh-VEHR?
How long is this weather going to last?	Quanto durará este tempo?	KWAHN-too doo-rah-RAH EHS-chee TEHM-poo?
Is it going to get hotter/colder?	Vai fazer mais calor/frio?	vahy fah-ZEER mahys kah-LOHR/FREE-oo?
Is the weather going to change?	O tempo vai mudar?	oo TEHM-poo vahy moo-DAHR?
It's . . . today, isn't it?	Hoje está . . ., não é?	OH-zhee ehs-TAH . . ., nown eh?
• hot	• quente	• KEHN-chee
• cold	• frio	• FREE-oo
• windy	• com vento	• kohn VEHN-too
• sunny	• ensolarado	• ehn-soh-lah-RAH-doo
• rainy	• chuvoso	• shoo-VOH-zoo

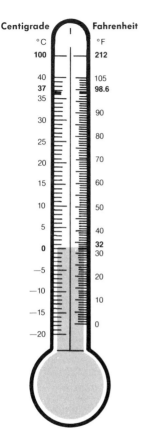

Centigrade / Fahrenheit

°C / °F

100	212
40	105
37	98.6
35	
30	90
25	80
20	70
15	60
10	50
5	40
0	32
	30
−5	20
−10	10
−15	0
−20	

TEMPERATURE CONVERSIONS

In Brazil and Portugal, temperature is measured in degrees Celsius, or centigrade, rather than in Fahrenheit, as in the United States.

To convert degrees Celsius into degrees Fahrenheit, use this formula and follow these steps:

$$\left(\frac{9}{5}\right) C + 32 = F$$

1. Divide by 5
2. Multiply by 9
3. Add 32

To convert Fahrenheit to Celsius, use this formula and follow these steps:

$$\frac{5}{9} (F - 32) = C$$

1. Subtract 32
2. Divide by 9
3. Multiply by 5

175

CONTINENTS, COUNTRIES, NATIONALITIES, AND LANGUAGES

Continents

Africa	**Africa**	AH-free-kah
Asia	**Asia**	AH-zyah
Australia	**Austrália**	ows-TRAH-lyah
Europa	**Europa**	ay-oo-ROH-pah
North America	**América do Norte**	ah-MEH-ree-kah doo NOHR-chee
South America	**América do Sul**	ah-MEH-ree-kah doo sool

Countries / Nationalities

Argentina	**Argentina** ahr-zhehn-CHEE-nah	**argentino(-a)** ahr-zhehn-CHEE-noo(-nah)
Australia	**Austrália** ows-TRAH-lyah	**Australiano** ows-trah-LYAH-noo (-nah)
Azores (Islands)	**Açores** ah-SOH-rehsh	**açoreano(-a)** ah-soh-RYAH-noh (-nah)
Bolivia	**Bolivia** boh-LEE-vyah	**boliviano(-a)** boh-lee-VYAH-noo (-nah)
Brazil	**Brasil** brah-ZEE-oo	**brasileiro(-a)** brah-zee-LAY-roo (-rah)
Canada	**Canadá** kah-nah-DAH	**canadense** kah-nah-DEHN-zee
Chile	**Chile** SHEE-lee	**chileno(-a)** shee-LAY-noo(-nah)
China	**China** SHEE-nah	**chinês(+a)** shee-NAYZ(-tah)
Colombia	**Colômbia** koh-LOHM-byah	**colombiano(-a)** koh-lohm-BYAH-noo (-nah)

176

Costa Rica	**Costa Rica** KOHS-tah HEE-kah	costarriquenho(-a) kohs-tah-hee-KAYN-yoo(-yah)
Cuba	**Cuba** KOO-bah	cubano(-a) koo-BAH-noo(-nah)
Denmark	**Dinamarca** jee-nah-MAHR-kah	dinamarquês(+a) dee-nah-mahr-KAYS(+zah)
Ecuador	**Equador** eh-kwah-DOHR	equatoriano(-a) eh-kwah-toh-RYAH-noo(-nah)
Egypt	**Egito** eh-ZHEE-too	egípcio(-a) eh-ZHEEP-syoo(-syah)
England	**Inglaterra** een-glah-TEH-hah	inglês(+a) een-GLAYS(+zah)
Finland	**Finlândia** feen-LAHN-dyah	finlandês(+a) feen-lahn-DAYS(+zah)
France	**França** FRAHN-syah	francês(+a) frahn-SAYS(+zah)
Germany	**Alemanha** ah-lay-MAH-nyah	alemão(-ã) ah-lay-MOWN (-MAHN)
Greece	**Grécia** GREH-syah	grego(-a) GRAY-goo(-gah)
Guatemala	**Guatemala** gwah-tay-MAH-lah	guatemalteco(-a) gwah-tay-mahl-TAY-koo(-kah)
Holland	**Holanda** oh-LAHN-dah	holandés(+a) oh-lahn-DAYS(+zah)
Iceland	**Islândia** eez-LAHN-dyah	islandês(+a) eez-lahn-DAYS(+zah)
Ireland	**Irlanda** eerr-LAHN-dah	irlandês(+a) eer-lahn-DAYS(+zah)
Israel	**Israel** eez-rah-AY-oo	israelense eez-rah-eh-LEHN-zee
Italy	**Itália** ee-TAH-lyah	italiano(-a) ee-tah-LYAH-noo (-nah)

177

Japan	**Japão**	japonês(+a)
	zhah-POWN	zhah-poh-NAYS(+zah)
Mexico	**México**	mexicano(-a)
	MEH-shee-koo	meh-zhee-KAH-noo (-nah)
Morocco	**Marracos**	marroquino(-a)
	mah-HAHK-oos	mah-hah-KEE-noo (-nah)
Paraguay	**Paraguai**	paraguaio(-a)
	pah-rah-GWAHY	pah-rah-GWAH-yoo(-yah)
Perú	**Perú**	peruano(-a)
	pay-ROO	peh-roo-AH-noo (-nah)
Poland	**Polonia**	polonês(+a)
	poh-LOH-nyah	poh-loh-NAYS(+zah)
Portugal	**Portugal**	português(+a)
	pohr-too-GOW	pohr-too-GAYS(+zah)
Russia	**Rússia**	russo(-a)
	HOO-syah	HOO-soo(-sah)
Spain	**Espanha**	espanhol(+a)
	ehs-PAHN-yah	ehs-pahn-YOHL(+ah)
Sweden	**Suécia**	sueco(-a)
	SWEH-see-ah	SWEH-koo(-kah)
Switzerland	**Suiça**	suiço(-a)
	SWEE-sah	SWEE-soo(-sah)
Thailand	**Tailândia**	tailandês(+a)
	tee-LAHN-dee-ah	thay-lahn-DEHZ(tah)
Turkey	**Turquia**	turco(-a)
	toor-KEE-ah	TOOR-koo(-kah)
United States	**Estados Unidos**	americano(-a)
	ehs-TAH-doos oo-NEE-doos	ah-meh-ree-KAH-noo(-nah)
Uruguay	**Uruguai**	uruguaio(-a)
	oo-roo-GWAHY	oo-roo-GWAH-yoo (-yah)
Venezuela	**Venezuela**	venezuelano(-a)
	veh-nay-ZWAY-lah	veh-nay-zway-LAH-noo(-nah)

Languages

Names of languages are usually based on the masculine form of the nationality given above. For example, the word for the German or Italian languages would be *alemão* (ah-lay-MOWN) or *italiano* (ee-tah-LYAH-noo). Likewise, to say, "I speak Portuguese," say "*Eu falo português*" (AY-oo FAH-loo pohr-too-GAYS) or, for "I speak English," say "*Eu falo inglês*" (AY-oo FAH-loo een-GLAYS).

PROFESSIONS AND OCCUPATIONS

Professions

architect	**arquiteto(-a)**	ahr-kee-TEH-too(-tah)
artist	**artista**	ahr-CHEES-tah
cardiologist	**cardiologista**	kahr-jyoh-loh-JEES-tah
dentist	**dentista**	dehn-CHEES-tah
doctor	**médico(-a)**	MEH-jee-koo(-kah)
engineer	**engenheiro(-a)**	ehn-zhehn-YAY-roo (-rah)
opthamologist	**oftalmologista**	ohf-tahl-moh-loh-ZHEES-tah
lawyer	**advogado(-a)**	ah-jee-voh-GAH-doo (-dah)
neurologist	**neurologista**	nay-oo-roh-loh-ZHEES-tah
professor (teacher)	**professor(+a)**	proh-feh-SOHR(+ah)
painter	**pintor(+a)**	peen-TOHR(+ah)
sculptor	**escultor(+a)**	ehs-kool-TOHR(+ah)

Occupations

accountant	**contabilista**	kohn-tah-bee-LEES-tah
baker	**padeiro(-a)**	pah-DAY-roo(-rah)
banker	**banquiero(-a)**	bahn-KAY-roo(-rah)
butcher	**açougueiro**	ah-soh-GAY-roo
	homen do talho (P)	OH-mehn doh TAHL-yoh
carpenter	**merceneiro**	mehr-sehn-NAY-roo
	carpinteiro (P)	kahr-peen-TAY-roh

179

clerk	**balconista**	bahl-koh-NEES-tah
	oficinista (P)	oh-fee-see-NEES-tah
cook	**cozinheiro(-a)**	koh-zeen-YAY-roo(-rah)
electrician	**electricista**	eh-lehk-tree-SEES-tah
jeweler	**joalheiro(-a)**	zwahl-YAY-roo(-rah)
maid	**empregada**	ehm-pray-GAH-dah
nurse	**enfermeiro(-a)**	ehn-fehr-MAY-roo(-rah)
salesperson	**vendedor(+a)**	vehn-day-DOHR(+ah)
shoemaker	**sapateiro**	sah-pah-TAY-roo
shopkeeper	**lojista**	loh-ZHEES-tah
	comerciante (P)	koh-mehr-SYAHN-teh
waiter	**garçom**	gahr-SOHN
	empregado(-a) (P)	ehm-pray-GAH-doh (-dah)
waitress	**garçonete**	gahr-soh-NEH-chee
writer	**escritor(+a)**	ehs-kree-TOHR(+a)

EMERGENCY EXPRESSIONS

Look!	**Olhe!**	OHL-yee!
Listen!	**Escute!**	ehs-KOO-chee!
Watch out!	**Cuidado!**	kwee-DAH-doo!
Fire!	**Fogo!**	FOH-goo!
Help!	**Socorro!**	soh-KOH-hoo!
Hurry!	**Depressa!**	jee-PRAY-sah!
Stop!	**Pare!**	PAH-ree!
I need help quick!	**Preciso de ajuda, urgente!**	pray-SEE-zoo jee ah-ZHOO-dah, oor-ZHEHN-chee!
Can you help me?	**Pode me ajudar?**	POH-jee mee ah-zhoo-DAHR?
Police!	**Policia!**	poh-LEE-syah!
I need a policeman!	**Preciso de um policial!**	pray-SEE-zoo jee oon poh-lee-SYOW!
It's an emergency!	**E uma emergência!**	eh OO-mah eh-mehr-ZHAYN-syah!
That man's a thief!	**Esse homen é um ladrão!**	EH-see OH-mehn eh oon lah-DROWN!
Stop him!	**Detenha-o!**	day-TEHN-yah-oo!
He stole my . . .	**Ele roubou . . .**	AY-lee hoh-BOH-oo . . .

• pocketbook.	• **a minha bolsa.**	• ah MEEN-yah BOHL-sah
• wallet.	• **a minha carteira.**	• ah MEEN-yah kahr-TAY-rah
• passport.	• **o meu passaporte.**	• oo MAY-oo pah-sah-POHR-chee
• watch.	• **o meu relógio.**	• oo MAY-oo hay-LOH-zhyoo
I've lost my . . .	**Perdi . . .**	pehr-JEE . . .
• suitcase.	• **a mala.**	• ah MAH-lah
• money.	• **o dinheiro.**	• oo jeen-YAY-roo
• glasses.	• **os óculos.**	• oos OH-koo-loos
• keys.	• **as chaves.**	• ahs SHAH-vees

SIGNS AND ANNOUNCEMENTS

Aberto	ah-BEHR-too	Open
Acima	ah-SEE-mah	Up
Aluga-se	ah-LOO-gah-see	For rent
Bemvindos	behn-VEEN-doos	Welcome
Caixa	KAY-zhah	Cashier
Câmbio	KAHM-byoo	Money exchange
Cheio	SHAY-yoo	Full
Cuidado	kwee-DAH-doo	Watch out
Elevador	eh-lay-vah-DOHR	Elevator
Empurre	em-POO-hee	Push
Entrada	ehn-TRAH-dah	Entrance
Entrada proibida (Proibida a entrada)	ehn-TRAH-dah proh-ee-BEE-dah	No entrance, keep out
Fechado	fay-SHAH-doo	Closed
Frio	FREE-oo	Cold
Homens	OH-mehns	Men
Leilão	lay-LOWN	Auction
Livre	LEEV-ree	Vacant
Liquidação	lee-kee-dah-SOWN	Close-out sale
Lotado	loh-TAH-doo	Full
Não entre	nown EHN-tree	Do not enter
Não mexa	nown MAY-shah	Do not touch

181

Ocupado	oh-koo-PAH-doo	Busy, occupied
Para alugar	PAH-rah ah-loo-GAHR	For rent
Pare	PAH-ree	Stop
Passe	PAH-see	Walk, cross
Perigo	peh-REE-goo	Danger
Proibido	proh-ee-BEE-doo	Forbidden
Proibido fumar	proh-ee-BEE-doo foo-MAHR	No smoking
Puxar	poo-SHAHR	Pull
Quente	KEEN-chee	Hot
Reservado	hay-zehr-VAH-doo	Reserved
Saida	sah-EE-dah	Exit
Senhoras	sehn-YOH-rahs	Ladies
Siga	SEE-gah	Walk, cross
Vende-se	VEHN-jee-see	For sale
Veneno	veh-NAY-noo	Poison

COMMON ABBREVIATIONS

a/c	ao cuidado de	c/o (in care of)
apart., apto.	apartamento	apartment
av.	avenida	avenue
cent.	centavo	cent
cia., C.ia	companhia	company
d., dto.	direito	direct
Dr.	Doutor	Doctor
E.U.A.	Estados Unidos da América	U.S.A.
esc.	escudo (P)	escudo (Portuguese currency)
Gov.	governo	government
h.	hora	hour
kg.	quilograma(s)	kilogram(s)
n.°	número	number
m.	metro	meter
Na. Sra.	Nossa Senhora	Our Lady
P.	praça	plaza/square
pág., pg.	página	page
Prof.	Professor	Professor
R.	rua	street
Rem.	remetente	sender

r/c	**res-do-chão (P)**	ground floor
S.A.	**Sociedade Anónima**	Ltd., Inc.
S.to/ta	**Santo/Santa**	Saint
Sr.	**Senhor**	Mr.
Sr.a	**Senhora**	Mrs.
Srta.	**Senhorita**	Miss/Ms.
Tel.	**telefone**	telephone

15. GRAMMAR IN BRIEF

With *Traveltalk™*, you can find and use essential phrases without formal study of Portuguese grammar. However, by learning some of the basic grammatical patterns, you will be able to construct an unlimited number of your own sentences and greatly increase your range of expression.

NOUNS

All Portuguese nouns are either masculine or feminine. Although there are some exceptions, as a general rule, most words ending in *-o* are masculine, while words ending in *-a, -dade,* or *-ção* are feminine. You will have to learn the gender of other nouns when you learn the words.

To form the plural of nouns, add *-s* after vowels or *-es* after consonants. Note, however, that words ending in *-m* first change to *-n* before adding the *-s.* Examples:

o passaporte (the passport)	**os passaportes** (the passports)
a mala (the suitcase)	**as malas** (the suitcases)
um homem (a man)	**uns homens** (some men)
uma mulher (a woman)	**umas mulheres** (some women)

Note the following irregular plural endings:

o animal (the animal)	**os animais** (the animals)
a lição (the lesson)	**as lições** (the lessons)

DEFINITE AND INDEFINITE ARTICLES

Portuguese has both indefinite and definite articles, the equivalents of the English "a" or "an" and "the," repectively. However, Portuguese articles have several different forms in order to agree with nouns in gender (masculine or feminine) and in number (singular or plural). For example, *passaporte* (passport) is masculine; hence the article it takes might be either *um* or *o* (*um passaporte* or *o passaporte*). Likewise, *mala* (suitcase) is feminine, and its articles might be *uma* or *a.* The corresponding plural form of the masculine or feminine article would be used if the word was plural (e.g., *uns, os, umas,* or *as*). Finally, definite articles often contract with prepositions, as shown in the chart below:

	Indefinite	Definite	Definite Article Contracted with: (de+)	(a+)
Masculine (singular)	**um** (a)	**o** (the)	**do** (from the)	**ao** (to the)
Feminine (singular)	**uma** (a)	**a** (the)	**da** (from the)	**à** (to the)
Masculine (plural)	**uns** (some)	**os** (the)	**dos** (from the)	**aos** (to the)
Feminine (plural)	**umas** (some)	**as** (the)	**das** (from the)	**às** (to the)

Defininite articles are used with

a. Abstract nouns	**a liberdade**
b. Countries and cities when qualified	**o Brasil romântico, a Lima senhorial**
c. Some countries and cities without adjectives	**o Japão, a China, o Rio**
d. Days of weeks, seasons	**chegou no sábado, vou na Primavera**
e. Infinitive nouns	**O cantar dos pássaros é muito bonito.**
f. Names of languages	**O português é muito fácil.**
g. Titles—not in address	**E o senhor Silva.**

ADJECTIVES

Adjectives agree in number and gender with the nouns they describe. Unlike in English, Portuguese adjectives often follow the noun, although the opposite is also possible. The choice is often a matter of style and emphasis:

o restaurante brasileiro (the Brazilian restaurant)
a mala nova (the new suitcase)

a boa viagem (the nice trip)

os restaurantes brasileiros (the Brazilian restaurants)
as malas novas (the new suitcases)
as boas viagens (the nice trips)

Adjectives ending in *-e* do not change according to gender. However, you would add *-s* for the plural:

o homen importante (the important man)
a mulher importante (the important woman)
os homens importantes (the important men)
as mulheres importantes (the important women)

Demonstrative Adjectives

	Singular	Plural
this, these	**este** (masc.), **esta** (fem.)	**estes, estas**
that, those	**esse, essa**	**esses, essas**
that, those (remote)	**aquele, aquela**	**aqueles, aquelas**

There are also three demonstrative adjectives that do not vary in form because they are used without an accompanying noun: *isto, isso,* and *aquilo:*

Deixa isto en paz, por favor. (Leave this alone, please.)
Quero comprar isso. (I want to buy that.)
Traga-me aquilo lá. (Bring me that over there.)

Possessive Adjectives

	Masculine	Feminine
my	**o meu**	**a minha**
your (informal)	**o teu (P)**	**a tua (P)**
his/her/its; your, in Brazil only	**o seu**	**a sua**
our	**o nosso**	**a nossa**
your	**o vosso (P)**	**a vossa (P)**
their	**o seu**	**a sua**

All these forms add -s to form the plural. Possessive adjectives must agree in gender and number with the nouns they accompany:

O meu carro é bonito.	**Os nossos carros são bonitos.**
A minha mala é preta.	**As nossas malas são pretas.**

COMPARISONS

Portuguese forms comparatives by placing the word *mais* (more) before the noun, adjective, or adverb compared, followed by *do que:*

é mais caro do que (it's more expensive than)
é mais antigo do que (it's older than)
é mais bonito do que (it's prettier than)

Some exceptions to this rule exist, as in *melhor* (better), *maior* (larger).

The superlative is formed by putting *o* or *a* before *mais* (depending on the gender of the noun being described) and *de* afterward:

Ela é a mais bonita de todas.
(She is the prettiest one of all.)

ADVERBS

In English *-ly* is added to the adjective to form an adverb. Portuguese does this by adding *-mente* to the feminine forms of adjectives:

Adjective			
(masc.)	**(fem.)**	**Adverb**	
claro	**clara**	**claramente**	clearly
rápido	**rápida**	**rapidamente**	rapidly

PRONOUNS

Pronouns in Portuguese have several possible forms, depending on whether they are subject pronouns or used as direct or indirect objects:

Subject	Direct Object	Indirect Object
eu (I)	**me** (me)	**me** (me)
você (you)	**lhe** (you)	**lhe** (you)
tu (P) (you)	**te (P)** (you)	**ti (P)** (you)
ele (he)	**lhe** (him)	**lhe** (him)
ela (she)	**lhe** (her)	**lhe** (him)
nós (we)	**nos** (us)	**nos** (us)
vocês (you)	**lhes** (you)	**lhes** (you)
vós (P) (you)	**vos (P)** (you)	**vos (P)** (you)
eles (they/m.)	**lhes** (them/m.)	**lhes** (them)
elas (they/f.)	**lhes** (them/f.)	**lhes** (them)

In Brazil, the intimate form of singular "you" is *você*. For formal address, use the title *o senhor/a senhora* etc., with the verb; for example:

A senhorita fala bem português. (You speak Portuguese well.)

Subject pronouns are optional and often omitted in speaking; for example:

(Ele) não foi antem. (He didn't go yesterday.)

REFLEXIVE PRONOUNS

Reflexive pronouns accompany a verb, indicating that the verb reflects or reacts upon the subject to express the idea of "oneself." The reflexive pronouns are

(eu)	**me**	**(nós)**	**nos**
(tu) (P)	**te**	**(vós) (P)**	**vos**
(você)	**te**	**(vocês)**	**se**
(ele/ela)	**se**	**(eles/elas)**	**se**

Some common verbs can become reflexive by adding *-se* to the infinitive, producing changes such as

lavar (to wash)	**lavar-se** (to wash oneself)
vestir (to dress)	**vestir-se** (to dress oneself)

188

Here are some common reflexive verbs:

alçar-se	to get up
banhar-se	to bathe oneself
deitar-se	to lie down
despir-se	to get undressed
lavar-se	to get washed
pentear-se	to get combed
vestir-se	to get dressed

RELATIVE PRONOUNS

Relative pronouns must always be expressed in Portuguese.
You will recognize the following pronouns used in this book:

que	who, whom, which (invariable, and refers to persons or things)
quem	whom (inflected for number only, and refers to persons only)
o/a qual (que), os/as quais (que)	whom, which (used for clarity)
onde	where (with place, *a, de, até, desde, em, por onde*)

PREPOSITIONS

Some of the most common prepositions in Portuguese are

a (at, to)
até (until, up to)
com (with)
contra (against)
de (from, of, about)
em (in, on)
entre (between, among)
para (for, in order to, to, toward)
por (for, by, through, because)
segundo (according to)
sem (without)
sobre (on, about)

Some compound prepositions are

acima de (on top of)
além de (besides, in addition to, beyond)
antes de (before, references to time)
ao lado de (beside, at the side of)
atrás de (behind, in back of)
debaixo de (under, beneath)
dentro de (inside of, within)
depois de (after)
em frente de (in front of)
em vez de (instead of)
frente a (in front of, facing, opposite)
fora de (outside of)
longe de (far from)
perto de (near)

THE NEGATIVE

To form the negative in Portuguese, place the word *não* in front of the verb. For example:

Eu falo português. (I speak Portuguese.)
Eu não falo português. (I don't speak Portuguese.)

When the personal subject pronoun is omitted, the sentence starts with *não*. Sometimes Brazilians end sentences with an extra negative for emphasis, as in the third example below:

Viajo amanhã. (I travel tomorrow.)
Não viajo amanhã. (I don't travel tomorrow.)
Não viajo amanhã, não. (I don't travel tomorrow.)

Other words of negation are
nada (nothing)
nenhum (no one/nobody)
nunca (never)
ninguém (none)
também (neither)

Unlike "no" in English, all of these words can go before or after the verb, and are used along *with* the negative *não,* as in

Ela não sabe nada. (She does not know anything.)

THE INTERROGATIVE

Questions are easy to form in Portuguese. Simply raise your voice at the end of a statement as you might do in English. For example: *Você vai ao Brasil.* (You are going to Brazil.) with a rising tone becomes *Você vai ao Brasil?* (You are going to Brazil?).

VERBS: *SER* and *ESTAR*

Portuguese expresses the concept "to be" by using two different verbs: *ser* and *estar.* In general, *ser* is used to refer to a permanent, unchanging state or fact, such as

Ela ẽ portuguesa. (She is Portuguese.)

Estar, on the other hand, is used to refer to a temporary condition or activity; for example:

Vocá está cansado. (You are tired.)

Adjectives agree with the gender of the subject in sentences with *ser* and *estar.*

OTHER VERBS

Most Portuguese verbs end in either *-ar, -er,* or *-ir* in the infinitive, forming three primary types of verb conjugations. These verbs follow fairly regular patterns in the present, past, and future tenses, as shown below. A few other verbs end in *-or,* and are best dealt with separately.

Present Tense

	falar (to speak)	**comer** (to eat)	**partir** (to leave)
eu	**falo**	**como**	**parto**
tu (P)	**falas (P)**	**comes (P)**	**partes (P)**
você	**fala**	**come**	**parte**
ele/ela	**fala**	**come**	**parte**
nós	**falamos**	**comemos**	**partimos**

191

vós (P)	falais (P)	comeis (P)	partis (P)
vocês	falam	comem	partem
eles/elas	falam	comem	partem

Past Tense

	(-ar)	(-er)	(-ir)
eu	falei	comi	parti
tu (P)	falaste (P)	comeste (P)	partiste (P)
você	falou	comeu	partiu
êle/ela	falou	comeu	partiu
nós	falamos	comemos	partimos
vós (P)	falasteis (P)	comestes (P)	partistes (P)
vocês	falaram	comeram	partiram
êles/elas	falaram	comeram	partiram

Future Tense

	(-ar)	(-er)	(-ir)
eu	falarei	comerei	partirei
tu (P)	falarás (P)	comerás (P)	partirás (P)
você	falará	comerá	partirá
êle/ela	falará	comerá	partirá
nós	falaremos	comeremos	partiremos
vós (P)	falareis (P)	comereis (P)	partireis (P)
vocês	falarão	comerão	partirão
êles/elas	falarão	comerão	partirão

Examples of other verbs which follow these regular patterns are *comprar* (to buy), *viajar* (to travel), *beber* (to drink), *compreender* (to understand), and *pedir* (to ask for).

IRREGULAR VERBS
Some commonly used verbs which do not follow the patterns above, and have slightly irregular forms, are *dar*, *fazer*, *dizer*, *ter*, *poder*, *ver*, *ir*, *vir*, and *pôr*.

Present Tense

dar (to give)	**fazer** (to do/make)	**dizer** (to tell/say)
dou	faço	digo
das (P)	fazes (P)	dizes (P)
dá	faz	diz
damos	fazemos	dizemos
dais (P)	fazeis (P)	dizeis (P)
dão	fazem	dizem

ter (to have)	**poder** (to be able/can)	**ver** (to see)
tenho	posso	vejo
tens (P)	podes (P)	ves (P)
tem	pode	vê
temos	podemos	vemos
tendes (P)	podeis (P)	vedes (P)
têm	podem	vêem

ir (to go)	**vir** (to come)	**pôr** (to put, place)
vou	venho	ponho
vais (P)	vens (P)	pões (P)
vai	vem	põe
vamos	vimos	pomos
ides (P)	vindes (P)	pondes (P)
vão	vêm	põem

Past Tense

dar (to give)	**fazer** (to do)	**dizer** (to say)
dei	fiz	disse
deste (P)	fizeste (P)	disseste (P)
deu	fez	disse
demos	fizemos	dissemos
destes (P)	fizestes (P)	dissestes (P)
deram	fizeram	disseram

ter (to have)	**poder** (to be able to)	**ver** (to see)
tive	pude	vi

193

tiveste (P)	pudeste (P)	viste (P)
teve	pôde	viu
tivemos	pudemos	vimos
tivestes (P)	pudestes (P)	vistes (P)
tiveram	puderam	viram

ir (to go)	**vir** (to come)	**pôr** (to place, put)
fui	vim	pus
foste (P)	vieste (P)	puseste (P)
foi	veio	pôs
fomos	viemos	pusemos
fostes (P)	viestes (P)	pusestes (P)
foram	vieram	puseram

FORMS OF THE FUTURE TENSE

Portuguese has two ways of forming the future tense: the simple future (above), or the verb "to go" plus infinitive:

Falarei com o turista. (I will speak with the tourist.)
Vou falar com o turista. (I will speak with the tourist.) (Or: I am going to speak with the tourist.)

SPECIAL USES OF *TER, HAVER,* AND *FAZER*

To express "there is/there are," Portuguese speakers use the third person of *ter* (to have): *Tem um livro no quarto./ Tem muitos livros no quarto.* (There is a book in the room./ There are many books in the room.) A more formal way to say this is with the third person of *haver* (to have): *Há um livro no quarto./Há muitos livros no quarto.*

Fazer (to make, to do) is sometimes used in the third person to express "to be," as in:

Faz frio. (Or: **Está frio.**) (It is cold.)
Faz calor. (It is hot/warm.)
Faz vento. (It is windy.)

ENGLISH-PORTUGUESE DICTIONARY

The gender of nouns is indicated by (m.) for masculine or (f.) for feminine. Nouns commonly used in the plural are shown in the plural and followed by (pl.) Adjectives are listed in the masculine singular form, and verbs are shown in the infinitive form. Luso Portuguese variations are indicated by (P); some adjectives are indicated, using (adj.), and some adverbs by (adv.). Refer to the chapter on grammar for information about the formation of feminine and plural adjectives, and verb conjugations.

A

a, an um (m.), uma (f.) (oon, OO-mah)

able to, to be poder (poh-DEHR)

about acerca de, em volta de (ah-SEHR-kah jee, em VOHL-tah jee)

above acima (de) (ah-SEE-mah) (jee)

abscess abscesso (m.) (ahb-SAY-soo)

accelerator acelerador (m.) (ah-say-lehr-ah-DOHR)

accept, to aceitar (ah-say-TAHR)

accident acidente (m.) (ah-see-DEHN-chee)

ache (head) dor de cabeça (f.) (dohr jee kah-BAY-sah)

(stomach) dor de estómago (dohr jee ehs-TOH-mah-goo)

(tooth) dor de dentes (dohr jee DEHN-chees)

across a través (de) (ah trah-VEHS) (jee)

address endereço (m.) (ehn-deh-RAY-soo)

adjust, to ajustar, arrumar (ah-zhoos-TAHR, ah-hoo-MAHR)

admittance (no) proibida a entrada (proh-ee-BEE-dah ah ehn-TRAH-dah)

afraid, to be estar com medo (ehs-TAHR kohn MEH-doo)

after depois (de) (deh-POYS) (jee)

afternoon tarde (f.) (TAHR-jee)

again outra vez, de novo (OH-trah vehz, jee NOH-voo)

against contra (KOHN-trah)

ago há (with time expressions) (ah)

agree, to estar de acordo (ehs-TAHR jee ah-KOHR-doo)

ahead adiante (ah-JYAHN-chee)

aid ajuda (f.) (ah-ZHOO-dah)

first aid primeiros auxílios (m.pl.) (pree-MAY-roos owk-SEE-lyoos)

air ar (m.) (ahr)

airmail correio aéreo (m.) (koh-HAY-yoo ah-EH-ryoo)

airline linha aérea (f.) (LEEN-yah ah-EH-ray-ah)

airplane avião (m.) (ah-vee-OWN)

airport aeroporto (m.) (ah-eh-roh-POHR-too)

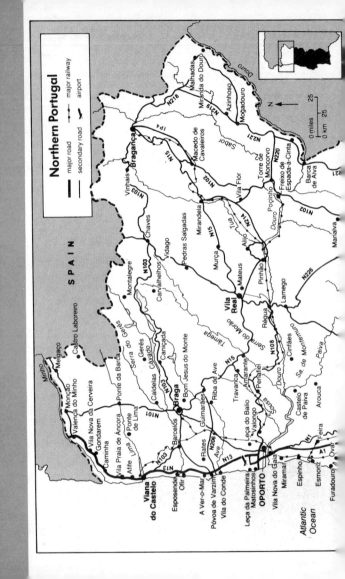

Southern Portugal

- — major road
- | secondary road
- major railway
- ✈ airport

0 miles 15
0 km 15

N

Atlantic Ocean

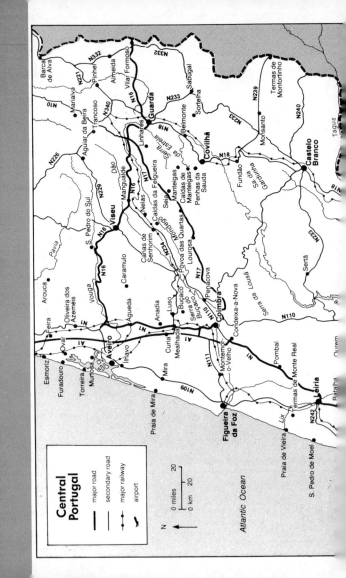

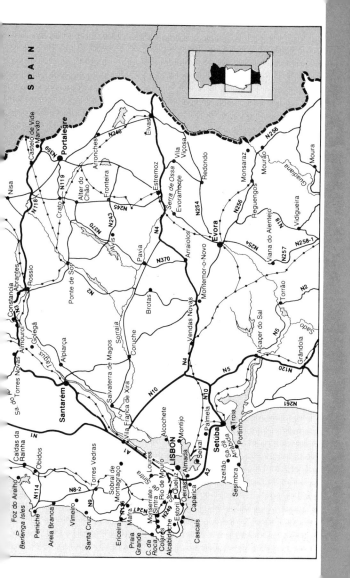

all tudo (*TOO-doo*)
  all right tudo bem, está bem (*TOO-doo behn, ehs-TAH behn*)
allow, to permitir (*pehr-mee-CHEER*)
almost quase (*KWAH-see*)
alone só (*SOH*)
already ja (*zhyah*)
also também (*tahm-BEHN*)
always sempre (*SEHM-pree*)
A.M. da manhã (*dah-mahn-YAHN*)
am sou, estou (*soh, ehs-TOH*)
American norteamericano(-a) (*nohr-chee-ah-meh-ree-KAH-noo*) (*-nah*)
among entre (*EHN-tree*)
and e (*ee*)
ankle tornozelo (m.) (*tohr-noh-ZAY-!oo*)
annoy, to molestar (*moh-lays-TAHR*)
another outro (*OH-troo*)
answer (response) resposta (f.) (*hays-POHS-tah*)
any algum, qualquer (*ahl-GOON, kwahl-KEHR*)
anybody, anyone alguem, qualquer um (*AHL-gehn, kwahl-KEHR oon*)
anything algo (*AHL-goo*)
  anything else? algo mais? (*AHL-goo-mahys?*)
apartment apartamento (m.) (*ah-pahr-tah-MEHN-too*)
aperitif aperitivo (m.) (*ah-peh-reh-CHEE-voo*)
apple maçã (f.) (*mah-SAHN*)
apricot damasco (m.) (*dah-MAHS-koo*)

April abril (*ah-BREE-oo*)
Arab árabe (*AH-rah-bee*)
are são, estão (*sown, ehs-TOWN*)
arm braço (m.) (*BRAH-soo*)
around em volta (de) (*ehn VOHL-tah*) (*jee*)
arrival chegada (f.) (*shay-GAH-dah*)
arrive, to chegar (v.) (*shay-GAHR*)
article artigo (m.) (*ahr-CHEE-goo*)
as como (*KOH-moo*)
ashtray cinzeiro (m.) (*seen-ZAY-roo*)
ask, to (a question) perguntar (*pehr-goon-TAHR*)
  to ask for pedir (*peh-JEER*)
asparagus aspargo (m.) (*ahs-PAHR-goo*)
aspirin aspirina (f.) (*ahs-pee-REE-nah*)
at em, a (*ehn, ah*)
attention atenção (f.) (*ah-tehn-SOWN*)
August agosto (*ah-GOHS-too*)
aunt tia (f.) (*CHEE-ah*)
automobile carro (m.) (*KAH-hoo*)
autumn Outuno (m.) (*oh-TOO-noo*)
avoid, to evitar (*eh-vee-TAHR*)
awful terrivel (*teh-HEE-vay-oo*)

B

baby bebê (m. or f.) (*beh-BAY*)
back (body) costas (f.pl.) (*KOHS-tahs*)

(direction) atrás (de) (ah-TRAHS) (jee)

(direction, movement) atrás (ah-TRAHS)

back, to be estar de volta (ehs-TAHR jee VOHL-tah)

bacon toucinho (m.) (toh-SEEN-yoo)

bad mau (MAY-oo)

bag mala (f.) (MAH-lah)

handbag mala de mão (f.) (MAH-lah jee mown)

baggage bagagem (m.) (bah-GAH-zhehn)

baked cozido no forno (koo-ZEE-doo noo FOHR-noo)

bakery padaria (pah-dah-REE-ah)

balcony (theater) galeria (f.) (gah-leh-REE-ah)

(house) balcão (m.) (bahl-KOWN)

ball bola (f.) (BOH-lah)

banana banana (f.) (bah-NAH-nah)

bandage (covering) atadura (f.) (ah-tah-DOO-rah)

bank banco (m.) (BAHN-koo)

bar bar (m.) (bahr)

barber barbeiro (m.) (bahr-BAY-roo)

barbershop barbearia (f.) (bahr-bay-ah-REE-ah)

bath banho (m.) (BAHN-yoo)

bathe, to banharse (bahn-YAHR-see)

bathroom banheiro (m.) (bahn-YAY-roo)

battery (automobile) bateria (f.) (bah-teh-REE-ah)

be, to ser, estar (sehr, ehs-TAHR)

beach praia (f.) (PRAHY-yah)

bean feijão (fay-ZHOWN)

beautiful belo, lindo, bonito (BAY-loo, LEEN-doo, boh-NEE-too)

beauty salon salão de beleza (sah-LOWN jee beh-LAY-zah)

because porque (poor-KEH)

bed cama (f.) (KAH-mah)

bedroom quarto (m.) (KWAHR-too)

beef bife (m.) (BEE-fee)

beer cerveja (f.) (sehr-VAY-zhah)

before antes (de) (AHN-chees) (jee)

begin, to começar (koh-may-SAHR)

behind atrás (de) (ah-TRAHS jee)

beige beige (BAY-zhee)

believe, to crer (krehr)

belong, to pertencer (pehr-tehn-SEHR)

belt cinto (m.) (SEEN-too)

best o/a melhor (oo ah mehl-YOHR)

better melhor (mehl-YOHR)

between entre (EHN-tree)

big grande (GRAHN-jee)

bill (restaurant check) conta (f.) (KOHN-tah)

bird pássaro (m.) (PAH-sah-roo)

bite mordida (f.) (mohr-JEE-dah)

to bite morder (mohr-DEHR)

bitter amargo (ah-MAHR-goo)

black preto (PRAY-too)

blank form formulário (m.) (fohr-moo-LAH-ryoo)

201

blood sangue (m.) (*SAHN-gee*)

blouse blusa (f.) (*BLOO-zah*)

blue azul (*ah-ZOOL*)

boat barco (m.) (*BAHR-koo*)

body corpo (m.) (*KOHR-poo*)

boiled fervido (*fehr-VEE-doo*)

bone osso (m.) (*OH-soo*)

book livro (m.) (*LEEV-roo*)

bookstore livraria (f.) (*leev-rah-REE-ah*)

born, to be nascer (*nah-SEHR*)

bother aborrecer (*ah-boh-hay-SEHR*)

bottle garrafa (f.) (*gah-HAH-fah*)

box caixa (f.) (*KAHY-shah*)

boy moço (m.), menino (m.) (*MOH-soo, mee-NEE-noo*)

bra, brassiere soutien (m.) (*soh-CHYEHN*)

braised guisado (*gee-ZAH-doo*)

brakes fréios (m.pl.) (*FRAY-yoos*)

Brazilian brasileiro(-a) (*brah-zee-LAY-roo*)(*-rah*)

bread pão (m.) (*pown*)

break, to romper, quebar (*hohm-PEHR, kay-BRAHR*)

breakfast café da manhã (m.) (*kah-FEH dah mahn-YAHN*)

breathe, to respirar (*hays-pee-RAHR*)

bridge ponte (m.) (*POHN-chee*)

bright brilhante (*breel-YAHN-chee*)

bring trazer (*trah-ZEHR*)

broil grelhar (*grehl-YAHR*)

broken quebrado (*kay-BRAH-doo*)

brother irmão (*eer-MOWN*)

brown castanho (*kahs-TAHN-yoo*)

bruise (injury) contusão (f.) (*kohn-too-ZOWN*)

brush escova (f.) (*ehs-KOH-vah*)
   to brush escovar (*ehs-koh-VAHR*)

building prédio (m.) (*PREH-joo*)

bulb lâmpada (f.) (*LAHM-pah-dah*)

bullfight tourada (f.) (*toh-RAH-dah*)

bumper (automobile) pára-choque (m.) (*pah-rah-SHOH-kee*)

burn (injury) queimadura (f.) (*kay-mah-DOO-rah*)
   to burn queimar (*kay-MAHR*)

bus ônibus (m.), autocarro (m.) (P) (*OH-nee-boos*) (*ow-toh-KAH-rroh*)

busy ocupado (*oh-koo-PAH-doo*)

but mas (*mahs*)

butcher açougeiro (m.) homen de talho (m.) (P) (*ah-soh-GAY-roo*) (*OH-mehn deh TAHL-yoh*)

butter manteiga (f.) (*mahn-CHAY-gah*)

button botão (m.) (*boh-TOWN*)

buy, to comprar (*kohm-PRAHR*)

by por (*poor*)

C

cab táxi (m.) (*TAHK-see*)

cabaret clube noturno (m.) (KLOO-bee noh-TOOR-noo)

cabbage couve (f.) (KOH-vee)

cable (telegram) telegrama (m.) (teh-lay-GRAH-mah)

cake bolo (m.) (BOH-loo)

call, to chamar, telefonar (shah-MAHR, teh-lay-foh-NAHR)

   telephone call telefonema (m.) (teh-lay-foh-NAY-mah)

camera máquina fotográfica (f.) (MAH-kee-nah foh-toh-GRAH-fee-kah)

camp acampamento (m.) (ah-kahm-pah-MEHN-too)

can (container) lata (f.) (LAH-tah)

   to be able to poder (poh-DEHR)

   can opener abridor de lata (m.) (ah-bree-DOHR jee LAH-tah)

cancel, to cancelar, anular (kahn-say-LAHR, ah-noo-LAHR)

candle vela (f.) (VAY-lah)

candy bombom (m.), rebuçado (m.) (P) (bohn-BOHN, hay-boo-SAH-doh)

cap boné (m.), chapéu (m.) (boh-NEH, shah-PAY-oo)

capital capital (f.) (kah-pee-TOW)

car (automobile) carro (m.) (KAH-hoo)

   streetcar bonde (m.) (BOHN-jee)

carburetor carburador (m.) (kahr-boo-rah-DOHR)

card cartão (m.) (kahr-TOWN)

postcard postal (m.) (pohs-TOW)

care (caution) cuidado (m.) (kwee-DAH-doo)

careful cuidadoso (kwee-dah-DOH-zoo)

   to be careful ter cuidado (tehr kwee-DAH-doo)

carefully com cuidado (kohn kwee-DAH-doo)

carrot cenoura (f.) (seh-NOH-rah)

carry, to levar (lay-VAHR)

cash (money) dinheiro (m.) (jeen-YAY-roo)

   to cash cobrar (koh-BRAHR)

   to pay in cash pagar à vista (pah-GAHR ah VEES-tah)

cashier caixa (m.) (KAHY-shah)

castle castelo (m.) (kahs-TEH-loo)

cat gato (m.) (GAH-too)

catch, to apanhar, tomar (ah-pahn-YAHR, toh-MAHR)

cathedral catedral (f.) (kah-tay-DROW)

Catholic católico(-a) (kah-TOH-lee-koo)(-kah)

cauliflower couve-flor (f.) (koh-vee-FLOHR)

caution cautela (f.) (kow-TEH-lah)

   to caution advertir (ah-jee-vehr-CHEER)

ceiling teto (m.) (TEH-too)

celery aipo (m.) (AHY-poo)

center centro (m.) (SEHN-troo)

certainly certo, pois não (SEHR-too, poys nown)

certificate certificado (m.) (sehr-chee-fee-KAH-doo)

chain cadeia (f.), corrente (f.) (*kah-DAY-yah, koh-HEHN-che*)

chair cadeira (f.), assento (m.) (*kah-DAY-rah, ah-SEHN-too*)

change (money) trôco (m.) (*TROH-koo*)
  to change trocar, mudar (*troh-KAHR, moo-DAHR*)

charge (cover) consumo mínimo (m.) (*kohn-SOO MEE-nee-moo*)
  charge preço (*PRAY-soo*)

cheap barato, económico (*bah-RAH-too, eh-koh-NOH-mee-koo*)

check (bill) conta (f.) (*KOHN-tah*)
  check (bank) cheque (*SHEH-kee*)

cheek bochecha (f.) (*boh-SHAY-shah*)

cheese queijo (m.) (*KAY-zhoo*)

cherry cereja (f.) (*seh-RAY-zhah*)

chest peito (m.) (*PAY-too*)

chestnut castanha (f.) (*kahs-TAHN-yah*)

chicken frango (m.) (*FRAHN-goo*)

child criança (f.) (*kree-AHN-sah*)

Chilean chileno(-a) (*shee-LAY-noo*)(*-nah*)

chill calafrio (m.), friagem (f.) (*kah-lah-FREE-oo, free-AH-zhehn*)

chin queixo (m.) (*KAY-shoo*)

Chinese chinês(+a) (*shee-NAYS*)(+*ah*)

chiropodist calista (m. or f.) (*kah-LEES-tah*)

chocolate chocolate (m.) (*shoh-koh-LAH-chee*)

choose, to escolher (*ehs-kohl-YEHR*)

chop, cutlet costeleta (f.) (*kohs-tay-LEH-tah*)

Christmas Natal (m.) (*nah-TOW*)

church igreja (f.) (*ee-GRAY-zhah*)

cigar charuto (m.) (*sha-ROO-too*)

cigarette cigarro (m.) (*see-GAH-hoo*)

city cidade (f.) (*see-DAH-jee*)

class classe (f.) (*KLAH-see*)

clean (spotless) limpo (*LEEM-poo*)
  to clean limpar (*leem-PAHR*)

cleaner's lavandaria a seco (f.) (*lah-vahn-dah-REE-ah ah SAY-koo*)

clear (transparent) claro, transparente (*KLAH-roo, trahns-pah-REHN-chee*)

climb subir (*soo-BEER*)

clock relógio (m.) (*hay-LOH-zhoo*)

close (near) perto, próximo (*PEHR-too, PROHK-see-moo*)
  to close fechar (*fay-SHAHR*)
  closed fechado (*fay-SHAH-doo*)

cloth tecido (m.) (*teh-SEE-doo*)

clothes, clothing roupa (f.) (*HOH-pah*)

cloud nuvem {f.) (*NOO-vehn*)

cloudy nublado (*noo-BLAH-doo*)

club clube (m.) (*KLOO-bee*)

clutch (car) embreagem (f.) (*ehm-bray-AH-zhehn*)

coat casaco (m.) (*kah-ZAH-koo*)

  coat hanger cabide (m.) (*kah-BEE-jee*)

cocktail coquetel (m.) (*koh-kee-TAY-oo*)

coffee café (m.) (*kah-FEH*)

coin (money) moeda (f.) (*moh-EH-dah*)

cold (temperature) frio (*FREE-oo*)

  (illness) resfriado (m.) (*hehs-FRYAH-doo*)

  to be cold fazer frio (*fah-ZEHR FREE-oo*)

collect, to colecionar (*koh-leh-syon-AHR*)

color cor (f.) (*kohr*)

  color film filme colorido (m.) (*FEEL-mee koh-loh-REE-doo*)

comb pente (m.) (*PEHN-chee*)

  to comb pentear (*pehn-chee-AHR*)

come, to vir (*veer*)

  to come in entrar (*ehn-TRAHR*)

comedy comédia (f.) (*koh-MEH-jyah*)

comfortable confortável (*kohn-fohr-TAH-vay-oo*)

companion companheiro (-a) (*kohm-pahn-YAY-roo*) (*-rah*)

company companhia (f.) (*kohm-pahn-YEE-ah*)

compartment compartimento (m.) (*kohm-pahr-chee-MEHN-too*)

complaint queixa (f.) (*KAY-zhah*)

concert concerto (m.) (*kohn-SEHR-too*)

congratulations parabéns (m.pl.) (*pah-rah-BEHNS*)

consul cônsul (m.) (*KOHN-sool*)

consulate consulado (m.) (*kohn-soo-LAH-doo*)

continue, to continuar, prosseguir (*kohn-chee-noo-WAHR, proh-seh-GEER*)

convent convento (m.) (*kohn-VEHN-too*)

cooked cozido (*koh-ZEE-doo*)

cool fresco (*FRAYS-koo*)

corn milho (m.) (*MEEL-yoo*)

corner esquina (f.) (*ehs-KEE-nah*)

cost (amount) custo (m.) (*KOOS-too*)

  to cost custar (*koos-TAHR*)

cotton algodão (m.) (*ahl-goh-DOWN*)

cough tosse (f.) (*TOH-see*)

  to cough tossir (*toh-SEER*)

count contar (*kohn-TAHR*)

country (nation) país (m.) (*pah-EES*)

countryside campo (m.) (*KAHM-poo*)

course (in meals) prato (m.) (*PRAH-too*)

crazy louco; doido (*LOH-koo; DOY-doo*)

cream creme (m.) (*KRAY-mee*)

crystal cristal (m.) (*krees-TOW*)

Cuban cubano(-a) (*koo-BAH-noo*)(*-nah*)

205

cucumber pepino (m.) (peh-PEE-noo)
cup xícara (f.), chávena (f.) (P) (SHEE-kah-rah, SHA-veh-nah)
curtain cortina (f.) kohr-CHEE-nah)
curve curva (f.) (KOOR-vah)
customs alfândega (f.) (ahl-FAHN-jeh-gah)
cut, to cortar (kohr-TAHR)
  cut it out! chega! (SHAY-gah!)
cutlet costeleta (f.) (kohs-tay-LEH-tah)
Czech checo(-a) (SHEH-koo (-kah)

D

daily diário (JYAH-ryoo)
  by the day por dia (poor JEE-ah)
damp úmido (OO-mee-doo)
dance dança (f.) (DAHN-sah)
  to dance dançar (dahn-SAHR)
danger perigo (m.) (peh-REE-goo)
dangerous perigoso (peh-ree-GOH-zoo)
Danish dinamarquês(+a) (jee-nah-mahr-KAYS)(+ah)
dark escuro (ehs-KOO-roo)
darn it! puxa vida! (POO-shah VEE-dah!)
date (today's) data (f.) (DAH-tah)
daughter filha (f.) (FEEL-yah)
day dia (m.) (JEE-ah)
dead morto (MOHR-too)
death morte (f.) (MOHR-chee)

December dezembro (jee-ZEHM-broo)
declaration declaração (f.) (day-klah-rah-SOWN)
declare, to declarar (day-klah-RAHR)
deep fundo (FOON-doo)
deliver, to entregar (ehn-tray-GAHR)
delivery entrega (f.) (ehn-TRAY-gah)
dentist dentista (m. or f.) (dehn-CHEES-tah)
denture dentadura (f.) (dehn-tah-DOO-rah)
deordorant desodorante (m.), desodorizante (m.) (P) (deh-zoh-doh-RAHN-chee, deh-zoh-doh-ree-ZAHN-teh)
department store loja de departamento (m.) (LOH-zhah jee day-pahr-tah-MEHN-too)
dessert sobremesa (f.) (soh-bree-MAY-zah)
detour desvio (m.) (dehz-VEE-oo)
develop, to (film) revelar (hay-vay-LAHR)
devil diabo (m.) (JYAH-boo)
diaper fralda (f.) (FRAHL-dah)
dictionary dicionário (m.) (dee-syoh-NAH-ryoo)
different diferente (dee-feh-REHN-chee)
difficult difícil (dee-FEE-see-oo)
difficulty dificuldade (f.) (dee-fee-kool-DAH-jee)
dining car carro-restaurante (m.) (KAH-hoo-hehs-tow-RAHN-chee)
dining room sala de jantar (f.)` (SAH-lah jee zhahn-TAHR)

dinner jantar (m.) (*zahn-TAHR*)
direct, to indicar, dirigir (*een-jee-KAHR, dee-ree-ZHEER*)
direction direção (f.) (*dee-reh-SOWN*)
dirty sujo (*SOO-zhoo*)
discount desconto (m.) (*dehs-KOHN-too*)
disease doença (f.) (*doh-EHN-sah*)
dish prato (m.) (*PRAH-too*)
district bairro (m.) (*BAHY-hoo*)
disturb, to incomodar (*een-koh-moh-DAHR*)
dizzy (to feel) ficar tonto (*fee-KAHR TOHN-too*)
do, to fazer (*fah-ZEHR*)
doctor médico(-a), doutor(+a) (*MEH-jee-joo*)(*-kah, doh-TOHR*)(*+ah*)
document documento (m.) (*doh-koo-MEHN-too*)
dog cachorro (m.) (*kah-SHOH-hoo*)
domestic doméstico (*doh-MEHS-chee-koo*)
door porta (f.) (*POHR-tah*)
doorman porteiro (m.) (*pohr-TAY-roo*)
down abaixo (*ah-BAHY-shoo*)
dozen dúzia (f.) (*DOO-zee-ah*)
draw, to (sketch) desenhar (*dee-zehn-YAHR*)
drawer gaveta (f.) (*gah-VEH-tah*)
dress (garment) vestido (m.) (*vehs-CHEE-doo*)
  to dress vestir-se (*vehs-CHEER-see*)

dressing gown robe (m.) (*HOH-bee*)
drink (beverage) bebida (f.) (*beh-BEE-dah*)
  to drink beber (*beh-BEHR*)
drinkable potável (*poh-TAH-vay-oo*)
drive (ride) passeio de carro (m.) (*pah-SAY-oo jee KAH-hoo*)
  to drive dirigir (*dee-ree-ZHEER*)
driver motorista (m.) (*moh-toh-REES-tah*)
drugstore farmácia (f.), drogaria (f.) (*fahr-MAH-syah, droh-gah-REE-ah*)
drunk bêbado (*BEH-bah-doo*)
dry seco (*SAY-koo*)
  to dry secar (*say-KAHR*)
  to dry-clean lavar a seco (*lah-VAHR ah SAY-koo*)
duck pato (m.) (*PAH-too*)
during durante (*doo-RAHN-chee*)
dysentery disenteria (f.) (*dee-sehn-teh-REE-ah*)

E

each cada (*KAH-dah*)
  each one cada um (*KAH-dah oon*)
ear orelha (f.) (*oh-REHL-yah*)
earache dor de ouvidos (m.) (*dohr jee oh-VEE-doos*)
early cedo (*SEH-doo*)
easy fácil (*FAH-see-oo*)
eat, to comer (*koh-MEHR*)
egg ovo (m.) (*OH-voo*)
eight oito (*OY-too*)
eighteen dezoito (*deh-ZOY-too*)

207

eighth oitavo (*oy-TAH-voo*)
eighty oitenta (*oy-TEHN-tah*)
either um ou outro (*oon oh OH-troo*)
elbow cotovelo (m.) (*koh-toh-VEH-loo*)
electric elêtrico (*eh-LAY-tree-koo*)
elevator elevador (m.) (*eh-lay-vah-DOHR*)
eleven onze (*OHN-zee*)
else (nothing) mais nada (*mahys NAH-dah*)
  what else? que mais? (*keh mahys*)?
embassy embaixada (*ehm-bahy-ZHAH-dah*)
emergency emergência (*eh-mehr-ZHAYN-syah*)
employee empregado(-a) (*ehm-pray-GAH-doo*)(*-dah*)
empty vazio (*vah-ZEE-oo*)
end (*conclusion*) fim (*feen*)
  to end terminar (*tehr-mee-NAHR*)
endorse, to endossar (*ehn-doh-SAHR*)
engine motor (m.) (*moh-TOHR*)
English inglês(+a) (*een-GLAYS*)(*+ah*)
enlargement ampliação (f.) (*ahm-plee-ah-SOWN*)
enough bastante (*bahs-TAHN-chee*)
enter, to entrar (*ehn-TRAHR*)
error erro (m.) (*eh-HOO*)
European europeu(-péia) (*ay-oo-roh-PAY-oo*)(*-yah*)
evening noite (f.) (*NOY-chee*)
every cada (*KAH-dah*)

everybody, everyone todos (m.pl.), todo o mundo (m.) (*TOH-doos, TOH-doh oo MOON-doo*)
everything tudo (*TOO-doo*)
examine, to examinar (*ehk-sah-mee-NAHR*)
exchange trocar (*troh-KAHR*)
  exchange rate câmbio (*KAHM-byoo*)
  exchange office casa de câmbio (*KAH-zah-jee KAHM-byoo*)
excursion excursão (f.) (*ehs-koor-SOWN*)
excuse, to desculpar (*days-kool-PAHR*)
exit saída (f.) (*sah-EE-dah*)
expect esperar (*ehs-peh-RAHR*)
expensive caro (*KAH-roo*)
express, to expresso (*ehks-PRAY-soo*)
extra extra, suplementar (*EHKS-trah, soo-play-mehn-TAHR*)
eye olho (m.) (*OHL-yoo*)
eyebrow sobrancelha (f.) (*soh-brahn-SEHL-yah*)
eyelash cílos (m.pl.) (*SEE-lyoos*)
eyelid pálpebra (m.) (*PAHL-pay-brah*)

F
face rosto (m.) (*HOHS-too*)
  face powder pó-de-arroz (m.) (*POH-jee-ah-HOHZ*)
facial massagem facial (f.) (*mah-SAH-zhehn fah-SYOW*)
fall (autumn) outuno (m.) (*oh-TOO-noo*)

to fall cair (*kah-EER*)
false falso (*FAHL-soo*)
family família (f.) (*fah-MEEL-yah*)
   family name sobrenome (m.) (*soh-bree-NOH-mee*)
fan ventilador (m.) (*vehn-chee-lah-DOHR*)
far longe (*LOHN-zhee*)
fare (fee) preço da viagem (m.) (*PRAY-soo dah vee-ah-ZHEHN*)
fast rápido (*HAH-pee-doo*)
father pai (m.) (*pahy*)
faucet torneira (f.) (*tohr-NAY-rah*)
fear medo (m.) (*MAY-doo*)
   to fear estar com medo (*ehs-TAHR kohn MAY-doo*)
February fevereiro (*feh-veh-RAY-roo*)
feel, to sentir (*sehn-CHEER*)
   to feel like estar com vontade de (*ehs-TAHR kohn vohn-TAH-jee jee*)
felt (cloth) feltro (*FEHL-troo*)
fender defesa (f.) (*deh-FAY-zah*)
festival festival (m.) (*fehs-chee-VOW*)
fever febre (f.) (*FEH-bree*)
few poucos (*POH-koos*)
fifteen quinze (*KEEN-zee*)
fifth quinto (*KEEN-too*)
fifty cinquenta (*seen-KWEHN-tah*)
fig figo (m.) (*FEE-goo*)
fill, to encher (*ehn-SHEHR*)
   to fill out preencher (*prehn-SHEHR*)
film filme (m.) (*FEEL-mee*)

find, to encontrar, achar (*ehn-kohn-TRAHR, ah-SHAHR*)
fine (good quality) fino (*FEE-noo*)
   fine (penalty) multa (f.) (*MOOL-tah*)
finger dedo (m.) (*DAY-doo*)
finish, to acabar, terminar (*ah-kah-BAHR, tehr-mee-NAHR*)
fire fogo (m.) (*FOH-goo*)
   (destructive) incêndio (m.) (*een-SAYN-jyoo*)
first primeiro (*pree-MAY-roo*)
   first aid primeiros socorros (m.pl.) (*pree-MAY-roos soh-KOH-hoos*)
fish peixe (m.) (*PAY-shee*)
   to fish pescar (*pehs-KAHR*)
fix, to consertar (*kohn-sehr-TAHR*)
flashlight lanterna (de mão) (f.) (*lahn-TEHR-nah*) (*jee mown*)
flat (level) plano (*PLAH-noo*)
   flat tire pneu furado (m.) (*pee-NAY-oo foo-RAH-doo*)
flight (plane) vôo (m.) (*VOH-oo*)
floor chão (m.), andar (m.) (*shown, ahn-DAHR*)
flower flor (f.) (*flohr*)
fog neblina (f.) (*neh-BLEE-nah*)
follow, to seguir (*seh-GEER*)
food alimento (m.), comida (f.) (*ah-lee-MEHN-too, kohn-MEE-dah*)
foot pé (m.) (*peh*)
for (purpose, destination) para (*PAH-rah*)
   (exchange) por (*poor*)
forbidden proibido (*proh-ee-BEE-doo*)

forehead testa (f.) (*TEHS-tah*)

foreign estrangeiro (*ehs-trahn-ZHAY-roo*)

forget, to esquecer (*ehs-koy-SEHR*)

fork garfo (m.) (*GAHR-foo*)

form (document) formulário (m.) (*fohr-moo-LAH-ryoo*)

forty quarenta (*kwah-REHN-tah*)

forward (direction) em frente (*ehn FREHN-chee*)

fountain fonte (f.) (*FOHN-chee*)

four quatro (*KWAH-troo*)

fourteen catorze (*kah-TOHR-zee*)

fourth quarto (*KWAHR-too*)

fracture (injury) fratura (f.) (*frah-TOO-rah*)

free (unattached) livre (*LEEV-ree*)
   fee of charge gratuito (*grah-TWEE-too*)

French francês(+a) (*frahn-SAYS*)(+*ah*)

Friday sexta-feira (f.) (*SEHS-tah FAY-rah*)

friend amigo(-a) (*ah-MEE-goo*)(-*gah*)

from de, desde (*jee, DAYS-jee*)

front (position) frente (*FREHN-chee*)
   in front of em frente de (*ehn FREHN-chee jee*)

fruit fruta (f.) (*FROO-tah*)

fry, to fritar (*free-TAHR*)

fuel pump bomba de combustível (f.) (*BOHM-bah jee kohm-boos-CHEE-vay-oo*)

full cheio (*SHAY-yoo*)

funny engraçado (*ehn-grah-SAH-doo*)

G

gain, to ganhar (*gahn-YAHR*)

game jogo (m.) (*ZHOH-goo*)

garage garagem (f.) (*gah-RAH-zhehn*)

garden jardim (m.) (*zhahr-JEEN*)

garlic alho (m.) (*AHL-yoo*)

gas gasolina (*gah-zoh-LEE-nah*)
   gas station posto de gasolina (m.) (*POHS-too jee gah-zoh-LEE-nah*)

gate portão (m.) (*pohr-TOWN*)

gauze gaze (f.) (*GAH-zee*)

gear (car) marcha (f.) (*MAHR-shah*)

gentleman cavalheiro, senhor (*kah-vahl-YAY-roo, sehn-YOHR*)

get, to obter (*oh-bee-TEER*)
   to get back (recover) recuperar (*hay-koo-pehr-AHR*)
   to get off descer (*day-SEHR*)
   to get on subir (*soo-BEER*)
   to get up levantar-se (*lay-vahn-TAHR-see*)

gift presente (m.) (*pray-SEHN-chee*)

girl menina (f.), rapariga (f.) (P) (*may-NEE-nah, rrah-pah-REE-gah*)

give, to dar (*dahr*)
   to give back devolver (*deh-vohl-VEHR*)

glad contente (*kohn-TEHN-chee*)

gladly com muito prazer (*kohn MWEE-too prah-ZEHR*)
glass (drinking) copo (*KOH-poo*)
  (material) vidro (*VEE-droo*)
glasses óculos (m.pl.) (*Oh-koo-loos*)
glove luva (f.) (*LOO-vah*)
go, to ir (*eer*)
  to go away ir-se embora (*EER-see ehm-BOH-rah*)
  to go shopping fazer compras (*fah-ZEHR KOHM-prahs*)
  to go down descer (*day-SEHR*)
  to go home ir para casa (*eer PAH-rah KAH-zah*)
  to go in entrar (*ehn-TRAHR*)
  to go out sair (*sah-EER*)
  to go up subir (*soo-BEER*)
god deus (m.) (*DAY-oos*)
gold ouro (m.) (*OH-roo*)
good bom (*bohn*)
good-bye até a vista, adeus, até logo, tchau (*ah-TEH ah VEES-tah, ah-DAY-oos, ah-TEH LOH-goo, chow*)
grain grão (m.) (*grown*)
gram grama (m.) (*GRAH-mah*)
grandfather/mother avô(-ó) (*ah-VO)(-VOH*)
grandson/daughter neto(-a) (*NAY-too)(-tah*)
grapefruit toranja (f.) (*toh-RAHN-zhah*)
grapes uvas (f.pl.) (*OO-vahs*)
grass grama (f.); erva (f.) (P) (*GRAH-mah*), (*EHR-vah*)

grateful agradecido (*ah-grah-day-SEE-doo*)
gravy (sauce) molho (m.) (*MOHL-yoo*)
gray cinza (*SEEN-zah*)
grease, to (lubricate) lubrificar (*loo-bree-fee-KAHR*)
Greek grego(-a) (*GRAY-goo)(-gah*)
green verde (*VEHR-jee*)
greeting saudação (f.) (*sah-oo-dah-SOWN*)
ground chão (m.) (*shown*)
  (floor) piso (m.), res-do-chão (m.) (P) (*PEE-zoo, rrehs-doh-shown*)
guest hóspede (m. or f.), convidado(-a) (*OHS-pee-jee, kohn-vee-DAH-doo[-dah]*)
guide guía (m. or f.) (*GEE-ah*)
  guidebook guía (m.) (*GEE-ah*)
gum (chewing) goma-de-mascar (m.) (*GOH-mah jee mahs-KAHR*)
guy tipo (m.), cara (m.) (*CHEE-poo, KAH-rah*)

H

hair cabelo (m.) (*kah-BAY-loo*)
hairbrush escova de cabelo (f.) (*ehs-KOH-vah jee kah-BAY-loo*)
haircut corte (m.) (*KOHR-chee*)
hairpin grampo de cabelo (m.) (*GRAHM-poo jee kah-BAY-loo*)
half (adj) meia, (n.) metade (f.) (*MAY-yoo, meh-TAH-jee*)

hall vestíbulo (m.); saguão (m.) (*vehs-CHEE-boo-loo, sah-GWOWN*)
ham presunto (m.) (*pray-ZOON-too*)
hammer martelo (m.) (*mahr-TAY-loo*)
hand mão (f.) (*mown*)
handbag bolsa (f.) (*BOHL-sah*)
handkerchief lenço (m.) (*LEHN-soo*)
handmade feito à mão (*FAY-too ah mown*)
hanger (coat) cabide (m.) (*kah-BEE-jee*)
happen, to suceder, acontecer (*soo-seh-DEHR, ah-kohn-tay-SEHR*)
happy feliz, contente (*feh-LEEZ, kohn-TEHN-chee*)
Happy New Year! Feliz Ano Novo! (*feh-LEEZ AH-noo NOH-voo*)
harbor porto (m.) (*POHR-too*)
hard (difficult) difícil (*jee-FEE-see-oo*)
  (tough) duro (*DOO-roo*)
hat chapéu (m.) (*shah-PAY-oo*)
have, to ter (*tehr*)
  to have to ter que (*ter keh*)
he ele (*AY-lee*)
head cabeça (f.) (*kah-BAY-sah*)
headache dor de cabeça (f.) (*dohr jee kay-BAY-sah*)
headlight farol (m.) (*fah-ROHL*)
headwaiter chefe da mesa (m.) (*SHEH-fee dah MAY-zah*)

health saúde (f.) (*sah-OO-jee*)
  health certificate atestado de saúde (m.) (*ah-tehs-TAH-doo jee sah-OO-jee*)
hear, to ouvir (*oh-VEER*)
  to hear from ter notícias de (*ter noh-CHEE-syahs jee*)
heart coração (m.) (*koh-rah-SOWN*)
heat calor (m.) (*kah-LOHR*)
heaven céu (m.) (*SEH-oo*)
heavy pesado (*pay-ZAH-doo*)
height altura (*ahl-TOO-rah*)
hell inferno (m.) (*een-FEHR-noo*)
hello! olá! (*oh-LAH*)
help ajudar (v.) (*ah-zhoo-DAHR*)
  help! socorro! (m.) (*soh-KOH-hoo*)
here aqui (*ah-KEE*)
high alto (*AHL-too*)
highway rodovia (f.), estrada principal (P) (*hoh-doh-VEE-ah, ehs-TRAH-dah preen-see-POW*)
hill colina (f.) (*koh-LEE-nah*)
hip quadril (m.) (*kwah-DREE-oo*)
hire, to alugar (*ah-loo-GAHR*)
his seu (*SAY-oo*)
holiday férias (f.pl.) (*FEH-ryahs*)
home lar (f.), morada (f.) (*lahr, moh-RAH-dah*)
  to go home ir para casa (*eer PAH-rah KAH-zah*)
  to be at home estar em casa (*ehs-TAHR ehn KAH-zah*)
hook gancho (m.) (*GAHN-shoo*)

hope, to esperar (*ehs-peh-RAHR*)

horn (car) buzina (f.) (*boo-ZEE-nah*)

hors d'oeuvre entradas (f.pl.), acepipes (m.pl.) (P) (*ehn-TRAH-dahs, ah-say-PEE-pees*)

horse cavalo (m.) (*kah-VAH-loo*)

hospital hospital (m.) (*ohs-pee-TOW*)

hostel pousada (f.) (*poh-ZAH-dah*)

hostess (plane) aeromoça (f.), hospedeira (f.) (P) (*ah-eh-roh-MOH-sah, ohs-pay-DAY-rah*)

hot quente (*KEHN-chee*)

hotel hotel (m.) (*oh-TAY-oo*)

hour hora (f.) (*OH-rah*)

house casa (f.) (*KAH-zah*)

housewife dona de casa (f.) (*DOH-nah jee KAH-zah*)

how como? (*KOH-moo?*)

    how far? a que distância? (*ah keh dees-TAHN-syah?*)

    how long? quanto tempo? (*KWAHN-too TEHM-poo?*)

    how many? quantos? (*KWAHN-toos?*)

    how much? quanto? (*KAWHN-too?*)

hundred cem (*sehn*)

hungry, to be estar com fome (*ehs-TAHR kohn FOH-mee*)

hurry, to apressar-se (*ah-pray-SAHR-see*)

hurt, to ferir (*feh-REER*)

husband marido (m.) (*mah-REE-doo*)

I

I eu (*AY-oo*)

ice gelo (m.) (*ZHAY-loo*)

    ice cream sorvete (m.), gelado (m.) (P) (*sohr-VAY-chee, zheh-LAH-doh*)

identification identificação (f.) (*ee-dehn-chee-fee-kah-SOWN*)

if se (*see*)

ignition (car) ignição (f.) (*eeg-nee-SOWN*)

ill doente (*DWEHN-chee*)

illness doença (f.) (*DWEHN-sah*)

imported importado (*eem-pohr-TAH-doo*)

in em, dentro de (*ehn, DEHN-troo jee*)

include incluir (*een-kloo-EER*)

indigestion indisposição(f.) (*een-dees-poh-zee-SOWN*)

indisposed indisposto (*een-dees-POHS-too*)

information informação (f.) (*een-fohr-mah-SOWN*)

injection injeção (f.) (*een-zheh-SOWN*)

inquire, to perguntar, indagar (*pehr-goon-TAHR, een-dah-GAHR*)

insect inseto (m.) (*een-SAY-too*)

insecticide inseticida (m.) (*een-say-chee-SEE-dah*)

inside dentro (de) (*DEHN-troo*) (*jee*)

instead of em vez de (*ehn vehz jee*)

institution instituição (f.) (*een-stee-too-ee-SOWN*)

insurance seguro (m.) (*say-GOO-roo*)

213

insure, to fazer seguro de
(fah-ZEHR say-GOO-roo jee)
interest interesse (m.) *(een-teh-RAY-see)*
interpreter intérprete (m. or f.) *(een-TEHR-pray-tee)*
interesection intersecção (f.) *(een-teer-sehk-SOWN)*
into dentro de, para dentro *(DEHN-troo jee, PAH-rah DEHN-troo)*
introduce, to apresentar *(ah-pray-zehn-TAHR)*
iodine iodo (m.) *(YOH-doo)*
iron (metal) ferro (m.) *(FEH-hoo)*
   flatiron ferro (m.) *(FEH-hoo)*
   to iron passar a ferro *(pah-SAHR ah FEH-hoo)*
is é, está *(eh, ehs-TAH)*
island ilha (f.) *(EEL-yah)*

J

jack (for car) macaco (m.) *(mah-KAH-koo)*
jam (fruit) geléia (f.), doce de fruta (m.) (P) *(zheh-LEH-yah, DOH-say deh FROO-tah)*
January janeiro *(zhah-NAY-roo)*
jaw maxilar (f.) *(mahk-see-LAHR)*
jewelry jóias (f.) *(ZHOY-yahs)*
   jewelry store jaolharia (f.) *(zhoh-ahl-yah-REE-ah)*
Jew judeu (judia) (m. or f.) *(zhoo-DAY-oo, zhoo-JEE-ah)*
journey (trip) viagem (f.) *(vee-AH-zhehn)*
juice suco (m.), sumo (m.) (P) *(SOO-koo, SOO-moo)*

July julho *(ZHOOL-yoo)*
June junho *(ZHOON-yoo)*

K

keep, to manter, guardar *(mahn-TEHR, gwahr-DAHR)*
key chave (f.) *(SHAH-vee)*
kilogram quilograma (m.) *(kee-loh-GRAH-mah)*
kilometer quilómetro (m.) *(kee-LOH-meh-troo)*
kind (nice) simpático, bom *(seem-PAH-chee-koo, bohn)*
kiss beijo (m.) *(BAY-zhoo)*
   to kiss beijar *(bay-ZHAHR)*
kitchen cozinha (f.) *(koh-ZEEN-yah)*
knee joelho (m.) *(zhoh-EHL-yoo)*
knife faca (f.) *(FAH-kah)*
knock bater *(bah-TEHR)*
know, to (a fact, know how) saber *(sah-BEHR)* **(a person or thing)** conhecer *(kohn-yay-SEHR)*

L

label etiqueta (f.) *(eh-chee-KEH-tah)*
lace renda (f.) *(HEHN-dah)*
lady senhora (f.) *(sehn-YOH-rah)*
lamb cordeiro (m.) *(kohr-DAY-roo)*
land terra (f.) *(TEH-hah)*
   to land aterrisar *(ah-teh-hee-ZAHR)*
language língua (f.) *(LEEN-gwah)*
large grande *(GRAN-jee)*
last último *(OOL-chee-moo)*
   to last durar *(doo-RAHR)*

late tarde, atrasado (*TAHR-jee, ah-trah-ZAH-doo*)
laugh, to rir, riso (m.) (*HEER, HEE-zoo*)
laundry lavanderia (f.) (*lah-vahn-deh-REE-ah*)
lavatory sanitário (m.) (*sah-nee-TAH-ryoo*)
laxative chefe (m. or f.), líder (m. or f.) (*SHEH-fee, LEE-dehr*)
leak, to pingar (*peen-GAHR*)
lean, to apoiar-se (*ah-poy-YAHR-see*)
learn, to aprender (*ah-prehn-DEHR*)
least (at . . .) pelo menos (*PEH-loo MAY-noos*)
leather couro (m.), cabedal (m.) (P) (*KOH-roo, kah-beh-DOWL*)
leave (behind), to deixar (*day-ZHAHR*)
    to depart partir (*pahr-CHEER*)
left (opposite of right) esquerda (*ehs-KEHR-dah*)
leg perna (f.) (*PEHR-nah*)
lemon limão (m.) (*lee-MOWN*)
lemonade limonada (f.) (*lee-moh-NAH-dah*)
lend, to emprestar (*ehm-prays-TAHR*)
length comprimento (*kohm-pree-MEHN-too*)
lens lente (f.) (*LEHN-chee*)
less menos (*MAY-noos*)
let, to deixar, permitir (*day-ZHAHR, pehr-mee CHEER*)
letter carta (f.) (*KAHR-tah*)
lettuce alface (f.) (*ahl-FAH-see*)

library biblioteca (f.) (*bee-blyoh-TAY-kah*)
lie, to (down) deitar-se (*day-TAHR-see*)
life vida (f.) (*VEE-dah*)
lift, to levantar (*lay-vahn-TAHR*)
light (color) claro (*KLAH-roo*)
    (brightness) luz (f.) (*loos*)
    to light acender (*ah-sehn-DEHR*)
lighter (cigarette) isqueiro (m.) (*ees-KAY-roo*)
lightning relâmpago (m.) (*hay-LAHM-pah-goo*)
like (as) como (*KOH-moo*)
    to like gostar (de) (*gohs-TAHR*) (*jee*)
line linha (f.) (*LEEN-yah*)
linen linho (m.), roupa branca (f.) (*LEEN-yoo, HOH-pah BRAHN-kah*)
lip lábio (m.) (*LAH-byoo*)
lipstick batom (m.) (*bah-TOHN*)
liqueur licor (m.) (*lee-KOHR*)
liquor bebidas alcoólicas (f.) (*beh-BEE-dahs ahl-KOH-lee-kahs*)
list (wine, food) carta (f.) (*KAHR-tah*)
listen to, to escutar (*ehs-koo-TAHR*)
liter litro (m.) (*LEE-troo*)
little pequeno (*pay-KEH-noo*)
live, to viver (*vee-VEHR*)
liver fígado (m.) (*FEE-gah-doo*)
living room sala de estar (f.) (*SAH-lah jee ehs-TAHR*)

215

lobby vestíbulo (m.) (vehs-CHEE-boo-loo)
lobster lagosta (f.) (lah-GOHS-tah)
local local (loh-KOW)
  local phone call chamada local (f.) (chah-MAH-dah, loh-KOW)
lock (fastening) fechadura (f.) (fay-shah-DOO-rah)
long long, comprido (LOHN-goo, kohm-PREE-doo)
look at, to olhar (ohl-YAHR)
  to look for procurar (proh-koor-AHR)
  to look out ter cuidado (tehr kwee-DAH-doo)
lose, to perder (pehr-DEHR)
lost and found achados e perdidos (ah-SHAH-doos ee pehr-JEE-doos)
lotion loção (f.) (loh-SOWN)
lots of, many muito (MWEE-too)
lounge salão (m.) (sah-LOWN)
low baixo (BAHY-shoo)
luck sorte (f.) (SOHR-chee)
lunch almoço (m.) (ahl-MOH-soo)
  to lunch almoçar (ahl-moh-SAHR)
lung pulmão (m.) (pool-MOWN)

M

madam senhora (f.) (sehn-YOH-rah)
maid empregada (f.) (ehm-pray-GAH-dah)
mail correio (m.) (koh-HAY-yoo)

mailbox caixa de correio (f.) (KAHY-shah jee koh-HAY-yoo)
magazine revista (f.) (hay-VEES-tah)
make, to fazer (fah-ZEHR)
man homem (m.) (OH-mehn)
manager diretor(+a) (m. or f.), gerente (m. or f.) (jee-reh-TOHR)(+ah), zheh-REHN-chee)
manicure manicure (f.) (mah-nee-KOO-ree)
many muitos (MWEE-toos)
map (road) mapa (m.) (MAH-pah)
March março (MAHR-soo)
market mercado (m.) (mehr-KAH-doo)
marry, to casar-se (kah-ZAHR-see)
mass (religious) missa (f.) (MEE-sah)
massage massagem (f.) (mah-SAH-zhehn)
match fósforo (m.) (FOHS-foh-roo)
matter (it doesn't matter) não faz mal (nown fahs mow)
  what's the matter? o que aconteceu? (oo keh ah-kohn-tay-SAY-oo?)
mattress colchão (m.) (kohl-SHOWN)
May maio (MAHY-yoo)
maybe talvez (tah-VEHZ)
meal refeição (f.) (hay-fahy-SOWN)
mean, to significar; querer dizer (see-gee-nee-fee-KAHR, keh-REHR jee-ZEHR)
measure, to medir (meh-JEER)
meat carne (f.) (KAHR-nee)

216

mechanic mecânico (m.) (*meh-KAH-nee-koo*)

medical médico (m.) (*MEH-jee-koo*)

medicine remédio (m.) (*heh-MEH-joo*)

meet, to encontrar (*ehn-kohn-TRAHR*)

(socially) conhecer (*kohn-yay-SEHR*)

melon melão (m.) (*meh-LOWN*)

mend remendar (*hay-mehn-DAHR*)

menu cardápio (m.), menú (m.) (P); ementa (f.) (P) (*kahr-DAH-pyoo, meh-NOO; eh-MEHN-tah*)

merry alegre (*ah-LEH-gree*)

Merry Christmas! Feliz Natal! (*feh-LEEZ nah-TOW!*)

message mensagem (f.) (*mehn-ZAH-zhehn*)

meter (length) metro (m.) (*MEH-troo*)

Mexican mexicano(-a) (*meh-zhee-KAH-noo)(-nah*)

middle (center) meio (m.) (*MAY-yoo*)

midnight meia-noite (f.) (*may-yah-NOY-chee*)

mild suave (*SWAH-vee*)

milk leite (m.) (*LAY-chee*)

mind (understanding) mente (f.) (*MEHN-chee*)

never mind não importa (*nown eem-POHR-tah*)

mine o meu, a minha (*oo MAY-oo, ah MEEN-yah*)

mineral water água mineral (f.)) (*AH-gwah mee-neh-ROW*)

minister ministro (m.) (*mee-NEES-troo*)

minute minuto (m.) (*mee-NOO-too*)

mirror espelho (m.) (*ehs-PEHL-yoo*)

Miss (woman) senhorita (f.) (*sehn-yoh-REE-tah*)

(young woman) menina (f.) (P) (*meh-NEE-nah*)

miss, to (a train) perder (*pehr-DEHR*)

mistake erro (m.) (*EH-hoo*)

monastery mosteiro (m.) (*mohs-TAY-roo*)

Monday segunda-feira (f.) (*say-GOON-dah FAY-rah*)

money dinheiro (m.) (*jeen-YAY-roo*)

money order ordem de pagamento (f.) (*OHR-dehn jee pah-gah-MEHN-too*)

month mês (m.) (*mays*)

monument monumento (m.) (*moh-noo-MEHN-too*)

moon lua (f.) (*LOO-ah*)

more mais (*mahys*)

morning amanhã (f.) (*ah-mahn-YAHN*)

mosquito mosquito (m.) (*mohs-KEE-too*)

mother mãe (f.) (*mahy*)

motor (car) motor (m.) (*moh-TOHR*)

mountain montanha (f.) (*mohn-TAHN-yah*)

mouth boca (f.) (*BOH-kah*)

move, to mover (*moh-VEHR*)

to change residence mudar-se (*moo-DAHR-see*)

movie filme (m.) (*FEEL-mee*)

Mr. senhor (m.) (*sehn-YOHR*)

Mrs. senhora (f.) (*sehn-YOH-rah*)

much muito (*MWEE-too*)

217

museum museu (m.) (*moo-ZAY-oo*)

mushroom cogumelo (m.) (*koh-goo-MAY-loo*)

music música (f.) (*MOO-zee-kah*)

must dever, ter de (*day-VEHR, tehr jee*)

N

nail (finger) unha (f.) (*OON-yah*)

name nome (m.) (*NOH-mee*)

napkin guardanapo (m.) (*gwahr-dah-NAH-poo*)

narrow estreito (*ehs-TRAY-too*)

nationality nacionalidade (f.) (*nah-syoh-nay-lee-DAH-jee*)

nausea náusea (f.) (*NOW-syah*)

near (adj) vizinho, (prep.) perto de (*vee-ZEEN-yoo, PEHR-too jee*)

nearly quase (*KWAH-zee*)

necessary necessário (*neh-say-SAH-ryoo*)

neck pescoço (m.) (*pehs-KOH-soo*)

necklace colar (m.) (*koh-LAHR*)

necktie gravata (f.) (*grah-VAH-tah*)

need, to necessitar, precisar (*neh-seh-see-TAHR, pray-see-ZAHR*)

needle agulha (f.) (*ah-GOOL-yah*)

nerve nervo (m.) (*NEHR-voo*)

net rede (f.) (*HEH-jee*)

never nunca (*NOON-kah*)

new novo (*NOH-voo*)

New Year Ano Novo (*AH-noo NOH-voo*)

newspaper jornal (m.) (*zhoor-NOW*)

newsstand banca (f.), quiosque (m.) (P) (*BAHN-kah, KYOHS-kee*)

next próximo, seguinte (*PROHK-see-moo, seh-GEEN-chee*)

night noite (f.) (*NOY-chee*)

nightclub clube noturno (m.), cabaret (m.) (P) (*KLOO-bee noh-TOOR-noh, kah-bah-REHT-chee*)

nightgown camisola (f.), camisa de dormir (f.) (P) (*kah-mee-ZOH-lah, kah-MEE-zah day dohr-MEER*)

nine nove (*NOH-vee*)

nineteen dezenove (*deh-zee-NOH-vee*)

ninety noventa (*noh-VEHN-tah*)

ninth nono (*NOH-noo*)

no não (*nown*)

no one ninguém (*neen-GEHN*)

noise ruído (m.) (*HWEE-doo*)

noisy barulhento, ruidoso (P) (*bah-rool-YEHN-too, rroo-ee-DOH-zoh*)

none nenhum (*neh-YOON*)

noon meio-dia (m.) (*may-yoo-JEE-ah*)

north norte (*NOHR-chee*)

nose nariz (m.) (*nah-REEZ*)

not não (*nown*)

nothing nada (*NAH-dah*)

nothing else mais nada (*mayhs NAH-dah*)

notice (announcement) aviso (m.) (*ah-VEE-zoo*)

novel romance (m.) *(hoh-MAHN-see)*
November novembro *(noh-VEHM-broo)*
now agora *(ah-GOH-rah)*
number número (m.) *(NOO-meh-roo)*
nurse enfermeira (f.) *(ehn-fehr-MAY-rah)*
nut noz (f.) *(nohz)*

O

occasion ocasião (f.) *(oh-kah-zee-OWN)*
occupied ocupado *(oh-koo-PAH-doo)*
occur acontecer *(ah-kohn-tay-SEHR)*
ocean oceano (m.) *(oh-say-AH-noo)*
October outubro *(oh-TOO-broo)*
oculist oculista (m. or f.) *(oh-koo-LEES-tah)*
of de *(jee)*
of course pois não, naturalmente *(poys nown, nah-too-row-MEHN-chee)*
office escritório (m.) *(ehs-kree-TOH-ryoo)*
often muitas vezes, frequentemente *(MWEE-tahs VEH-zees, fray-kwehn-teh-MEHN-chee)*
oil óleo (m.) *(OH-lee-oo)*
okay (it's) está bem, de acordo! óquei (O.K.) *(ehs-TAH behn, jee ah-KOHR-doo, oh-KAY)*
old velho *(VEHL-yoo)*
olive azeitona (f.) *(ah-zay-TOH-nah)*

omelette omelete (f.) *(oh-meh-LEH-chee)*
on em, sobre *(ehn, SOH-bree)*
once uma vez *(OO-mah vehz)*
at once já *(zhah)*
one um, uns, uma, umas *(oon, oons, OO-mah, OO-mahs)*
onion cebola (f.) *(say-BOH-lah)*
only só, somente *(soh, soh-MEHN-chee)*
open aberto *(ah-BEHR-too)*
to open abrir *(ah-BREER)*
opera ópera (f.) *(OH-peh-rah)*
operator (phone) telefonista (f.) *(teh-lay-foh-NEES-tah)*
optician oculista (m. or f.) *(oh-koo-LEES-tah)*
orange laranja (f.) *(lah-RAHN-zhah)*
orangeade laranjada (f.) *(lah-rahn-ZHAH-dah)*
orchestra (band) orquestra (f.)) *(ohr-KEHS-trah)*
order ordem (f.), encomenda (f.) *(OHR-dehn, ehn-koh-MEHN-dah)*
to order encomendar *(ehn-koh-mehn-DAHR)*
other outro *(OH-troo)*
ought dever *(day-VEHR)*
our, ours nosso, nossa *(NOH-soo, NOH-sah)*
out fora (de) *(FOH-rah) (jee)*
outside (adv.) de fora *(jee FOH-rah)*
over (above) sobre, por cima de *(SOH-bree, pohr SEE-mah jee)*
(finished) acabado *(ah-kah-BAH-doo)*
overcoat sobretudo *(soh-bree-TOO-doo)*

219

overnight por uma noite (*poor oo-mah NOY-chee*)
owe dever (*day-VEHR*)

P

pack, to (luggage) fazer as malas (*fah-ZEHR ahs MAH-lahs*)
package pacote (m.), volume (m.) (P) (*pah-KOH-chee, voh-LOO-meh*)
page (of book) página (f.) (*PAH-zhee-nah*)
pain dor (f.) (*dohr*)
paint, to pintar (*peen-TAHR*)
pair par (m.) (*pahr*)
palace palácio (m.) (*pah-LAH-syoo*)
panties calcinhas (f.pl.) (*kahl-SEEN-yahs*)
pants calças (f.pl.), cuecas (f.pl.) (P) (*KAHL-sahs, KWAY-kahs*)
paper papel (m.) (*pah-PAY-oo*)
   wrapping paper papel de embrulho (m.) (*pah-PAY-oo jee ehm-BROOL-yoo*)
parcel embrulho (m.) (*ehm-BROOL-yoo*)
pardon perdão (m.) (*pehr-DOWN*)
park, to estacionar (*ehs-tah-syoh-NAHR*)
parking lot estacionamento (m.) (*ehs-tah-syoh-nah-MEHN-too*)
   (no . . .) proibido estacionar (*proh-ee-BEE-doo ehs-tah-syoh-NAHR*)
part parte (f.) (*PAHR-chee*)

to separate separar, dividir (*seh-pah-RAHR, jee-vee-JEER*)
part (spare) peça, sobressalente (f.) (*PAY-sah, soh-bree-sah-LEHN-chee*)
pass, to passar (*pah-SAHR*)
passenger passageiro(-a) (*pah-sah-ZHAY-roo*)(*-rah*)
passport passaporte (m.) (*pah-sah-POHR-chee*)
past passado (m.) (*pah-SAH-doo*)
pastry pastelaria (f.) (*pahs-teh-lah-REE-ah*)
pay, to pagar (*pah-GAHR*)
pea ervilha (f.) (*ehr-VEEL-yah*)
peach pêssego (m.) (*PAY-say-goo*)
pear pêra (f.) (*PAY-rah*)
pedestrian pedeste (m.), peão (m.) (P) (*pay-DEHS-tree, pee-OWN*)
pen caneta (f.) (*kah-NAY-tah*)
pencil lápis (m.) (*LAH-pees*)
people gente (f.) (*ZHEHN-chee*)
pepper (black) pimenta (f.) (*pee-MEHN-tah*)
percent porcento (m.) (*pohr-SEHN-too*)
perfect perfeito (*pehr-FAY-too*)
performance espetáculo (m.) (*ehs-pay-TAH-koo-loo*)
perfume perfume (m.) (*pehr-FOO-mee*)
perhaps talvez (*tahl-VEHZ*)
permanent (wave) permanente (f.) (*pehr-mah-NEHN-chee*)

permit licença (f.) (*lee-SEHN-sah*)
   to permit permitir (*pehr-mee-CHEER*)
Persian persa (m. or f.) (*PEHR-sah*)
personal pessoal (*peh-soh-OW*)
pharmacy farmácia (f.) (*fahr-MAH-syah*)
phone telefone (m.) (*teh-lay-FOH-nee*)
   to phone telefonar (*teh-lay-foh-NAHR*)
phone booth cabine telefónica (f.) (*kah-BEE-nee teh-lay-FOH-nee-kah*)
photograph fotografia (f.) (*foh-toh-grah-FEE-ah*)
pick, to escolher (*ehs-kohl-YEHR*)
pickle picle (m.) (*PEEK-lee*)
picnic piquenique (m.) (*pee-keh-NEE-kee*)
picture (art) quadro (m.), pintura (f.) (*KWAH-droo, peen-TOO-rah*)
piece peça (f.) (*PAY-sah*)
pier cais (m.), molhe (m.) (P) (*KAH-ees, MOHL-yeh*)
pill pílula (f.) (*PEE-loo-lah*)
pillow travasseiro (m.), almofada (f.) (P) (*trah-vah-SAY-roo, ahl-moh-FAH-dah*)
pillowcase fronha (f.) (*FROHN-yah*)
pilot piloto (m.) (*pee-LOH-too*)
pin alfinete (m.) (*ahl-fee-NAY-chee*)
pineapple abacaxi (m.), ananás (m.) (P) (*ah-bah-kah-SHEE, ah-nah-NAHS*)

pink cor-de-rosa (*kohr jee HOH-zah*)
pipe (smoking) cachimbo (f.) (*kah-SHEEM-boo*)
pity (what a pity!) que pena! (*keh PAY-nah!*)
place lugar (m.) (*loo-GAHR*)
   to place colocar (*koh-loh-KAHR*)
plane (air) avião (m.) (*ah-vee-OWN*)
plate prato (m.) (*PRAH-too*)
platform plataforma (f.) (*plah-tah-FOHR-mah*)
play peça teatral (f.) (*PAY-sah chyah-TROWL*)
   to play (a game) jogar (*zhoh-GAHR*)
   to play (an instrument) tocar (*toh-KAHR*)
playing cards cartas de jogar (f.) (*KAHR-tahs jee zhoh-GAHR*)
pleasant agradável (*ah-grah-DAH-vay-oo*)
   (a person) simpático(-a) (*seem-PAH-chee-koo*)(*-kah*)
please faz favor, por favor (*fahs fah-VOHR, poor fah-VOHR*)
pleasure prazer (m.) (*prah-ZEHR*)
pliers alicate (m.) (*ah-lee-KAH-chee*)
plum ameixa (f.) (*ah-MAY-zhah*)
P.M. da tarde, da noite (*dah TAHR-jee, dah NOY-chee*)
pocket bolso (m.) (*BOHL-soo*)
pocketbook bolsa (f.) (*BOHL-sah*)

221

point (place) ponto (m.) (*POHN-too*)

poison veneno (m.) (*veh-NAY-noo*)

police polícia (f.) (*poh-LEE-syah*)

policeman policial (m.) (*poh-lee-SYOW*)

Polish polonês(+a) (*poh-loh-NAYS*)(+ah)

polite educado (*eh-doo-KAH-doo*)

politeness cortesia (*kohr-tay-ZEE-ah*)

poor pobre (*POH-bree*)

population população (f.) (*poh-poo-lah-SOWN*)

pork carne de porco (f.) (*KAHR-nee jee POHR-koo*)

port (harbor) porto (m.) (*POHR-too*)

porter carregador (m.), porteiro (m.) (*kah-hay-gah-DOHR, pohr-TAY-roo*)

portion porção (f.) (*pohr-SOWN*)

Portugal Portugal (*pohr-too-GOW*)

possible possível (*poh-SEE-vay-oo*)

postage porte (m.) (*POHR-chee*)

postcard cartão postal (m.) (*kahr-TOWN pohs-TOW*)

post office box caixa de correio (f.) (*KAY-shah jee koo-HAY-yoo*)

potato batata (f.) (*bah-TAH-tah*)

pour, to servir (*sehr-VEER*)

powder pó (m.) (*poh*)

power energia (f.) (*eh-nehr-ZHEE-ah*)

practice prática (f.) (*PRAH-chee-kah*)

to practice practicar (*prah-chee-KAHR*)

prefer, to preferir (*pray-feh-REER*)

prepare, to preparar (*pray-pahr-AHR*)

prescription receita (f.) (*hay-SAY-tah*)

present, to apresentar (*ah-pray-zehn-TAHR*)

press (iron), to passar a ferro (*pah-SAHR ah FEH-hoo*)

pretty bonito (*boh-NEE-too*)

price preço (m.) (*PRAY-soo*)

priest padre (m.) (*PAH-dree*)

to print imprimir (*eem-pree-MEER*)

problem problema (m.) (*proh-BLAY-mah*)

program programa (m.) (*proh-GRAH-mah*)

to promise prometer (*proh-meh-TEHR*)

pronunciation pronúncia (f.) (*proh-NOON-syah*)

Protestant protestante (m. or f.) (*proh-tehs-TAHN-chee*)

prune ameixa (f.) (*ah-MAY-shah*)

publication publicação (f.) (*poob-lee-kah-SOWN*)

pull puxar (*poo-ZHAHR*)

pump bomba (f.) (*BOHM-bah*)

punctured (tire) furado (m.) (*foo-RAH-doo*)

purchase, to comprar (*kohm-PRAHR*)
(an item) compra (f.) (*KOHM-prah*)

purple roxo, purpúreo (P) (*HOH-shoo, poor-POOR-ay-oh*)

purse bolsa (f.) (*BOHL-sah*)

push, to empurrar (*ehm-poo-HAHR*)

put, to pôr (*pohr*)
 to put in colocar (*koh-loh-KAHR*)
 to put on vestir (*vehs-CHEER*)

Q

quality qualidade (f.) (*kwah-lee-DAH-jee*)

quarter quarto (m.) (*KWAHR-too*)

question pergunta (f.) (*pehr-GOON-tah*)

quick rápido (*HAH-pee-doo*)

quiet calmo (*KAHL-moo*)

quinine quinino (m.) (*kee-NEE-noo*)

quit, to dessistir (*deh-sees-CHEER*)

quite bastante (*bahs-TAHN-chee*)

quota quota (f.), cota (f.) (*KWOH-tah, KOH-tah*)

R

rabbit coelho (m.) (*KWEHL-yoo*)

radiator radiador (m.) (*hah-jyah-DOHR*)

radio rádio (m.) (*HAH-joo*)

radish rabanete (m.) (*hah-bah-NAY-chee*)

railroad estrada de ferro (f.) (*ehs-TRAH-dah jee FEH-hoo*)

rain chuva (f.) (*SHOO-vah*)

raincoat capa de chuva (f.), impermeável (m.) (P) (*KAH-pah jee SHOO-vah, eem-pehr-may-AH-vay-oo*)

rare raro (*HAH-roo*)

rate of exchange taxa de câmbio (*TAH-zhah jee KAHM-byoo*)

rather (have), to preferir (*pray-feh-REER*)

razor barbeador (m.) (*bahr-byah-DOHR*)

razor blade gilete (f.), lámina (f.) (P) (*zhee-LEH-chee, LAH-mee-nah*)

read, to ler (*lehr*)

ready (to be) (*ehs-TAHR PROHN-too*)

real verdadeiro (*vehr-dah-DAY-roo*)

really realmente (*hay-ahl-MEHN-chee*)

reasonable razoável (*hah-zoh-AH-vay-oo*)

receipt recibo (m.) (*hay-SEE-boo*)

receive, to receber (*hay-seh-BEHR*)

recommend, to recomendar (*heh-koh-mehn-DAHR*)

record (phonograph) disco (m.) (*DEES-koo*)

recover (get back), to recuperar (*hay-koo-pehr-AHR*)
 (health) curar-se (*koo-RAHR-see*)

red vermelho (*vehr-MEHL-yoo*)

refund reembolso (m.) (*hay-ehm-BOHL-soo*)
 to refund reembolsar (*hay-ehm-bohl-SAHR*)

refuse, to recusar (*hay-koo-ZAHR*)

223

regards lembranças (f.pl.) (*lehm-BRAHN-sahs*)

registered letter carta registrada (f.) (*KAHR-tah hay-jees-TRAH-dah*)

regular (ordinary) regular, normal (*heh-goo-LAHR, nohr-MOW*)

remedy remédio (m.) (*heh-MEH-jyoo*)

remember, to lembrar-se (*lehm-BRAHR-see*)

rent, to alugar (*ah-loo-GAHR*)

repair, to consertar (*kohn-sehr-TAHR*)

repeat, to repetir (*heh-pay-CHEER*)

reply, to responder (*hays-pohn-DEHR*)

reservation reserva (f.) (*hay-ZEHR-vah*)

reserve, to reservar (*hay-zehr-VAHR*)

reserved seat lugar reservado (m.) (*loo-GAHR hay-zehr-VAH-doo*)

to rest repousar, descansar (*hay-poh-ZAHR, dehs-kahn-SAHR*)

restaurant restaurante (m.) (*hehs-tow-RAHN-chee*)

return, to voltar (*vohl-TAHR*)

rib costela (f.) (*kohs-TAY-lah*)

ribbon fita (f.) (*FEE-tah*)

rice arroz (m.) (*ah-HOHZ*)

rich rico (*HEE-koo*)

ride passeio (m.) (*pah-SAY-yoo*)

right direito (*jee-RAY-too*)
   to be right ter razão (*tehr hah-ZOWN*)
   all right está bem (*ehs-TAH behn*)

ring anel (m.) (*ah-NAY-oo*)

to rinse enxuagar (*ehn-zhwah-GAHR*)

river rio (m.) (*HEE-oo*)

road estrada (f.) (*ehs-TRAH-dah*)
   (highway) rodovia (f.) (*hoh-doh-VEE-ah*)

roast, to assar (*ah-SAHR*)

rob, to roubar (*hoh-BAHR*)

robe roupão (m.), bata (f.) (P) (*hoh-POWN, BAH-tah*)

roll (bread) pão francês (m.) (*pown frahn-SAYS*)

room quarto (m.) (*KWAHR-too*)
   room service serviço de quarto (m.) (*sehr-VEE-soo jee KWAHR-too*)

root raiz (f.) (*hah-EEZ*)

rope corda (f.) (*KOHR-dah*)

rouge ruge (m.) (*HOO-zhee*)

round redondo (*hay-DOHN-doo*)
   round trip viagem de ida e volta (f.) (*vee-AH-zhehn jee EE-dah ee VOHL-tah*)

row (theater) fileira (f.), fila (f.)(P) (*fee-LAY-rah, FEE-lah*)

rubber borracha (f.) (*boh-HAH-shah*)
   rubber band elástico (m.) (*eh-LAHS-chee-koo*)

rug tapete (m.) (*tah-PEH-chee*)

Rumanian romeno(-a) (*hoh-MEH-noo*)(*-nah*)

run correr (*koh-HEHR*)

Russian russo(-a) (*HOO-soo*)(*-sah*)

S

sad triste (*TREES-chee*)

safe seguro (*say-GOO-roo*)

saint santo(-a) (*SAHN-too*) (*-tah*)

salad salada (f.) (*sah-LAH-dah*)

sale venda (f.) (*VEHN-dah*)
(clearance) liquidação (f.) (*lee-kee-dah-SOWN*)

salon (beauty) salão de beleza (m.) (*sah-LOWN jee beh-LAY-zah*)

saloon bar (m.) (*bahr*)

salt sal (m.) (*sow*)

same mesmo (*MAYZ-moo*)

sand areia (f.) (*ah-RAY-yah*)

sandwich sanduiche (f.) (*sahn-DWEE-shee*)

sardine sardinha (f.) (*sahr-DEEN-yah*)

Saturday sábado (*SAH-bah-doo*)

sauce molho (m.) (*MOHL-yoo*)

saucer pires (m.) (*PEE-rees*)

sausage salsicha (f.) (*sahl-SEE-shah*)

say dizer (*jee-ZEHR*)

scarf lenço (da cabeça) (m.) (*LEHN-soo dah kah-BAY-sah*)

school escola (f.) (*ehs-KOH-lah*)

scissors tesoura (f.) (*teh-SOH-rah*)

sea mar (m.) (*mahr*)

seafood frutas do mar (m.p.), mariscos (m.pl.) (P) (*FROO-tahs doo mahr, mah-REES-kohs*)

seasickness enjoo (m.) (*ehn-ZHOH-oo*)

season estação (f.) (*ehs-tah-SOWN*)

seat assento (m.) (*ah-SEHN-too*)

second segundo (m.) (*say-GOON-doo*)

secretary secretária(-o) (*seh-kray-TAH-ryah*)(*-ryoo*)

see, to ver (*vehr*)

seem, to parecer (*pah-ray-SEHR*)

select, to escolher (*ehs-kohl-YEHR*)

sell, to vender (*vehn-DEHR*)

send, to enviar, mandar (*ehn-VYAHR, mahn-DAHR*)

separate, to separar (*say-pah-RAHR*)

September setembro (*seh-TEHM-broo*)

serve, to servir (*sehr-VEER*)

service serviço (m.) (*sehr-VEE-soo*)

seven sete (*SAY-chee*)

seventeen dezessete (*deh-zee-SEH-chee*)

seventh sétimo (*SEH-chee-moo*)

seventy setenta (*seh-TEHN-tah*)

several vários (*VAH-ryoos*)

shade (not sun) sombra (f.) (*SOHM-brah*)

shampoo xampu (m.), champó (m.) (P) (*shahm-poo, shahm-POH*)
to shampoo lavar a cabeça (*lah-VAHR ah kah-BEH-sah*)

shave, to fazer a barba (*fah-ZEHR ah BAHR-bah*)

shawl xale (m.) (*SHAH-lee*)

she ela (*EH-lah*)

sheet (paper) folha (f.) (*FOHL-yah*)

225

(bed) lençol (m.) (*lehn-SOHL*)

shine, to brilhar (*breel-YAHR*)

ship navio (m.) (*nah-VEE-oo*)
  to ship enviar (*ehn-VYAHR*)

shirt camisa (f.) (*kah-MEE-zah*)

shoe sapato (m.) (*sah-PAH-too*)

shop loja (f.) (*LOH-zhah*)

short curto (*KOOR-too*)

shorts (underwear) cuecas (f.pl.), calções (m.pl.) (P) (*KWAY-kahs, kahl-SOWN-eesh*)

shoulder ombro (m.) (*OHM-broo*)

show, to mostrar (*mohs-TRAHR*)

shower chuveiro (m.), ducha (f.) (P) (*shoo-VAY-roo, DOO-sheh*)

shrimp camarão (m.) (*kah-mah-ROWN*)

shrine santuário (m.) (*sahn-TWAH-ryoo*)

shut fechar (*fay-SHAHR*)

sick doente (*DWEHN-chee*)

sickness doença (f.) (*DWEHN-sah*)

side lado (m.) (*LAH-doo*)

sidewalk calçada (f.) (*kahl-SAH-dah*)

sign aviso (m.) (*ah-VEE-zoo*)
  to sign assinar (*ah-see-NAHR*)

silk seda (f.) (*SEH-dah*)

silver prata (f.) (*PRAH-tah*)

since desde (*DAYZ-jee*)

sing, to cantar (*kahn-TAHR*)

single (room) quarto individual (m.) (*KWAHR-too een-jee-vee-doo-OW*)

sink (basin) pia (f.), lava-louça (m.) (P) (*PEE-ah, LAH-vah LOH-sah*)

sir senhor (m.) (*sehn-YOHR*)

sister irmã (f.) (*eer-MAHN*)

sit, to sentar-se (*sehn-TAHR-see*)

six seis (*says*)

sixteen dezesseis (*deh-zee-SAYS*)

sixth sexto (*SAYKS-too*)

size tamanho (m.) (*tah-MAHN-yoo*)

skin pele (f.) (*PEH-lee*)

skirt saia (f.) (*SAHY-yah*)

sky céu (m.) (*SEH-oo*)

sleep, to dormir (*dohr-MEER*)

sleeping car vagão-leito (m.), carruagem-cama (f.) (P) (*vah-GOWN LAY-too, kah-rroo-AH-zhehn KAH-mah*)

slip (garment) combinaçao (f.), saia de baixo (f.) (P) (*kohm-bee-nah-SOWN, SAHY-yah deh BAHY-shoh*)

slippers chinelos (m.pl.), pantufas (f.pl.) (P) (*shee-NAY-loos, pahn-TOO-fahsh*)

slow lento (*LEHN-too*)

slowly devagar (*jee-vah-GAHR*)

small pequeno (*pay-KEH-noo*)

smoke, to fumar (*foo-MAHR*)

snow neve (f.) (*NAY-vee*)
  to snow nevar (*neh-VAHR*)

so então, portanto (*ehn-TOWN, pohr-TAHN-too*)

soap sabão (m.), sabonete (m.) (*sah-BOWN, sah-boh-NAY-chee*)

soccer futebol (m.) (*foo-chee-BOHL*)

sofa sofá (m.) (*soh-FAH*)

soft mole (*MOH-lee*)

  soft drink refrigerante (m.), bebida não alcoólica (f.) (P) (*heh-free-zheh-RAHN-chee, beh-BEE-dah nown ahl-KOH-lee-kah*)

some alguns (*ahl-GOONS*)

someone alguém (*ahl-GEHN*)

something alguma coisa (*ahl-GOO-mah KOY-zah*)

sometimes as vezes (*ahs VAY-zees*)

son filho (m.) (*FEEL-yoo*)

song canção (f.) (*kahn-SOWN*)

soon em breve (*ehn BRAY-vee*)

sore throat dor de garganta (m.) (*dohr jee gahr-GAHN-tah*)

sorry! perdão!, desculpa! (*pehr-DOWN, dehs-KOOL-pah*)

soup sopa (f.) (*SOH-pah*)

sour azedo (*ah-ZEH-doo*)

south sul (*sool*)

souvenir lembrança (f.), recordação (f.) (P) (*lehm-BRAHN-sah, rray-kohr-dah-SOWN*)

Spanish espanhol(+a) (*ehs-pahn-YOHL*)(*+ah*)

spare part peça sobresselente (f.) (*PAY-sah soh-bree-seh-LEHN-chee*)

spark plug vela de ignição (f.) (*VAY-lah jee eeg-nee-SOWN*)

speak, to falar (*fah-LAHR*)

special especial (*ehs-peh-SYOW*)

speed limit límite de velocidade (m.) (*lee-MEE-chee jee veh-loh-see-DAH-jee*)

spend, to (money) gastar (*gahs-TAHR*)

  (time) passar (*pah-SAHR*)

spinach espinafre (m.) (*ehs-pee-NAH-free*)

spoon colher (f.) (*kool-YEHR*)

sprain, to torcer (*tohr-SEHR*)

spring (mechanical) mola (f.) (*MOH-lah*)

  (season) primavera (f.) (*pree-mah-VEH-rah*)

square (adj.) quadrado (*kwah-DRAH-doo*)

  main square praça principal (f.) (*PRAH-sah preen-see-POW*)

stairs escada (f.) (*ehs-KAH-dah*)

stamp (postage) selo (m.) (*SAY-loo*)

stand, to ficar em pé (*fee-KAHR-ehn peh*)

star estrela (f.) (*ehs-TRAY-lah*)

starch (laundry) goma (f.) (*GOH-mah*)

start, to começar (*koh-may-SAHR*)

station estação (f.) (*ehs-tah-SOWN*)

stay estadia (f.) (*ehs-tah-JEE-ah*)

  to stay ficar (*fee-KAHR*)

steak bife (m.) (*BEE-fee*)

steal roubar (*hoh-BAHR*)

steel aço (m.) (*AH-soo*)

steering wheel volante (m.) (*voh-LAHN-chee*)

227

stew cosido (m.), guisado (m.) (P) (*koh-ZEE-doo, gee-ZAH-doh*)

stewardess aeromoça (f.), hospedeira (f.) (P) (*ah-eh-roh-MOH-sah, ohs-pay-DAY-rah*)

stockings meias (f.pl.) (*MAY-yahs*)

stomach estômago (m.) (*ehs-TOH-mah-goo*)

 stomachache dor de estômago (f.) (*dohr jee ehs-TOH-mah-goo*)

stop (bus) ponto de ônibus (m.), parada de autocarro (f.) (P) (*POHN-too jee OH-nee-boos, pah-RAH-dah deh ow-toh-KAH-rroh*)

store loja (f.) (*LOH-zhah*)

straight direto (*jee-RAY-too*)

strap correia (f.), tira (f.) (*koh-HAY-yah, CHEE-rah*)

straw palha (f.) (*PAHL-yah*)

strawberry morango (m.) (*moh-RAHN-goo*)

street rua (f.) (*HOO-ah*)

streetcar bonde (m.) (*BOHN-jee*)

string barbante (m.), cordel (m.) (P) (*bahr-BAHN-chee, kohr-DAY-oo*)

strong forte (*FOHR-chee*)

style estilo (m.) (*ehs-TEE-loo*)
 (fashion) moda (f.) (*MOH-dah*)

sudden repentino (*hay-pehn-CHEE-noo*)

suddenly de repente (*jee heh-PEHN-chee*)

sugar açúcar (m.) (*ah-SOO-kahr*)

suit terno (m.) (*TEHR-noo*)

suitcase mala (f.) (*MAH-lah*)

summer verão (m.) (*veh-ROWN*)

sun sol (m.) (*sohl*)

Sunday domingo (*doh-MEEN-goo*)

sunglasses óculos-de-sol (m.pl.) (*OH-koo-loos jee sohl*)

sunny ensolarado, soalheiro (P) (*ehn-soh-lah-RAH-doo, soh-ahl-YAY-roh*)

supermarket supermercado (m.) (*soo-pehr-mehr-KAH-doo*)

supper jantar (m.), ceia (f.) (P) (*zhahn-TAHR, SAY-yah*)

sure certo (*SEHR-too*)

surgeon cirugião (m.) (*see-roor-ZHOWN*)

sweater malha (f.) (*MAHL-yah*)

Swedish sueco(-a) (*SWEH-koo*)(*-kah*)

sweet doce (*DOH-see*)
 sweet wine vinho doce (m.) (*VEEN-yoo DOH-see*)

swell, to inchar (*een-SHAHR*)

swim, to nadar (*nah-DAHR*)

swimming pool piscina (f.) (*pee-SEE-nah*)

Swiss suíço(-a) (*SWEE-soo*) (*-sah*)

switch (electric) interruptor (m.) (*een-teh-hoop-TOHR*)

synagogue sinagoga (f.) (*see-nah-GOH-gah*)

syrup xarope (m.) (*shal-ROH-pee*)

T

table mesa (f.) (*MAY-zah*)

tablecloth toalha de mesa (f.) (*TWAHL-yah jee MAY-zah*)

tablespoon colher de sopa (f.) (*kool-YEHR jee SOH-pah*)
tablet pastilha (f.) (*pahs-TEEL-yah*)
taillight farol traseiro (m.) (*fah-ROHL trah-ZAY-roo*)
tailor alfaiate (m.) (*ahl-FAHY-yah-chee*)
take, to levar (*lay-VAHR*)
  (a thing) tomar (*toh-MAHR, ah-gah-HAHR*)
  take off, to (a garment) tirar a roupa (*chee-RAHR ah HOH-pah*)
taken (occupied) ocupado (*oh-koo-PAH-doo*)
tall alto (*AHL-too*)
tangerine mexerica (f.); tangerina (f.) (P) (*may-sheh-REE-kah*); (*tahn-zheh-REE-nah*)
tank tanque (m.) (*TAHN-kee*)
tap torneira (f.) (*tohr-NAY-rah*)
tape (adhesive) fita adesiva (f.) (*FEE-tah ah-deh-ZEE-vah*)
tasty saboroso (*sah-boh-ROH-zoo*)
tax imposto (m.) (*eem-POHS-too*)
taxi taxi (m.) (*TAHK-see*)
tea chá (m.) (*shah*)
teach, to ensinar (*ehn-see-NAHR*)
teaspoon colher de chá (f.) (*kool-YEHR jee shah*)
teenager adolescente (m. or f.) (*ah-doh-lay-SEHN-chee*)
telegram telegrama (m.) (*teh-lay-GRAH-mah*)
telephone telefone (m.) (*teh-lay-FOH-nee*)
  to telephone telefonar (*teh-lay-foh-NAHR*)

telephone book lista telefônica (*LEES-tah teh-lay-FOH-nee-kah*)
tell, to dizer, contar (*jee-ZEER, kohn-TAHR*)
temporary temporário (*tehm-poh-RAH-ryoo*)
ten dez (*days*)
tenth décimo (*DEH-see-moo*)
terminal terminal (m.) (*tehr-mee-NOW*)
thank agradecer (*ah-grah-day-SEHR*)
  thank you! obrigado(-a)! (*oh-bree-GAH-doo!)(-dah!*)
that (conj.) que, (adj.) esse, aquele, (pron.) isso (*keh, EH-see, ah-KAY-lee, EE-soo*)
the o (m.), a (f.), os (m.pl.), as (f.pl.) (*oo, ah, oos, ahs*)
theater teatro (m.) (*chee-AH-troo*)
their deles, o seu (P) (*DAY-lees, oo SAY-oo*)
then então, depois (*ehn-TOWN, jee-POYS*)
there lá, para lá (*lah, PAH-rah lah*)
thermometer termómetro (m.) (*tehr-MOH-meh-troo*)
these estes (*EHS-chees*)
they eles (m.pl.), elas (f.pl.) (*AY-lees, EH-lahs*)
thick grosso, espesso (*GROH-soo, ehs-PAY-soo*)
thief ladrão (m.) (*lah-DROWN*)
thigh coxa (f.) (*KOH-shah*)
thing coisa (f.) (*KOY-zah*)
think, to pensar (*pehn-SAHR*)
third terceiro (*tehr-SAY-roo*)
thirsty estar com sede (*ehs-TAHR kohn SAY-jee*)

229

thirteen treze (*TRAY-zee*)

thirty trinta (*TREEN-tah*)

this este (*EHS-chee*)

those esses, aqueles (*AY-sees, ah-KAY-lees*)

thousand mil (*MEE-oo*)

thread fio (m.), linha (f.) (*FEE-oo, LEEN-yah*)

three três (*trays*)

throat garganta (f.) (*gahr-GAHN-tah*)

through através (*ah-trah-VEHS*)

thumb polegar (m.) (*poh-lee-GAHR*)

thunder trovão (m.) (*troh-VOWN*)
  to thunder trovejar (*troh-vay-ZHAHR*)

Thursday quinta-feira (f.) (*KEEN-tah FAY-rah*)

ticket bilhete (m.), ingresso (m.) (*beel-YEH-chee, een-GRAY-soo*)

tie (neck) gravata (f.) (*grah-VAH-tah*)

tighten, to apertar (*ah-pehr-TAHR*)

till até (*ah-TEH*)

time tempo (m.) (*TEHM-poo*)
  on time na hora (*nah OH-rah*)
  at what time a que horas? (*ah keh OH-rahs*)

timetable horário (m.) (*oh-RAH-ryoo*)

tip (gratuity) gorjeta (f.) (*gohr-ZHEH-tah*)

tire pneu (m.) (*peh-NAY-oo*)
  to tire cansar-se (*kahn-ZAHR-see*)

tissue paper lenço de papel (m.) (*LEHN-soo jee pah-PAY-oo*)

230

to a, para (*ah, PAH-rah*)

toast (bread) torrada (f.) (*toh-HAH-dah*)
  (drink) brinde (m.) (*BREEN-jee*)

tobacco tabaco (m.) (*tah-BAH-koo*)

today hoje (*OH-zhee*)

toe dedo (do pé) (m.) (*DEH-doo*) (*doo peh*)

together juntos (*ZHOON-toos*)

toilet toalete (m.), retretes (f.pl.) (P) (*twah-LEH-chee, rreh-TRAY-tehsh*)
  toilet paper papel higiênico (m.) (*pah-PAY-oo ee-ZHAY-nee-koo*)

tomato tomate (m.) (*toh-MAH-chee*)

tomorrow amanhã (f.) (*ah-mahn-YAHN*)

tongue língua (f.) (*LEEN-gwah*)

tonight esta noite (*EHS-tah NOY-chee*)

too também (*tahm-BEHN*)
  too bad! que pena! (*keh PEH-nah!*)
  too much demais (*jee-MAHYS*)

tooth dente (m.) (*DEHN-chee*)

toothache dor-de-dente (f.) (*dohr jee DEHN-chee*)

toothbrush escova de dentes (f.) (*ehs-KOH-vah jee DEHN-chees*)

top cume (m.) (*KOO-mee*)

touch, to tocar (*toh-KAHR*)

tough duro (*DOO-roo*)

tourist turista (m. or f.) (*too-REES-tah*)

tow, to rebocar (*hay-boh-KAHR*)

toward para, em direção a (*PAH-rah, ehn jee-reh-SOWN ah*)

towel toalha (f.) (*TWAHL-yah*)

town cidade (f) (*see-DAH-jee*)

track via (f.), pista (f.) (*VEE-ah; PEES-tah*)

traffic trânsito (m.) (*TRAHN-see-too*)

(light) sinaleira (f.) (*see-nah-LAY-rah*)

train trem (m.), comboio (m.) (P) (*trehn, kohn-BOY-yoh*)

transfer transferir (*trahns-feh-REER*)

translate, to traduzir (*trah-doo-ZEER*)

travel, to viajar (*vee-ah-ZHAHR*)

travel insurance seguro de viagem (m.) (*say-GOO-roo jee VYAH-zhehn*)

traveler viajante (*m.* or *f.*) (*vyah-ZHAHN-chee*)

traveler's check cheque de viagem (m.) (*SHEH-kee jee VYAH-zhehn*)

tree árvore (f.) (*AHR-voh-ree*)

trouble, to incomodar (*een-koh-moh-DAHR*)

trousers calças (f.pl.) (*KOWL-sahs*)

truck caminhão (m.) (*kah-meen-YOWN*)

true verdadeiro (*vehr-dah-DAY-roo*)

try on, to provar (*proh-VAHR*)

try to, to tentar (*tehn-TAHR*)

Tuesday terça-feria (f.) (*TEHR-sah FAY-rah*)

Turkish turco(-a) (*TOOR-koo*)(*-kah*)

turn, to virar (*vee-RAHR*)

to turn back voltar atrás (*vohl-TAHR ah-TRAHS*)

tuxedo smoking (m.) (*ehs-MOH-keeng*)

twelve doze (*DOH-zee*)

twenty vinte (*VEEN-chee*)

twice duas vezes (*DOO-ahs VAY-zees*)

twin beds camas iguais (f.pl.) (*KAH-mahs ee-GWAHYS*)

two dois (*doys*)

typical típico (*CHEE-pee-koo*)

U

ugly feio (*FAY-yoo*)

umbrella guarda-chuva (m.) (*GWAHR-dah-SHOO-vah*)

uncertain incerto (*een-SEHR-too*)

uncle tío (*CHEE-oo*)

uncomfortable descomfortável (*dehs-kohm-fohr-TAH-vay-oo*)

under debaixo de (*day-BAHY-shoo jee*)

undershirt camiseta (f.) (*kah-mee-ZEH-tah*)

understand, to compreender, entender (*kohm-pree-ehn-DEHR, ehn-tehn-DEHR*)

underwear roupa íntima (f.) (*HOH-pah EEN-chee-mah*)

undress despir-se (*dehs-PEER-see*)

unhappy infeliz (*een-fay-LEEZ*)

United States Estados Unidos (*ehs-TAH-doos oo-NEE-doos*)

university universidade (f.) (*oo-nee-vehr-see-DAH-jee*)

231

unless a não ser que (*ah nown sehr keh*)
until até (*ah-TEH*)
up em cima, acima, para cima (*ehn SEE-mah, ah-SEE-mah, PAH-rah SEE-mah*)
upon sobre (*SOH-bree*)
upper superior (*soo-pehr-YOHR*)
upstairs andar acima (*ahn-DAHR ah-SEE-mah*)
urgent urgente (*oor-ZHEHN-chee*)
us nós (*nohs*)
use uso (m.) (*OO-zoo*)
  to use usar (*oo-ZAHR*)

V

vaccination vacinação (f.) (*vah-see-nah-SOWN*)
valley vale (m.) (*VAH-lee*)
valuable valioso (*vah-lee-OH-zoo*)
vanish desaparecer (*dehs-ah-pah-ray-SEHR*)
various diversos (*jee-VEHR-soos*)
veal vitela (f.) (*vee-TAY-lah*)
vegetable verdura (f.) (*vehr-DOO-rah*)
vehicle veículo (m.) (*vay-EE-koo-loo*)
very muito (*MWEE-too*)
vest colete (m.) (*koh-LAY-chee*)
veterinarian veterinário (m.) (*veh-teh-ree-NAH-ryoo*)
view vista (f.) (*VEES-tah*)
vinegar vinagre (m.) (*vee-NAH-gree*)
visa visto (m.) (*VEES-too*)
visit (sojourn) visita (f.) (*vee-ZEE-tah*)

to visit visitar (*vee-zee-TAHR*)
visitor visitante (m. or f.) (*vee-zee-TAHN-chee*)
vocabulary vocabulário (m.) (*voh-kah-boo-LAH-ryoo*)
voice voz (f.) (*vohz*)
voyage viagem (f.) (*vee-AH-zhehn*)

W

waist cintura (f.) (*seen-TOO-rah*)
wait for, to esperar (*ehs-peh-RAHR*)
waiter garçom (m.) (*gahr-SOHN*)
waiting list lista de espera (f.) (*LEES-tah jee ehs-PEH-rah*)
waiting room sala de espera (f.) (*SAH-lah jee ehs-PEH-rah*)
waitress garçonete (f.) (*gahr-soh-NAY-chee*)
wake up, to despertar, acordar (*dehs-pehr-TAHR, ah-kohr-DAHR*)
walk, to andar, passear (*ahn-DAHR, pah-say-AHR*)
wall (inside wall) parede (f.) (*pah-REH-jee*)
  (outside wall) muro (m.) (*MOO-roo*)
wallet carteira (f.) (*kahr-TAY-rah*)
want, to querer, desejar (*keh-REHR, deh-zay-ZHAR*)
warm quente (*KEHN-chee*)
to wash lavar-se (*lah-VAHR-see*)
washroom lavabo (m.) (*lah-VAH-boo*)

232

watch (clock) relógio (m.) (*hay-LOH-zhyoo*)

  to watch observar (*oh-bee-sehr-VAHR*)

  to watch out! cuidado! (*kwee-DAH-doo!*)

water água (f.) (*AH-gwah*)

watermelon melancia (f.) (*meh-lahn-SEE-ah*)

way (path) caminho (m.) (*kah-MEEN-yoo*)

  (mode) maneira (f.), modo (m.) (*mah-NAY-rah, MOH-doo*)

by the way a propósito, aliás (*ah pro-POH-zee-too, ah-LYAHS*)

  one way sentido único (*sehn-CHEE-doo OO-nee-koo*)

  which way? por onde? (*poor OHN-jee?*)

we nós (*nohs*)

weak fraco (*FRAH-koo*)

wear, to usar (*oo-ZAHR*)

weather tempo (m.) (*TEHM-poo*)

wedding casamento (m.) (*kah-zah-MEHN-too*)

Wednesday quarta-feira (f.) (*KWAHR-tah FAY-rah*)

week semana (f.) (*say-MAH-nah*)

  weekend fim-de-semana (*feen jee say-MAH-nah*)

weigh, to pesar (*pay-ZAHR*)

weight peso (m.) (*PAY-zoo*)

welcome bemvindo (*behn-VEEN-doo*)

  welcome (you are) de nada (*jee NAH-dah*)

well (adv.) bem, (adj.) bom (*behn, bohn*)

west oeste (m.) (*oh-EHS-chee*)

wet molhado (*mohl-YAH-doo*)

what o quê? (*oo keh?*)

wheel roda (f.) (*HOH-dah*)

when quando? (*KWAHN-doo?*)

where onde? (*OHN-jee?*)

which qual? (*kwow?*)

while enquanto (*ehn-KWAHN-too*)

white branco (*BRAHN-koo*)

who quem? (*kehn?*)

why porquê? (*poor-KEH?*)

wide largo (*LAHR-goo*)

width largura (*lahr-GOO-rah*)

wife esposa (f.), mulher (f.) (P) (*ehs-POH-zah, mool-YEHR*)

wind vento (m.) (*VEHN-too*)

window janela (f.) (*zhah-NEH-lah*)

windshield para-brisas (m.) (*pah-rah-BREE-zahs*)

wine vinho (m.) (*VEEN-yoo*)

  wine list lista dos vinhos (f.) (*LEES-tah doos VEEN-yoos*)

  sparkling wine vinho espumante (m.) (*VEEN-yoo ehs-poo-MAHN-chee*)

winter inverno (m.) (*een-VEHR-noo*)

wish, to desejar, querer (*deh-zay-ZHAHR, keh-REHR*)

with com (*kohn*)

without sem (*sehn*)

woman mulher (f.) (*mool-YEHR*)

wood madeira (f.) (*mah-DAY-rah*)

wool lã (f.) (*lahn*)

word palavra (f.) (*pah-LAHV-rah*)

work trabalho (m.) (*trah-BAHL-yoo*)

233

to work trabalhar (*trah-bahl-YAHR*)

to worry preocupar-se, (n.) preocupação (f.) (*pray-oh-koo-PAHR-see, pray-oh-koo-pah-SOWN*)

worse pior (*pee-OHR*)

worst o(a) pior (*oo/ah pee-OHR*)

worth, to be valer (*vah-LEHR*)

wounded ferido (*feh-REE-doo*)

to wrap embrulhar (*ehm-brool-YAHR*)

wrench (tool) chave inglesa (f.) (*SHAH-vee een-GLAY-zah*)

wrist pulso (m.) (*POOL-soo*)

wristwatch relógio de pulso (m.) (*hay-LOH-zhyoo jee POOL-soo*)

write, to escrever (*ehs-kray-VEHR*)

wrong errado (*eh-HAH-doo*)

to be wrong estar errado (*ehs-TAHR eh-HAH-doo*)

X

X-ray radiografia (f.), raio-X (*hah-jyoh-grah-FEE-ah, HAHY-yoo shees*)

Y

year ano (m.) (*AH-noo*)

yellow amarelo (*ah-mah-RAY-loo*)

yes sim (*seen*)

yesterday ontem (*OHN-tehn*)

yet ainda (*ah-EEN-dah*)

not yet ainda não (*ah-EEN-dah nown*)

you você (informal), tu (informal) (P), o senhor (a senhora) (formal), vocês (pl.) (*voh-SAY, too, oo sehn-YOHR, ah sehn-YOH-rah, voh-SAYS*)

young jovem (*ZHOH-vehn*)

your, yours o seu (m.), sua (f.), vosso(-a) (P) (*oo SAY-oo, ah SOO-ah, VOH-soh*)(*-sah*)

youth hostel albergue de juventude (m.) (*ahl-BEHR-gee jee zhoo-vehn-TOO-jee*)

Z

zero zero (*ZAY-roo*)

zip code código postal (m.) (*KOH-jee-goo pohs-TOW*)

zipper zíper (m.), fecho ecler (m.) (*ZEE-pehr, FAY-shoo eh-KLEHR*)

zone zona (f.) (*ZOH-nah*)

PORTUGUESE-ENGLISH DICTIONARY

See usage note under English-Portuguese, page 195.

A

a (f.) (*ah*) the, at, on
abaixo (*ah-BAHY-shoo*) below, down
abcesso (m.) (*ahb-SEH-soo*) abscess
aberto (*ah-BEHR-too*) open
aborrecer (*ah-boh-hay-SEHR*) to annoy
abril (*ah-BREE-oo*) April
abrir (*ah-BREER*) to open, unlock
acabar (*ah-kah-BAHR*) to finish, end, stop
acampamento (m.) (*ah-kahm-pah-MEHN-too*) camp
achar (*ah-SHAHR*) to consider, to think (*opinion*)
acontecer (*ah-kohn-tay-SEHR*) to occur, happen
acordar (*ah-kohr-DAHR*) to awake, wake up
acordo (m.) (*ah-KOHR-doo*) agreement
acreditar (*ah-kray-jee-TAHR*) to believe
açúcar (m.) (*ah-SOO-kahr*) sugar
acumulador (m.) (*ah-koo-moo-lah-DOHR*) battery (car)
adiante (*ah-JYAHN-chee*) ahead, forward
adeus (*ah-DAY-oos*) goodbye, farewell
aeroporto (m.) (*ah-ehr-oh-POHR-too*) airport

agora (*ah-GOH-rah*) now
agosto (*ah-GOHS-too*) August
agradável (*ah-grah-DAH-vay-oo*) pleasant, nice
agradecer (*ah-grah-day-SEHR*) to thank
água (m.) (*AH-gwah*) water
 corrente (*koh-HEHN-chee*) running water
 potável (*poh-TAH-vay-oo*) drinking water
 mineral (*mee-neh-ROW*) mineral water
agulha (f.) (*ah-GOOL-yah*) needle
aí (*ah-EE*) there
ainda (*ah-EEN-dah*) still, yet
ajudar (*ah-zhoo-DAHR*) to help
ajustar (*ah-zhoos-TAHR*) to adjust
alcachofra (f.) (*ahl-kah-SHOH-frah*) artichoke
álcool (m.) (*AHL-kool*) alcohol
alegre (*ah-LAY-gree*) glad, merry, jolly
além (*ah-LEHN*) beyond
 além disso (*al-LEHN JEE-soo*) besides
alface (f.) (*ahl-FAH-see*) lettuce
alfinete (m.) (*ahl-fee-NAY-chee*) pin
algo (*AHL-goo*) something, anything

235

algodão (m.) (ahl-goh-DOWN) cotton

alguém (AHL-gehn) someone, somebody

algum (ahl-GOON) some, any

   algumas vezes (ahl-GOO-mahs VAY-zees) sometimes

alicate (m.) (ah-lee-KAH-chee) pliers

alimento (m.) (ah-lee-MEHN-too) food

almoçar (ahl-moh-SAHR) to eat lunch

almoço (m.) (ahl-MOH-soo) dinner, lunch

almofada (f.) (ahl-moh-FAH-dah) cushion

altitude (ahl-chee-TOO-jee) altitude

alto (AHL-too) tall, high, loud

alugar (ah-loo-GAHR) to rent

aluno (m. or f.) (ah-LOO-noo) pupil, student

amanhã (f.) (ah-mahn-YAHN) tomorrow

amarelo (ah-mah-REH-loo) yellow

amargo (ah-MAHR-goo) bitter

amigo (m. or f.) (ah-MEE-goo) friend

amor (m.) (ah-MOHR) love

amplo (AHM-ploo) broad, extensive

andar (ahn-DAHR) go, walk

anel (m.) (ah-NAY-oo) ring

ano (m.) (AH-noo) year

anterior (ahn-teh-RYOHR) former, previous

antes (AHN-chees) before

antigo (ahn-CHEE-goo) former, antique, ancient

antipático (ahn-chee-PAH-chee-koo) unpleasant, not likable, nasty

apagar (ah-pah-GAHR) to extinguish; to erase

apelido (m.) (ah-pay-LEE-doo) nickname

aprender (ah-prehn-DEHR) to learn

apresentar (ah-pray-zehn-TAHR) to introduce, present

aquele (ah-KAY-lee) that

aqui (ah-KEE) here

árabe (m. or f.) (AH-rah-bee) Arab

areia (f.) (ah-RAY-yah) sand

arranjar (ah-hahn-ZHAHR) to arrange, to get

arroz (m.) (ah-HOHZ) rice

arrumar (ah-hoo-MAHR) to tidy up

árvore (m.) (AHR-voh-ree) tree

assegurar (ah-say-goo-RAHR) to assure

assim (ah-SEEN) so, thus

assento (m.) (ah-SEHN-too) seat

assinar (ah-see-NAHR) to sign

assustar (ah-soos-TAHR) to frighten

até (ah-TEH) until, till, to

aterrisar (ah-teh-hee-ZAHR) to land

atrás (ah-TRAHS) back, behind

auto-serviço (m.) (ow-too-sehr-VEE-soo) self-service

autocarro (m.) (P) (ow-toh-KAH-rroh) bus

avançar (ah-vahn-SAHR) to advance, get on with

avião (m.) (ah-VYOWN) airplane

aviso (m.) (ah-VEE-zoo) notice, sign, warning

azeite (m.) (ah-ZAY-chee) olive oil

azeitona (f.) (ah-zay-TOH-nah) olive

azul (ah-ZOOL) blue

B

bacalhau (m.) (bah-kahl-YAH-oo) codfish

bagagem (f.) (bah-GAH-zhehn) baggage, luggage

baixar (bahy-ZHAHR) to lower

baixo (BAHY-zhoo) low, short

balcão (m.) (bahl-KOWN) counter

banco (m.) (BAHN-koo) bench, bank

banhar-se (bahn-YAHR-see) to bathe, to take a bath

banheiro (m.) (bahn-YAY-roo) bathroom

barato (bah-RAH-too) cheap, inexpensive

barba (f.) (BAHR-bah) beard

barco (m.) (BAHR-koo) boat

barulho (m.) (bah-ROOL-yoo) noise

barulhento (bah-rool-YEHN-too) noisy

bastante (bahs-TAHN-chee) enough, sufficient

bata (f.) (BAH-tah) smock

bater (bah-TEHR) beat, knock

bateria (f.) (bah-teh-REE-ah) battery

baú (m.) (bah-OO) trunk

bebê (beh-BEH) baby

beber (beh-BEHR) to drink

bebida (f.) (beh-BEE-dah) drink, beverage

beijo (m.) (BAY-zhoo) kiss

belga (m. or f.) (BEHL-gah) Belgian

belo (BAY-loo) beautiful, handsome

bem (behn) well

bemvindo (behn-VEEN-doo) welcome

biblioteca (f.) (bee-blyoh-TAY-kah) library

bigode (m.) (bee-GOH-jee) moustache

bilhete (m.) (beel-YEH-chee) ticket, note

blusa (f.) (BLOO-zah) blouse

boca (f.) (BOH-kah) mouth

bochecha (f.) (boh-SHEH-sha) cheek

bolsa (f.) (BOHL-sah) bag, pouch, stock market

bom (bohn) good, kind, well

bombom (m.) (bohn-BOHN) candy

bonde (m.) (BOHN-jee) streetcar

bonito (boh-NEE-too) pretty

botão (m.) (boh-TOWN) button

braço (m.) (BRAH-soo) arm

branco (BRAHN-koo) white

breve (BRAY-vee) brief, soon

brilhar (breel-YAHR) to shine

237

brinde (m.) *(BREEN-jee)* toast

buffet (m.) *(boo-FEH-chee)* buffet

buraco (m.) *(boo-RAH-koo)* hole

buscar *(boos-KAHR)* to look for, to search

buzina (f.) *(boo-ZEE-nah)* horn

C

cá *(kah)* here

cabeça (f.) *(kah-BAY-sah)* head

cabelo (m.) *(kah-BAY-loo)* hair

cabine (f.) *(kah-BEE-nee)* phone booth

cada *(KAH-dah)* each, every
   cada um *(KAH-dah oon)* each one

cadeia (f.) *(kah-DAY-yah)* chain

cadeira (f.) *(kah-DAY-rah)* chair

caderno (m.) *(kah-DEHR-noo)* notebook

café (m.) *(kah-FEH)* coffee, café
   café-da-manhã (m.) *(kah-FEH dah mahn-YAHN)* breakfast

cair *(kah-EER)* to fall

caixa (f.) *(KAHY-shah)* box, case, cashier

calafrio (m.) *(kah-lah-FREE-oo)* chill

calar *(kah-LAHR)* to silence

calças (f. pl.) *(KAHL-sahs)* pants

calcular *(kahl-koo-LAHR)* to calculate

calmo *(KAHL-moo)* calm, quiet

calor (m.) *(kah-LOHR)* heat, warmth

cama (f.) *(KAH-mah)* bed

camarão (m.) *(kah-mah-ROWN)* shrimp

câmbio (m.) *(KAHM-byoo)* exchange rate

caminhão (m.) *(kah-meen-YOWN)* truck

caminhar *(kah-meen-YAHR)* to walk

caminho (m.) *(kah-MEEN-yoo)* road

camisa(f.) *(kah-MEE-zah)* shirt

camiseta (f.) *(kah-mee-ZEH-tah)* undershirt

campo (m.) *(KAHM-poo)* countryside

canção (f.) *(kahn-SOWN)* song

caneta (f.) *(kah-NAY-tah)* pen

cansado *(kahn-SAH-doo)* tired

cantar *(kahn-TAHR)* to sing

cantina (f.) *(kahn-CHEE-nah)* saloon

capital (f.) *(kah-pee-TOW)* capital

cara (f.) *(KAH-rah)* face

carne (f.) *(KAHR-nee)* flesh; meat

caro *(KAH-roo)* expensive, dear

carta (f.) *(KAHR-tah)* letter

cartão (m.) *(kahr-TOWN)* cardboard, card

carteira (f.) *(kahr-TAY-rah)* pocketbook, wallet

casa (f.) *(KAH-zah)* house, home

casaco de chuva (m.) *(kah-ZAH-koo jee SHOO-vah)* raincoat

casal (m.) *(kah-ZOW)* (married) couple

casar-se *(kah-ZAHR-see)* to marry

caso (m.) *(KAH-zoo)* case, instance, affair

castanho *(kahs-TAHN-yoo)* brown

castelo (m.) *(kahs-TAY-loo)* castle

catorze *(kah-TOHR-zee)* fourteen

causa (f.) *(KOW-zah)* reason, cause

cavalheiro (m.) *(kah-vahl-YAY-roo)* gentleman

cavalo (m.) *(kah-VAH-loo)* horse

cebola (f.) *(say-BOH-lah)* onion

ceder *(seh-DEHR)* to yield, give in

cedo *(SAY-doo)* early

ceia (f.) *(SAY-yah)* (late) supper

cem *(sehn)* hundred

centro (m.) *(SEHN-troo)* center, middle

cereja (f.) *(seh-RAY-zhah)* cherry

certificado *(sehr-chee-fee-KAH-doo)* certificate, registered

certo *(SEHR-too)* sure, certain, right

cerveja (f.) *(sehr-VAY-zhah)* beer

cessar *(say-SAHR)* to stop, discontinue

cesta (m.) *(SAYS-tah)* basket

céu (m.) *(SEH-oo)* sky, heaven

chá (m.) *(shah)* tea

chamar *(shah-MAHR)* to call, name

chão (m.) *(shown)* ground, floor

chapéu (m.) *(shah-PAY-oo)* hat

chave (f.) *(SHAH-vee)* key

chefe (m. or f.) *(SHEH-fee)* boss, leader, manager

chegar *(shay-GAHR)* to arrive

chegada (f.) *(shay-GAH-dah)* arrival

cheio *(SHAY-yoo)* full

cheiro *(SHAY-roo)* smell

cheque (m.) *(SHEH-kee)* check

chocolate (m.) *(shoh-koh-LAH-chee)* chocolate

cidade (f.) *(see-DAH-jee)* city

cima (f.) *(SEE-mah)* peak, summit

cinco *(SEEN-koo)* five

cinema (m.) *(see-NAY-mah)* movie theater

cinquenta *(seen-KWEHN-tah)* fifty

cinto (m.) *(SEEN-too)* belt

cinzeiro (m.) *(seen-ZAY-roo)* ashtray

cirurgião (m. or f.) *(see-roor-ZHOWN)* surgeon

claro *(KLAH-roo)* clear, bright

cobrir *(koh-BREER)* to cover

239

colher (f.) (*kool-YEHR*) spoon, to pick, gather

colocar (*koh-loh-KAHR*) to place, put

com (*kohn*) with

começar (*koh-may-SAHR*) to begin, initiate

comer (*koh-MEHR*) to eat

comida (f.) (*koh-MEE-dah*) food

como (*KOH-moo*) like, as

cômodo (*KOH-moh-doo*) comfortable, convenient

companheiro (m. or f.) (*kom-pahn-YAY-roo*) companion

companhia (f.) (*kohm-pahn-YEE-ah*) company, firm

comparar (*kohm-pahr-AHR*) to compare

completo (*kohm-PLAY-too*) complete, full

compra (f.) (*KOHM-prah*) purchase

comprar (*kohm-PRAHR*) to buy

compreender (*kohm-pray-ehn-DEHR*) to understand

comprido (*kohm-PREE-doo*) long

concerto (m.) (*kohn-SEHR-too*) concert

concordar (*kohn-kohr-DAHR*) to agree, approve of

conduzir (*kohn-doo-ZEER*) to drive, conduct, carry

conferência (f.) (*kohn-feh-RAYN-syah*) conference, lecture

conhecer (*kohn-yay-SEHR*) to know, to make the acquaintance of

conseguir (*kohn-say-GEER*) to get, obtain

conta (f.) (*KOHN-tah*) bill, account

contar (*kohn-TAHR*) to count, to tell

contestar (*kohn-tays-TAHR*) to dispute

contra (*KOHN-trah*) against, versus

contradizer (*kohn-trah-jee-SEHR*) to contradict

contudo (*kohn-TOO-doo*) however, yet

contusão (f.) (*kohn-too-ZOWN*) bruise

convidar (*kohn-vee-DAHR*) to invite

cópia (f.) (*KOH-pyah*) copy

cor (f.) (*kohr*) color

coração (m.) (*koh-rah-SOWN*) heart

corpo (m.) (*KOHR-poo*) body

correio (m.) (*koh-HAY-yoo*) mail

correr (*koh-HEHR*) to run

cortar (*kohr-TAHR*) to cut

corte (de cabelo) (m.) (*KOHR-chee*) (*jee kah-BAY-loo*) haircut

cortês (*kohr-TAYS*) polite

costela (f.) (*kohs-TAY-lah*) rib

cozinha (f.) (*koh-ZEEN-yah*) kitchen

creme(m.)(*KRAY-mee*) cream

crer (*krehr*) to believe

criança (f.) (*kree-AHN-sah*) child

cru (*kroo*) raw

cruzamento (m.) (*kroo-zah-MEHN-too*) junction, crossroad

cuidar (*kwee-DAHR*) to care for

cunhado (m. or f.) (*koon-YAH-doo*) brother-in-law

curar (*koo-RAHR*) to cure

curto (*KOOR-too*) short

curva (f.) (*KOOR-vah*) turn, bend

custar (*koos-TAHR*) to cost

D

dançar (*dahn-SAHR*) to dance

dar (*dahr*) to give

data (f.) (*DAH-tah*) date

de (*jee*) from, of, out of

debaixo (*day-BAHY-zhoo*) below, beneath

decidir (*day-see-JEER*) to decide

décimo (*DEH-see-moo*) tenth

declarar (*deh-klahr-AHR*) to declare

dedo (m.) (*DAY-doo*) finger

deitar-se (*day-TAHR-see*) to lie down

deixar (*day-ZHAHR*) to leave, to let, to permit

demais (*dee-MAHYS*) too much

demora (f.) (*jee-MOH-rah*) delay

dentadura (f.) (*dehn-tah-DOO-rah*) denture

dentista (m. or f.) (*dehn-CHEES-tah*) dentist

dentro (*DEHN-troo*) inside, in

depósito (m.) (*day-POH-zee-too*) deposit

depressa (*jee-PRAY-sah*) fast, quickly

descansar (*days-kahn-SAHR*) to rest

descobrir (*days-koh-BREER*) to discover, uncover

desconto (m.) (*days-KOHN-too*) discount

desculpar (*days-kool-PAHR*) to pardon, to excuse

desde (*(DAYS-jee*) since, as

desejar (*deh-zay-ZHAHR*) to wish, want

desembarcar (*dehz-ehm-bahr-KAHR*) to disembark

desenvolver (*dehs-ehn-vohl-VEHR*) to develop

desfrutar (*dehs-froo-TAHR*) to enjoy

desodorante (m.) (*dehs-oh-doh-RAHN-chee*); also **desodorizante (m.) (P)** (*dehs-oh-doh-ree-ZAHN-teh*) deodorant

despertador (m.) (*dehs-pehr-tah-DOHR*) alarm clock

despertar-se (*dehs-pehr-TAHR-see*) to wake up

destinatário (m.) (*dehs-chee-nah-TAH-ryoo*) addressee

desvio (m.) (*dehs-VEE-oo*) detour

deus (*DAY-oos*) god

dever (*day-VEHR*) to owe, have to

devolver (*deh-vohl-VEHR*) to return

dez (*dehs*) ten

dezenove (*deh-zee-NOH-vee*) nineteen

dezesseis (*deh-zee-SAYS*) sixteen

dezessete (*deh-zee-SEH-chee*) seventeen

241

dezembro (*jee-ZEHM-broo*) December

dezoito (*deh-ZOY-too*) eighteen

dia (m.) (*JEE-ah*) day
  bom dia (*bohn JEE-ah*) good morning, good day

dicionário (m.) (*dee-syo-NAH-ryoo*) dictionary

difícil (*jee-FEE-see-oo*) difficult

dinheiro (m.) (*jeen-YAY-roo*) money, cash

direção (f.) (*dee-ray-SOWN*) direction

direita (f.) (*jee-RAY-tah*) right side

direito (*jee-RAY-too*) right

direto (*jee-REH-too*) straight

dirigir (*dee-ree-ZHEER*) to direct, to drive

disco (m.) (*JEES-koo*) (phonograph) record

discurso (m.) (*dees-KOOR-soo*) speech

dispor (de) (*jees-POHR*) (*jee*) to have, make available

distância (f.) (*jees-TAHN-syah*) distance

dizer (*jee-ZEHR*) to say, tell

dobrar (*doh-BRAHR*) to fold, turn, bend, to double

doce (*DOH-see*) sweet

doente (*DWEHN-chee*) sick, ill

dois (*doys*) two

dólar (*DOH-lahr*) dollar

domingo (*doh-MEEN-goo*) Sunday

dor (f.) (*dohr*) pain

dormir (*dohr-MEER*) to sleep

dormitório (m.) (*dohr-mee-TOH-ryoo*) bedroom

doze (*DOH-zee*) twelve

drogaria (f.) (*droh-gah-REE-ah*) pharmacy

durante (*doo-RAHN-chee*) during

durar (*doo-RAHR*) to last, to continue

duro (*DOO-roo*) hard, tough

dúzia (f.) (*DOO-zyah*) dozen

E

e (*ee*) and

edição (f.) (*ay-dee-SOWN*) edition

educação (f.) (*ed-doo-kah-SOWN*) education

educado (*eh-doo-KAH-doo*) polite, well mannered

educar (*ed-doo-KAHR*) to educate, raise, bring up

ela (*EH-lah*) she

ele (*AY-lee*) he

eles, elas (*AY-lees, EH-lahs*) they

elevador (m.) (*eh-lay-vah-DOHR*) elevator

em (*ehn*) in, on

embora (*ehm-BOH-rah*) off, away, although

embreagem (f.) (*ehm-BRYAH-zhehn*) (car) clutch

embrulhar (*ehm-brool-YAHR*) to wrap

empregada (*ehm-pray-GAH-dah*) employee, maid

emprego (m.) (*ehm-PRAY-goo*) employment; job

empresa (f.) (*ehm-PRAY-zah*) firm, business

242

emprestar (*ehm-prays-TAHR*) to lend

empurrar (*ehm-poo-HAHR*) to push

encher (*ehn-SHEHR*) to fill

encontrar (*ehn-kohn-TRAHR*) to find, to meet, to come across

encurtar (*ehn-kohr-TAHR*) to shorten

endereço (m.) (*ehn-deh-RAY-soo*) address

enfermeira (f.) (*ehn-fehr-MAY-rah*) nurse

enganar (*ehn-gah-NAHR*) to deceive, cheat

enjoado (*ehn-zhoo-AH-doo*) seasick, nauseated

ensinar (*ehn-see-NAHR*) to teach

entender (*ehn-tehn-DEHR*) to understand

entrar (*ehn-TRAHR*) to enter, come in

entre (*EHN-tree*) between, among

entrega (f.) (*ehn-TRAY-gah*) delivery

entregar (*ehn-tray-GAHR*) to deliver, to hand over

enviar (*ehn-VYAHR*) to send, to mail

errado (m.) (*eh-HAH-doo*) mistaken, wrong

erro (m.) (*EH-hoo*) error, mistake

escada (f.) (*ehs-KAH-dah*) stairs, ladder

escandinavo(-a) (m. or f.) (*ehs-kahn-dee-NAH-voo*) (*-vah*) Scandinavian

escapar (*ehs-kah-PAHR*) to escape

esclarecer (*ehs-klah-ray-SEHR*) to clarify

escola (f.) (*ehs-KOH-lah*) school

escolher (*ehs-kohl-YEHR*) to pick, choose

escova (f.) (*ehs-KOH-vah*) brush

escrever (*ehs-kray-VEHR*) to write

escuro (*ehs-KOO-roo*) dark

escutar (*ehs-koo-TAHR*) to listen to

esparadrapo (m.) (*ehs-pah-rah-DRAH-poo*) adhesive tape, bandage

espelho (m.) (*ehs-PEHL-yoo*) mirror

esperar (*ehs-peh-RAHR*) to hope, to expect, to wait for

espesso (*ehs-PAY-soo*) thick

espinafre (f.) (*ehs-pee-NAH-free*) spinach

esposa (f.) (*ehs-POH-zah*); or **mulher (f.) (P)** (*mool-YEHR*) wife

esposo (m.) (*ehs-POH-zoo*) husband

esse (*EH-see*) this

esses (*EH-sees*) those

está bem (*ehs-TAH behn*) all right, O.K.

estação (f.) (*ehs-tah-SOWN*) season, station

estacionar (*ehs-tah-syoh-NAHR*) to park

Estados Unidos (*ehs-TAH-doos oo-NEE-doos*) United States

243

estar (*ehs-TAHR*) to be

este (m.) (*EHS-chee*) this

estômago (m.) (*ehs-TOH-mah-goo*) stomach

estrada (f.) (*ehs-TRAH-dah*) road, highway

estrangeiro (m. or f.) (*ehs-trahn-ZHAY-roo*) foreigner

estranho (*ehs-TRAHN-yoo*) strange

estreito (*ehs-TRAY-too*) narrow, tight

estrela (f.) (*ehs-TREH-lah*) star

estudante (m. or f.) (*ehs-too-DAHN-chee*) student

estudar (*ehs-too-DAHR*) to study

etiqueta (f.) (*eh-chee-KEH-tah*) label, tag

evitar (*eh-vee-TAHR*) to avoid, prevent

exato (*eh-ZAH-too*) exact, precise

excelente (*ehk-seh-LEHN-chee*) excellent

expressar (*ehks-pray-SAHR*) to express

F

faca (f.) (*FAH-kah*) knife

fácil (*FAH-see-oo*) easy

fala (f.) (*FAH-lah*) speech

falar (*fah-LAHR*) to speak

falta (f.) (*FAHL-tah*) lack, error

família (f.) (*fah-MEEL-yah*) family

farmácia (f.) (*fahr-MAH-syah*) pharmacy

farol (m.) (*fah-ROHL*) headlight, lighthouse

faturar (*fah-too-RAHR*) to bill, invoice

favor (m.) (*fah-VOHR*) favor

por favor (*poor . . .*) please

faça o favor (*FAH-sah oo . . .*) please

fazenda (f.) (*fah-ZEHN-dah*) farm

fechado (*fay-SHAH-doo*) closed

feio (*(FAY-yoo)*) ugly

felicidade (f.) (*fay-lee-see-DAH-jee*) happiness

felicidades (f. pl.) (*feh-lee-see-DAH-jees*) congratulations

feliz (*fay-LEEZ*) happy

feliz aniversário (*. . . ah-nee-vehr-SAH-ryoo*) happy birthday

Feliz Ano Novo (*. . . AH-noo NOH-voo*) Happy New Year

Feliz Natal (*. . . nah-TOW*) Merry Christmas

feriado (m.) (*feh-RYAH-doo*) holiday

ferir (*feh-REER*) to hurt, injure

festa (f.) (*FEHS-tah*) party

fevereiro (*feh-veh-RAY-roo*) February

ficha (f.) (*FEE-shah*) token (bus or phone)

fila (f.) (*FEE-lah*) row, queue, line

filho(-a) (m. or f.) (*FEEL-yoo*)(*-yah*) son, daughter

filme (m.) (*FEEL-mee*) film

fim (m.) *(feen)* end

fino *(FEE-noo)* fine, sheer

fita (f.) *(FEE-tah)* ribbon, tape

flor (f.) *(flohr)* flower

fogo (m.) *(FOH-goo)* fire

fonte (f.) *(FOHN-chee)* fountain

fora *(FOH-rah)* outside

forte *(FOHR-chee)* strong

fósforo (m.) *(FOHS-foh-roo)* match

fotografia (f.) *(foh-toh-grah-FEE-ah)* photograph

frango (m.) *(FRAHN-goo)* chicken

frente (f.) *(FREHN-chee)* front

frequente *(fray-KWEHN-chee)* frequent

fresco *(FREHS-koo)* fresh, cool

frio *(FREE-oo)* cold
  fazer frio *(fah-ZEHR . . .)* to be cold (weather)
  ter frio *(tehr . . .)* to be cold (person)

fritar *(free-TAHR)* to fry

fumar *(foo-MAHR)* to smoke

funcionar *(foon-syoh-NAHR)* to function, work

futebol (m.) *(foo-chee-BOHL)* soccer

futuro (m.) *(foo-TOO-roo)* future

G

gancho (m.) *(GAHN-shoo)* hook, peg

ganhar *(gahn-YAHR)* to earn

garagem (f.) *(gah-RAH-zhehn)* garage

garçom (m.) *(gahr-SOHN)* waiter

garçonete (f.) *(gahr-soh-NAY-chee)* waitress

garfo (m.) *(GAHR-foo)* fork

garganta (f.) *(gahr-GAHN-tah)* throat

gastar *(gahs-TAHR)* to spend

gasto (m.) *(GAHS-too)* worn, worn out

gato (m.) *(GAH-too)* cat

gelado (m.) *(zheh-LAH-doo)* cold

gêmeos (m. pl or f. pl.) *(ZHAY-mee-oos)* twins

gente (f.) *(ZHEHN-chee)* people

geral *((zheh-ROW)* general

gorjeta (f.) *(gohr-ZHEH-tah)* tip

gostar (de) *(gohs-TAHR) (jee)* to like, to be fond of

grande *(GRAHN-jee)* large, big, great

gratuito *(grah-TWEE-too)* free

gravata (f.) *(grah-VAH-tah)* necktie

grave *(GRAH-vee)* serious, grave

grelhar *(grehl-YAHR)* to grill, roast

grupo (m.) *(GROO-poo)* group, bunch

guardar *(gwahr-DAHR)* to keep, put away

H

há *(ah)* ago

hebraico *(eh-BRAHY-koo)* Hebrew (language)

245

higiene (f.) (ee-ZHEH-nee) hygiene

hoje (m.) (OH-zhee) today

homem (m.) (OH-mehn) man

hora (f.) (OH-rah) hour

horário (m.) (oh-RAH-ryoo) schedule, timetable

hóspede (m. or f.) (OHS-peh-jee) guest

hospital (m.) (ohs-pee-TOW) hospital

hotel (m.) (oh-TAY-oo) hotel

I

idéia (f.) (ee-DAY-yah) idea

idioma (m.) (ee-DYOH-mah) language

ignição (f.) (eeg-nee-SOWN) ignition

igreja (f.) (ee-GRAY-zhah) church

ilha (f.) (EEL-yah) island

impermeável (m.) (eem-pehr-may-AH-vay-oo) raincoat

importante (eem-pohr-TAHN-chee) important

importar (eem-pohr-TAHR) to be important, to import

imposto (m.) (eem-POHS-too) tax

incêndio (m.) (een-SAYN-dyoo) fire

incômodo (een-KOH-moh-doo) nuisance, inconvenience

indagar (een-dah-GAHR) to investigate, inquire

indicar (een-jee-KAHR) to point out, indicate

indígena (m. or f.) (een-DEE-zheh-nah) native

infeccionar (een-fehk-syo-NAHR) to infect

inferno (m.) (een-FEHR-noo) hell

informação (f.) (een-fohr-mah-SOWN) information

inglês (een-GLAYS) English

início (m.) (ee-NEE-syoo) beginning

inseto (m.) (een-SEH-too) insect

instrumento (m.) (een-stroo-MEHN-too) instrument

inteiro (een-TAY-roo) whole, intact

interessante (een-teh-ray-SAHN-chee) interesting

interpretar (een-tehr-pray-TAHR) to interpret

inverno (m.) (een-VEHR-noo) winter

ir (eer) to go

irmã (f.) (eer-MAHN) sister

irmão (m.) (eer-MOWN) brother

isso (EE-soo) that

itinerário (m.) (ee-tee-neh-RAH-ryoo) itinerary

J

já (zhah) at once, already

jamais (zhah-MAHYS) never

janeiro (zhah-NAY-roo) January

janela (f.) (zhah-NAY-lah) window

jantar (m.) (zhahn-TAHR), **(v.)** (zhahn-TAHR) dinner, to dine

jardim (m.) (zhahr-JEEN) garden

246

jarra (f.) (*ZHAH-hah*) jar
jarro (m.) (*ZHAH-hoo*) jug
jogar (*zhoh-GAHR*) to play
jornal (m.) (*zhohr-NOW*) newspaper
jovem (*ZHOH-vehn*) youngster
judeu (m.) (*zhoo-DAY-oo*); or **judia (f.)** (*zhoo-JEE-ah*) Jew
julho (*ZHOOL-yoo*) July
junho (*ZHOON-yoo*) June
junto (*ZHOON-too*) together

L

lá (*lah*) there
lã (*lahn*) wool
lábio (m.) (*LAH-byoo*) lip
lado (m.) (*LAH-doo*) side
ladrão (m.) (*lah-DROWN*) thief
lago (m.) (*LAH-goo*) lake
lagosta (f.) (*lah-GOHS-tah*) lobster
lâmpada (f.) (*LAHM-pah-dah*) light bulb
lanche (m.) (*LAHN-shee*) snack
lápis (m.) (*LAH-pees*) pencil
laranja (f.) (*lah-RAHN-zhah*) orange
largo (*LAHR-goo*) broad, wide
lata (f.) (*LAH-tah*) can, tin
lavabo (m.) (*lah-VAH-boo*) washroom
lavanderia (f.) (*lah-vahn-deh-REE-ah*) laundry
lavar (*lah-VAHR*) to wash
lavar-se (*lah-VAHR-see*) to wash oneself
laxante (m.) (*lah-SAHN-chee*) laxative

legume (m.) (*lay-GOO-mee*) vegetable
leite (m.) (*LAY-chee*) milk
lembrança (f.) (*lehm-BRAHN-sah*) remembrance
lembrar (*lehm-BRAHR*) to remember
lenço (m.) (*LEHN-soo*) handkerchief
lente (m.) (*LEHN-chee*) lens
lento (*LEHN-too*) slow
ler (*lehr*) to read
leste (m.) (*LEHS-chee*) (the) east
levantar (*lay-vahn-TAHR*) to raise, life
lhe (*yee*) him, her
libra (f.) (*LEE-brah*) pound
lição (f.) (*lee-SOWN*) lesson
ligar (*lee-GAHR*) to bind, connect, plug in
limpo (*LEEM-poo*) clean
língua (f.) (*LEEN-gwah*) tongue, language
linha (*LEEN-yah*) line, thread
litro (m.) (*LEE-troo*) liter
livraria (f.) (*leev-rah-REE-ah*) bookstore
livre (*LEEV-ree*) free
livro (m.) (*LEEV-roo*) book
loção (f.) (*loh-SOWN*) lotion
logo (*LOH-goo*) soon
loiro (*LOY-roo*) blond
loja (f.) (*LOH-zhah*) store
longe (*LOHN-zhee*) far
longo (*LOHN-goo*) long
louco (*LOH-koo*) crazy
lua (f.) (*LOO-ah*) moon
lugar (m.) (*loo-GAHR*) place, spot
luz (f.) (*looz*) light

247

M

machucar (mah-shoo-KAHR) to hurt, injure

madeira (f.) (mah-DAY-rah) wood

maduro (mah-DOO-roo) ripe, mature

mãe (f.) (mahy) mother

maestro(-a) (m. or f.) (mah-EHS-troo) (-trah) conductor

magro (MAH-groo) thin

Maio ((MAY-yoo) May

maior (may-YOHR) major, superior, bigger

mais (mahys) more, most

mala (f.) (MAH-lah) suitcase, bag

manchar (mahn-SHAHR) to stain

mandar (mahn-DAHR) order, command

maneira (f.) (mah-NAY-rah) manner, way

manga (m.) (MAHN-gah) sleeve

manhã (f.) (mahn-YAHN) morning

manteiga (f.) (mahn-CHAY-gah) butter

mão (f.) (mown) hand

mapa (m.) (MAH-pah) map

máquina (f.) (MAH-kee-nah) machine

mar (m.) (mahr) sea

março (MAHR-soo) March

marido (m.) (mah-REE-doo) husband

mas (mahs) but, yet

massagem (f.) (mah-SAH-zhehn) massage

mau (m.) (mow); or **má** (f.) (mah) wrong, evil, bad

mecânico (m.) (meh-KAH-nee-koo) mechanic

médico (m.) (MEH-jee-koo) doctor, medical doctor

medida (f.) (meh-JEE-dah) measure, size

medo (m.) (MAY-doo) fear **estar com . . .** (ehs-TAHR kohn . . .) to be afraid

meia-noite (f.) (MAY-yah-NOY-chee) midnight

meio (MAY-yoo) half

meio-dia (m.) (MAY-yoo-JEE-ah) noon, midday

melhor (mehl-YOHR) better, superior

menino(-a) (m. or f.) (meh-NEEN-noo) (-nah) boy, girl

menor (may-NOHR) minor, inferior, smaller

menos (MAY-noos) less, fewer

mensagem (f.) (mehn-SAH-zhehn) message

mercado (m.) (mehr-KAH-doo) market

mês (m.) (mays) month

mesa (f.) (MAY-zah) table

mesmo (MAYZ-moo) same, even, really

mestre (m. or f.) (MEHS-tree) teacher

metade (f.) (meh-TAH-jee) half

meter (meh-TEHR) to put (into)

mexicano(-a) (m. or f.) (meh-shee-KAH-noo)(-nah) Mexican

mexilhão (m.) (*meh-sheel-YOWN*) mussel

mil (*MEE-oo*) thousand

mínimo (*MEE-nee-moo*) minimum

minuto (m.) (*mee-NOO-too*) minute

missa (f.) (*MEE-sah*) mass

moda (f.) (*MOH-dah*) fashion

modo (m.) (*MOH-doo*) way, manner

moeda (f.) (*moh-EH-dah*) coin, currency

mole (*MOH-lee*) soft

molhado (*mohl-YAH-doo*) wet, damp

molhar-se (*mohl-YAHR-see*) to get wet

molho (m.) (*MOHL-yoo*) gravy, sauce

montanha (f.) (*mohn-TAHN-yah*) mountain

monumento (m.) (*mah-noo-MEHN-too*) monument

morar (*moh-RAHR*) to live

moreno (*moh-RAY-noo*) brunette, dark complexion

morrer (*moh-HEHR*) to die

mosquiteiro (m.) (*mohs-kee-TAY-roo*) mosquito net

mostarda (f.) (*mohs-TAHR-dah*) mustard

mostrar (*mohs-TRAHR*) to show

motor (m.) (*moh-TOHR*) motor, engine

mudar (*moo-DAHR*) to vary, change

muito (*MWEE-too*) much, very, quite

muito prazer (*MWEE-too prah-ZEHR*) much pleasure (acquaintance)

muitos (*MWEE-tos*) many, lots of

mulher (f.) (*mool-YEHR*) woman, wife (P)

mundo (m.) (*MOON-doo*) world

muro (m.) (*MOO-roo*) wall (outside)

músculo (m.) (*MOOS-koo-loo*) muscle

museu (m.) (*moo-ZAY-oo*) museum

música (f.) (*MOO-zee-kah*) music

N

nacionalidade (f.) (*nah-syo-nah-lee-DAH-jee*) nationality

nada (*NAH-dah*) nothing **de nada** (*jee . . .*) you're welcome (thanks)

nadar (*nah-DAHR*) to swim

não (*nown*) no, not

nariz (m.) (*nah-REEZ*) nose

nascer (*nah-SEHR*) to be born

Natal (m.) (*nah-TOW*) Christmas

navio (m.) (*nah-VEE-oo*) ship, boat

necessitar (*neh-seh-see-TAHR*) to need

negócio (m.) (*neh-GOH-syoo*) business, deal

nem . . . nem (*nehn . . . nehn*) neither . . . nor

neto(-a) (m. or f.) (*NAY-too*)(*-tah*) grandson, granddaughter

249

nevar (*nay-VAHR*) to snow
neve (f.) (*NAY-vee*) snow
ninguém (*neen-GEHN*) no one, nobody
noite (f.) (*NOY-chee*) night
  boa noite (*BOH-ah NOY-chee*) good evening, good night
nome (m.) (*NOH-mee*) name
nono (*NOH-noo*) ninth
norte (m.) (*NOHR-chee*) north
nos (*nohs*) us, to us
nós (*nohs*) we
nave (*NOH-vee*) nine
novela (f.) (*noh-VAY-lah*) soap opera
novembro (*noh-VEHM-broo*) November
noventa (*noh-VEHN-tah*) ninety
novo (*NOH-voo*) new
noz (f.) (*nohz*) walnut, nut
número (m.) (*NOO-meh-roo*) number
nunca (*NOON-kah*) never

O

o (*oo*) the, it, him
obra (f.) (*OH-brah*) (artistic) work
obrigado (m. or f.) (*oh-bree-GAH-doo*)(*-dah*) thank you, obliged
obter (*oh-bee-TEHR*) to get, obtain
ocasião (f.) (*oh-kah-zee-OWN*) occasion, chance
oceano (m.) (*oh-see-AH-noo*) ocean

oculista (m. or f.) (*oh-koo-LEES-tah*) optician, oculist
óculos (m. pl.) (*OH-koo-loos*) glasses
ocupação (f.) (*oh-koo-pah-SOWN*) business, occupation
ocupado (*oh-koo-PAH-doo*) occupied, busy, taken
oeste (m.) (*oh-EHS-chee*) west
oferta (f.) (*oh-FEHR-tah*) gift, offer
oitenta (*oy-TEHN-tah*) eighty
oito (*OY-too*) eight
olá (*oh-LAH*) hello
olho (m.) (*OHL-yoo*) eye
onde (*OHN-jee*) where
ônibus (m.) (*OH-nee-boos*) bus
ontem (m.) (*OHN-tehn*) yesterday
onze (*OHN-zee*) eleven
oposto (*oh-POHS-too*) opposite
ordem (f.) (*OHR-dehn*) order
orelha (f.) (*oh-REHL-yah*) ear (external)
os (*oos*) them
ostra (f.) (*OHS-trah*) oyster
ou (*ow*) or
ouro (m.) (*OH-roo*) gold
outro (*OH-troo*) other, another
outubro (*oh-TOO-broo*) October
ouvir (*oh-VEER*) to hear

P

pacote (m.) (*pah-KOH-chee*) packet

padaria (f.) (*pah-dah-REE-ah*) bakery

padre (m.) (*PAH-dree*) priest

pagamento (m.) (*pah-gah-MEHN-too*) payment

pagar (*pah-GAHR*) to pay

página (f.) (*PAH-zhee-nah*) page

pai (m.) (*pahy*) father

país (m.) (*pah-EES*) country, nation

paisagem (f.) (*pah-ee-ZAH-zhehn*) landscape

palácio (m.) (*pah-LAY-syoo*) palace

palavra (f.) (*pah-LAHV-rah*) word

paletó (m.) (*pah-leh-TOH*) jacket

palha (f.) (*PAHL-yah*) straw

pão (m.) (*pown*) bread

pãozinho (m.) (*pown-ZEEN-yoo*) roll

papel (m.) (*pah-PAY-oo*) paper
    papel de carta (*. . . jee KAHR-tah*) notepaper
    papel de embrulho (*. . . jee ehm-BROOL-yoo*) wrapping paper
    papel higiénico (*. . . ee-ZHYAY-nee-koo*) toilet paper

papelaria (f.) (*pah-peh-lah-REE-ah*) stationery store

par (m.) (*pahr*) pair

para (*PAH-rah*) for, to, at, in order to

parabéns (m. pl.) (*pah-rah-BEHNS*) congratulations

pára-brisas (m.) (*pah-rah-BREE-zahs*) windshield

pára-choques (m.) (*pah-rah-SHOH-kees*) bumper, fender

paragem (f.) (*pah-RAH-zhehn*) stop (bus, taxi)

parar (*pah-RAHR*) to stop

parecer (*pah-ray-SEHR*) to seem, to appear

parede (f.) (*pah-REH-jee*) wall (inside)

parente (m. or f.) (*pah-REHN-chee*) relative

parque (m.) (*PAHR-kee*) park

parte (f.) (*PAHR-chee*) part, share

partida (f.) (*pahr-CHEE-dah*) departure

partir (*pahr-CHEER*) to break, crack, leave

passado (*pah-SAH-doo*) last, past
    o ano passado (*oo AH-noo . . .*) last year

passageiro(-a) (m. or f.) (*pah-sah-ZHAY-roo*)(*-rah*) passenger

passagem (f.) (*pah-SAH-zhehn*) passage, aisle

passaporte (m.) (*pah-sah-POHR-chee*) passport

passar (*pah-SAHR*) to pass, to happen, to spend (time)

passear (*pah-say-AHR*) to take a walk, stroll

passeio (m.) (*pah-SAY-yoo*) walk, stroll

pastelaria (f.) (*pahs-teh-lah-REE-ah*) pastry shop

pato (m.) (*PAH-too*) duck

251

pé (*peh*) foot
pedestre (m. or f.) (*peh-DEHS-tree*); or **peão (m.) (P)** (*pay-OWN*) pedestrian
pedaço (m.) (*peh-DAH-soo*) piece, bit
pedir (*peh-JEER*) to ask for, charge
peito (m.) (*PAY-too*) chest, bosom
peixe (m.) (*PAY-shee*) fish
pensar (*pehn-SAHR*) to think, to intend
pente(m.)(*PEHN-chee*) comb
pepino (m.) (*peh-PEE-noo*) cucumber
pequeno (*peh-KEH-noo*) small, little
pêra (f.) (*PAY-rah*) pear
perdão (*pehr-DOWN*) pardon, excuse me
perder (*pehr-DEHR*) to lose, to miss (bus, train)
perdoar (*pehr-doh-AHR*) to forgive, to pardon
perfume (m.) (*pehr-FOO-mee*) perfume
perguntar (*pehr-goon-TAHR*) to ask, inquire
permitir (*pehr-mee-CHEER*) to permit, to allow
perna (f.) (*PEHR-nah*) leg
pertencer (*pehr-tehn-SEHR*) to belong (to)
pesado (*pay-ZAH-doo*) heavy
pesar (*pay-ZAHR*) to weigh
pescoço (m.) (*pehs-KOH-soo*) neck
peso (m.) (*PAY-zoo*) weight
pessoa (f.) (*peh-SOH-ah*) person

picada (f.) (*pee-KAH-dah*); or **picadela (f.) (P)** (*pee-kay-DAY-lah*) sting
pior (*pee-OHR*) worse
piscina (f.) (*pees-SEE-nah*) swimming pool
piso (m.) (*PEE-zoo*) floor
pista (f.) (*PEES-tah*) trail, track
plataforma (f.) (*plah-tah-FOHR-mah*) platform
pneu (m.) (*pee-NAY-oo*) tire
pobre (*POH-bree*) poor
poder (*poh-DEHR*) to be able, may, might
pois (*poys*) because
polícia (m.) (*poh-LEE-syah*) policeman
ponte (f.) (*POHN-chee*) bridge
ponto (m.) (*POHN-too*) stop (bus, taxi)
por (*poor*) by, for
pôr (*pohr*) to put, set, lay
porque (*poor-KEH*) because, as, for
porquê? (*pohr-KAY?*) why?
porta (f.) (*POHR-tah*) door, gate
portão (m.) (*pohr-TOWN*) gate
porteiro (m.) (*pohr-TAY-roo*) porter, doorman
porto (m.) (*POHR-too*) sea-port
possível (*poh-SEE-vay-oo*) possible
possuir (*poh-soo-EER*) to possess, own
postal (m.) (*pohs-TOW*) card

252

potável (*poh-TAH-vay-oo*) for drinking; potable

pouco (*POH-koo*) little, few

pousada (f.) (*poh-ZAH-dah*) inn

praça (f.) (*PRAH-sah*) square, plaza

praia (f.) (*PRAHY-yah*) beach

prata (f.) (*PRAH-tah*) silver

praticar (*prah-chee-KAHR*) to practice

prato (m.) (*PRAH-too*) dish

prazer (m.) (*prah-ZEHR*) pleasure, joy

precisar (*pray-see-ZAHR*) to need

preço (m.) (*PRAY-soo*) price

prédio (m.) (*PREH-joo*) building

preferir (*pray-feh-REER*) to prefer

preocupado (*pray-oh-koo-PAH-doo*) worried

pressa (f.) (*PRAY-sah*) haste, hurry

presunto (m.) (*pray-SOON-too*) ham

preto (*PRAY-too*) black

primavera (f.) (*pree-mah-VEH-rah*) spring (season)

primeiro (*pree-MAY-roo*) first

primo (m. or f.) (*PREE-moo*) cousin

privado (*pree-VAH-doo*) private

problema (m.) (*proh-BLAY-mah*) problem

procurar (*proh-koo-RAHR*) to search, look for

professor(+a) (m. or f.) (*proh-feh-SOHR*)(*+ah*) teacher, professor

profissão (f.) (*proh-fee-SOWN*) profession

programa (m.) (*proh-GRAH-mah*) program

proibido (*proh-ee-BEE-doo*) prohibited, forbidden

proibir (*proh-ee-BEER*) to forbid, prohibit

prometer (*proh-meh-TEHR*) to promise

pronto (*PROHN-too*) prompt, ready

próprio (*PROH-pryoo*) own

provar (*proh-VAHR*) to try on, taste

próximo (*PROHK-see-moo*) next, nearby, close

público (*POO-blee-koo*) public

pulmão (m.) (*pool-MOWN*) lung

pulseira (f.) (*pool-SAY-rah*) bracelet

puro (*POO-roo*) pure, sheer, clean

puxar (*poo-ZHAHR*) to draw, pull

Q

quadro (m.) (*KWAH-droo*) picture, board

qual (*kwow*) which

qualquer (*kwow-KEHR*) any, whichever

quando (*KWAHN-doo*) when

quanto (*KWAHN-too*) how much

quarenta (*kwah-REHN-tah*) forty

quarta-feira (f.) (*KWAHR-tah-FAY-rah*) Wednesday

quarto (*KWAHR-too*) fourth, room

quase (*KWAH-zee*) almost

quatro (*KWAH-troo*) four

(o) que (*oo keh*) that, which, who

quebrar (*kay-BRAHR*) to break, crack, fracture

queimar (*kay-MAHR*) to burn

queixa (f.) (*KAY-shah*) complaint

quem (*kehn*) who

quente (*KEHN-chee*) hot

querer (*keh-REHR*) to desire, to want, to wish

quinto (*KEEN-too*) fifth

quinze (*KEEN-zee*) fifteen

quota (f.) (*KWOH-tah; or* **cota** (*KOH-tah*) quota

R

rabanete (m.) (*hah-bah-NAY-chee*) radish

raça (f.) (*HAH-sah*) race, breed

radiador (m.) (*hah-jyah-DOHR*) radiator

radio (m.) (*HAH-jyoo*) radio

radiografia (f.) (*hah-dyoh-grah-FEE-ah*) X-ray

raiz (f.) (*hah-EEZ*) root

rapariga (f.)(P) (*rrah-pah-REE-gah*) girl

rapaz (m.) (*hah-PAHZ*) boy

rápido (*HAH-pee-doo*) rapid, quick, fast

raro (*HAH-roo*) rare, strange

realmente (*hay-ow-MEHN-cee*) really, actually

rebuçado (m.) (P) (*rray-boo-SAH-doh*) sweet, candy

receber (*hay-say-BEHR*) to receive

receita (f.) (*hay-SAY-tah*) prescription, recipe

recente (*heh-SEHN-chee*) recent

recibo (m.) (*hay-SEE-boo*) receipt

recommendar (*hay-koh-mehn-DAHR*) to recommend

reconhecer (*hay-kohn-yay-SEHR*) to recognize

recordar-se (*hay-kohr-DAHR-see*) to remember

rede (f.) (*HEH-jee*) net, network

redondo (*hay-DOHN-doo*) round

refeição (f.) (*hay-fay-SOWN*) meal

refresco (m.) (*hah-FRAYS-koo*) refreshment

regressar (*hay-gray-SAHR*) to go back, return

relâmpago (m.) (*hay-LAHM-pah-goo*) lightning

religião (f.) (*hay-lee-ZHOWN*) religion

relógio (m.) (*hay-LOH-zhoo*) clock, watch

remédio (m.) (*hay-MEH-joo*) remedy

reparar (*hah-pah-RAHR*) to repair, mend

repetir (*hay-peh-CHEER*) to repeat

requerer (*hay-keh-REHR*) to require, request

reserva (f.) (*hay-ZEHR-vah*) reservation

resistir (*hay-sees-CHEER*) to resist

respirar (*hays-pee-RAHR*) to breathe

responder (*hays-pohn-DEHR*) to answer, to respond

resposta (f.) (*hays-POHS-tah*) answer, response

resto (*HEHS-too*) rest, remainder

resultado (ter) (*hay-zool-TAH-doo*) (*tehr*) to result, to have a result

reto (*HAY-too*) straight

retretes (f. pl.) (P) (*rray-TRAY-tehsh*) toilet

revelar (*hay-vay-LAHR*) to develop (film); reveal

reverso (*hay-VEHR-soo*) reverse

revista (f.) (*hay-VEES-tah*) magazine

rico (*HEE-koo*) rich

rio (m.) (*HEE-oo*) river

rir (*heer*) to laugh

roda (f.) (*HOH-dah*) wheel

romper (*hohm-PEHR*) to break

rosto (m.) (*HOHS-too*) face

roubar (*hoh-BAHR*) to rob, steal

roupa (f.) (*HOH-pah*) clothes

   roupa de baixo (. . . *jee BAHY-zhoo*) underwear

rua (f.) (*HOO-ah*) street

ruído (m.) (*hoo-EE-doo*) noise

ruidoso (*hoo-ee-DOH-zoo*) noisy

russo(-a) (m. or f.) (*HOO-soo*)(*-sah*) Russian

S

sábado (m.) (*SAH-bah-doo*) Saturday

sabão (m.) (*sah-BOWN*) soap

saber (*sah-BEHR*) to know (a fact), to know how to

saboroso (*sah-boh-ROH-zoo*) tasty

saco (m.) (*SAH-koo*) bag

saia (f.) (*SAHY-yah*) skirt

saída (f.) (*sah-EE-dah*) exit

sair (*sah-EER*) to go out, check out

sal (m.) (*sowl*) salt

sala (f.) (*SAH-lah*) room, classroom

salada (f.) (*sah-LAH-dah*) salad

salão (m.) (*sah-LOWN*) lounge

   salão de beleza (. . . *jee beh-LAY-zah*) beauty parlor

salsicha (f.) (*sahl-SEE-shah*) sausage

sangue (m.) (*SAHN-gee*) blood

sanitário (m.) (*sah-nee-TAH-ryoo*) sanitary, lavatory

santo(-a) (m. or f.) (*SAHN-too*)(*-tah*) saint

santuário (m.) (*sahn-TWAH-ryoo*) sanctuary, shrine

sapataria (*sah-pah-tah-REE-ah*) shoe store

sapateiro (m.) (*sah-pah-TAY-roo*) shoemaker

255

sardinha (f.) (*sahr-JEEN-yah*) sardine

saudação (f.) (*sow-dah-SOWN*) greeting

saúde (f.) (*sah-OO-jee*) health

se (*see*) self, himself, herself, itself, themselves

seco (*SAY-koo*) dry

seda (f.) (*SAY-dah*) silk

sede (f.) (*SEH-jee*) thirst
  estar com sede (*ehs-TAHR kohn . . .*) to be thirsty

seguir (*seh-GEER*) to follow, to continue

segunda-feira (f.) (*say-GOON-dah-FAY-rah*) Monday

segundo (m.) (*say-GOON-doo*) second, according to

seguro (*say-GOO-roo*) safe, secure
  seguro de viagem (*. . . jee vee-AH-zhehn*) travel insurance

seis (*says*) six

selo (m.) (*SAY-loo*) seal, postage stamp

sem (*sehn*) without

semáforo (m.) (P) (*seh-MAH-foh-roo*) traffic light

semana (f.) (*say-MAH-nah*) week

sempre (*SEHM-pree*) always

senhor (m.) (*sehn-YOHR*) sir, Mr.

senhora (f.) (*sehn-YOH-rah*) madam, Mrs.

senhorita (f.) (*sehn-yoh-REE-tah*) Miss, Ms.

sentar-se (*sehn-TAHR-see*) to sit down

sentir (*sehn-CHEER*) to feel, sense

separar (*say-pah-RAHR*) to separate

ser (*sehr*) to be

serviço (m.) (*sehr-VEE-soo*) service

servir (*sehr-VEER*) to serve

sessenta (*seh-SEHN-tah*) sixty

setembro (*seh-TEHM-broo*) September

setenta (*seh-TEHN-tah*) seventy

sétimo (*SEH-chee-moo*) seventh

sexta-feira (f.) (*SEHKS-tah-FAY-rah*) Friday

sexto (*SEHKS-too*) sixth

seu (*SAY-oo*) his, her, your, its

significar (*seeg-nee-fee-KAHR*) to signify, to mean

sim (*seen*) yes

sinagoga (f.) (*see-nah-GOH-gah*) synagogue

sinal (m.) (*see-NOW*) sign

sinaleira (f.) (*see-nah-LAY-rah*) traffic light

sítio (m.) (*SEE-choo*) site, seat, place, spot

smoking (m.) (*SMOH-keen*) tuxedo, dinner jacket

só (*soh*) only

sob (*sohb*) under

sobre (*SOH-bree*) on, above, over

sobremesa (f.) (*soh-bree-MAY-zah*) dessert

sobretudo (*soh-bree-TOO-doo*) above all, especially

sobretudo (m.) (*soh-bree-TOO-doo*) overcoat, topcoat

sogro(-a) (m. or f.) (*SOH-groo*) (*-grah*) father-in-law, mother-in-law

sol (m.) (*sohl*) sun

sombra (f.) (*SOHM-brah*) shade

sorvete (m.) (*sohr-VEH-chee*) ice cream

suave (*SWAH-vee*) mild, gentle

subir (*soo-BEER*) to rise, mount

suceder (*soo-say-DEHR*) to happen, occur

sueco(-a) (m. or f.) (*SWAY-koo*)(*-kah*) Swedish

suéter (m.) (*SWEH-tehr*) sweater

suiço(-a) (m. or f.) (*SWEE-soo*)(*-sah*) Swiss

sujo (*SOO-zhoo*) dirty, soiled

sul (m.) (*sool*) south

T

tabaco (m.) (*tah-BAH-koo*) tobacco

tabefe (m.) (*tah-BEH-fee*) buffet

taberna (f.) (*tah-BEHR-nah*) tavern, pub

taça (f.) (*TAH-sah*) cup (glass)

tal (*tow*) such

talvez (*tow-VEHZ*) perhaps, maybe

tamanho (m.) (*tah-MAHN-yoo*) size

também (*tahm-BEHN*) also, too

tanto (*TAHN-too*) as much

tão (*town*) such, so

tarde (f.) (*TAHR-jee*) afternoon

  boa tarde (*BOH-ah TAHR-jee*) good afternoon

tarifa (f.) (*tah-REE-fah*) fare, rate

taxa (f.) (*TAH-shah*) customs duty

táxi (m.) (*TAHK-see*) taxicab

te (*chee*) you, yourself

telefone (m.) (*teh-lay-FOH-nee*) telephone

telefonema (m.) (*teh-lay-foh-NEH-mah*) telephone call

tempo (m.) (*TEHM-poo*) time, weather

ter (*tehr*) to have

terça-feira (f.) (*TEHR-sah-FAY-rah*) Tuesday

terceiro (*tehr-SAY-roo*) third

terminal (m.) (*tehr-mee-NOW*) terminal

terra (f.) (*TEH-hah*) earth, soil

teu (*TAY-oo*) your

tio(-a) (m. or f.) (*CHEE-oo*) (*-ah*) uncle, aunt

tinta (f.) (*CHEEN-tah*) ink, dye

tinturaria (f.) (*teen-too-rah-REE-ah*) dry cleaner's

toalete (m.) (*twah-LEH-chee*) toilet

toalha (f.) (*TWAHL-yah*) towel

tocar (*toh-KAHR*) to touch, to play (an instrument)
todo (*TOH-doo*) all, entire
  todo o mundo (*. . . oo MOON-doo*) everybody, everyone
tomar (*toh-MAHR*) to take
tosse (f.) (*TOH-see*) cough
trabalhar (*trah-bahl-YAHR*) to work
trabalho (m.) (*trah-BAHL-yoo*) work
traduzir (*trah-doo-ZEER*) to translate
tratar (*trah-TAHR*) to treat
  tratar com (*. . . kohn*) to deal with
travesseiro (m.) (*trah-vay-SAY-roo*) pillow
trazer (*trah-ZEHR*) to bring
trem (m.) (*trehn*) train
três (*trays*) three
treze (*TRAY-zee*) thirteen
trinta (*TREEN-tah*) thirty
triste (*TREES-chee*) sad
trocar (*troh-KAHR*) to change
troco (m.) (*TROH-koo*) change
tu (*too*) you
tudo (*TOO-doo*) everything
turco(-a) (m. or f.) (*TOOR-koo*)(*-kah*) Turkish
turismo (m.) (*too-REEZ-moo*) tourism
turista (m. or f.) (*too-REES-tah*) tourist

U

último (*OOL-chee-moo*) last, ultimate

um, uma (*oon, OO-mah*) one, a, an
  uma vez (*OO-mah vehz*) once (one time)
unha (f.) (*OON-yah*) nail (finger, toe)
único (*OO-nee-koo*) sole, only
unir (*oo-NEER*) join, connect, unite
uns (*oons*) some
usar (*oo-ZAHR*) to use, employ
uso (m.) (*OO-zoo*) use (purpose)
útil (*OO-chee-oo*) useful, helpful
utilizar (*oo-chee-lee-ZAHR*) to employ, use
uvas (f. pl.) (*OO-vahs*) grapes

V

vaca (f.) (*VAH-kah*) cow
vagão (m.) (*vah-GOWN*) railway car
valer (*vah-LEHR*) to be worth
válido (*VAH-lee-doo*) valid
valor (m.) (*vah-LOHR*) value, worth
variedade (f.) (*vah-ryay-DAH-jee*) variety
vários (*VAH-ryoos*) several
vaso (m.) (*VAH-zoo*) vase, pot
vazio (*vah-ZEE-oo*) empty
velho (*VEHL-yoo*) old, aged
velocidade (f.) (*vay-loh-see-DAH-jee*) velocity, speed
venda (f.) (*VEHN-dah*) sale
vender (*vehn-DEHR*) to sell

veneno (m.) (veh-NAY-noo) poison

vento (f.) (VEHN-too) wind

ventilador (m.) (vehn-chee-lah-DOHR) fan, ventilator

ver (vehr) to see

verão (m.) (veh-ROWN) summer

verdade (f.) (vehr-DAH-jee) truth

verdadeiramente (vehr-dah-day-rah-MEHN-chee) really, truly

verdadeiro (vehr-dah-DAY-roo) true, real, actual

verde (VEHR-jee) green

vermelho (vehr-MEHL-yoo) red

vestido (m.) (vehs-CHEE-doo) dress

vestir-se (vehs-CHEER-see) to get dressed

vez (f.) (vehz) time (occasion)

  uma vez (OO-mah . . .) once

  em vez de (ehn . . . jee) instead of, in place of

via (VEE-ah) via, track, lane

viagem (f.) (vee-AH-zhehn) trip, voyage

  boa viagem (BOH-ah vee-AH-zhehn) bon voyage

viajar (vee-ah-ZHAHR) to travel

vida (f.) (VEE-dah) life

vidro (m.) (VEE-droo) glass (material)

vinho (m.) (VEEN-yoo) wine

vinte (VEEN-chee) twenty

vir (veer) to come

virar (vee-RAHR) to turn

visitar (vee-zee-TAHR) to visit

vista (f.) (VEES-tah) sight, view

visto (m.) (VEES-too) visa

viúvo(-a) (m. or f.) (vee-OO-voo) (-vah) widower, widow

viver (vee-VEHR) to live

voar (voh-AHR) to fly

você (voh-SAY) you

volante (m.) (voh-LAHN-chee) steering wheel

volta (f.) (VOHL-tah) turn, way back

voltar (vohl-TAHR) to return, turn around

vôo (m.) (VOH-oo) flight

voz (f.) (vohz) voice

X

xarope (m.) (shah-ROH-pee) syrup

xeque (m.) (SHEH-kee) check

xícara (f.) (SHEE-kah-rah) cup

Z

zangado (zahn-GAH-doo) angry, cross

zero (ZAY-roo) zero

zona (f.) (ZOH-nah) zone, area